Everyman, I will go with thee,
and be thy guide

This vo
or, if re
If it

THE EVERYMAN
LIBRARY

*The Everyman Library was founded by J. M. Dent
in 1906. He chose the name Everyman because he wanted
to make available the best books ever written in every
field to the greatest number of people at the cheapest possible
price. He began with Boswell's 'Life of Johnson';
his one thousandth title was Aristotle's 'Metaphysics',
by which time sales exceeded 40 million.*

*Today Everyman paperbacks remain true to
J. M. Dent's aims and high standards, with a wide range
of titles at affordable prices in editions which address
the needs of today's readers. Each new text is reset to give
a clear, elegant page and to incorporate the latest thinking
and scholarship. Each book carries the pilgrim logo,
the character in 'Everyman', a medieval morality play,
a proud link between Everyman
past and present*

R. L. Stevenson

TRAVELS WITH A DONKEY
AN INLAND VOYAGE
THE SILVERADO SQUATTERS

Edited by
TREVOR ROYLE

EVERYMAN
J. M. DENT · LONDON
CHARLES E. TUTTLE
VERMONT

Introduction, Chronology, Note on the Text and all endmatter
© J. M. Dent, 1993

This title first published in Everyman 1925
First published in paperback in Everyman 1984
This edition first published 1993
Reprinted 1994, 1996, 1999

J. M. Dent
Orion Publishing Group
Orion House
5 Upper St Martin's Lane, London WC2H 9EA
and
Charles E. Tuttle Co. Inc.
28 South Main Street, Rutland, Vermont
05701, USA

Printed in Great Britain by
The Guernsey Press Co. Ltd,
Guernsey, C.I.

British Library Cataloguing-in-Publication Data
for this title is available upon request.

ISBN 0 460 87278 8

CONTENTS

NOTE ON THE AUTHOR AND EDITOR

ROBERT LOUIS STEVENSON was born in Edinburgh on 13 November 1850, and educated at Edinburgh Academy and University. He studied law but his main interest was in literature and he had already contributed to various periodicals. In 1876 he made a trip through France by canoe and wrote of it in his first book, *An Inland Voyage* (1878); a later tour, made by land, was described in *Travels with a Donkey* (1879). During these journeys he met Fanny Osbourne, an American ten years his senior who was estranged from her husband. When she secured a divorce in 1879, he sailed to America to marry her. They honeymooned in the mountains of San Francisco which provided the setting for *The Silverado Squatters* (1883). He returned to Europe with his wife and stepson in 1880 and began writing *Treasure Island* which was published in 1883. Its success was a turning-point in Stevenson's career, and he moved first to Switzerland and then to the Riviera in search of a cure for his ill-health. Back in England from 1884 to 1887, he wrote *Kidnapped* and *The Strange Case of Dr Jekyll and Mr Hyde*. The family left England again in search of a more congenial climate and eventually settled at Apia in Samoa. It was here that Stevenson wrote *The Master of Ballantrae* (1889), and *Catriona*, a sequel to *Kidnapped*, (1893). He then began *St Ives* and *Weir of Hermiston*, both of which were unfinished when he died suddenly of a brain haemorrhage on 3 December 1894 at the age of forty-four.

TREVOR ROYLE was born in Mysore, India in 1945 and educated in St Andrews and Aberdeen. He was a Visiting Fellow at the Institute for Advanced Studies in the Humanities at the University of Edinburgh in 1998 and he is now Associate Editor of the *Sunday Herald*. His many publications include *The Mainstream Companion to Scottish Literature* (1993).

CHRONOLOGY OF STEVENSON'S LIFE

Year	Age	Life
1850		13 November, born at 8 Howard Place, Edinburgh, the son of Thomas Stevenson and Margaret Isabella Balfour
1852	2	Alison Cunningham ('Cummy') becomes his nurse and a major influence on his development
1853	3	Move to 1 Inverleith Terrace, Edinburgh
1857	7	Move to 17 Heriot Row, Edinburgh. Privately educated at Henderson's Preparatory School
1858	8	First period of illness
1861	11	Enters Edinburgh Academy
1863	13	Visits France, Italy and Germany with his parents. Leaves Edinburgh Academy due to illness and is educated privately
1866	16	*The Pentland Rising*, a 16-page pamphlet privately printed

CHRONOLOGY OF HIS TIMES

Year	Literary Context	Historical Events
1850	Alfred, Lord Tennyson becomes Poet Laureate; Death of Honoré de Balzac	First Public Libraries Act passed
1852	William Makepeace Thackeray publishes *Henry Esmond* Nathaniel Hawthorne publishes *Tanglewood Tales*	The Earl of Derby becomes prime minister Napoleon III becomes emperor of France
1853	Charles Dickens publishes *Bleak House* Giuseppe Verdi produces *La Traviata* and *Il Trovatore*	
1857	Charles-Pierre Baudelaire publishes *Les Fleurs du Mal* Anthony Trollope publishes *Barchester Towers*	Indian Mutiny breaks out
1858	George Macdonald publishes *Phantastes* Dean Ramsay publishes *Reminiscences of Scottish Life* R. M. Ballantyne publishes *Coral Island*	
1861		Death of Prince Albert, husband of Queen Victoria Victor Emmanuel II becomes first king of a united Italy American Civil War breaks out
1863	Count Leo Tolstoy begins publication of *War and Peace* Margaret Oliphant publishes *Salem Chapel*	
1866	Feodor Dostoevsky publishes *Crime and Punishment* John Henry Newman publishes *The Dream of Gerontius*	Atlantic telegraph cable is laid

Year	Age	Life
1867	17	November: Enters Faculty of Engineering, University of Edinburgh
1869	19	March: elected to Speculative Society
1871	21	Gives up engineering for law. Enters Edinburgh firm of W. F. Skene and Peacock, Writers to the Signet
1872	22	July: visits Germany; November: passes preliminary examinations for Scottish Bar
1873	23	January: confrontation with parents over his agnosticism; July: visits Sussex and meets and falls in love with Fanny Sitwell, wife of Sidney Colvin; December: first published essay 'Roads' in *Portfolio* magazine
1874	24	April: visits Menton, France; Summer: visits Sidney Colvin in London. Elected to Savile Club. Cruises Inner Hebrides with Walter Simpson
1875	25	February: meets W. E. Henley in Edinburgh; Spring: visits France with cousin Bob Stevenson; July: called to Scottish Bar
1876	26	Summer: canoe trip in France with Simpson. Meets and falls in love with Fanny Osbourne in artists' colony at Grez
1877	27	Summer in Paris with Fanny Osbourne; October: 'A Lodging for the Night', first short story published in *Temple Bar*
1878	28	April: *An Inland Voyage*; June: secretary to Professor Fleeming Jenkin at Paris Exhibition; August: Fanny Osbourne returns to the United States; September: walking tour in the Cévennes; December: Edinburgh, *Picturesque Notes*
1879	29	February: works with Henley on *Deacon Brodie*; June: *Travels with a Donkey in the Cévennes*; August: travels to United States of America; Autumn: with Fanny Osbourne and her family in Monterey, California

Year	Literary Context	Historical Events
1867	Matthew Arnold publishes *Culture and Anarchy*	Second Reform Act passed
1869		Imprisonment for debt abolished
		Bedford College for women incorporated in University of London
		First railway across America completed
1871	George Eliot publishes *Middlemarch*	Bank holidays introduced
		William I becomes first German emperor
		Henry Morton Stanley meets Dr Livingstone at Ujiji
1872	Samuel Butler publishes *Erewhon*	First University College opens at Aberystwyth
1873	Arthur Rimbaud publishes *Une Saison d'Enfer*	Ashanti War breaks out
		Death of Dr David Livingstone
1874	Johann Strauss produces *Die Fledermaus*	Benjamin Disraeli becomes prime minister
	James Thomson publishes *The City of Dreadful Night*	
1875	Death of Hans Christian Andersen	Disraeli purchases Suez Canal shares on Britain's behalf
1876	Mark Twain publishes *The Adventures of Tom Sawyer*	Queen Victoria becomes Empress of India
		Bulgarian Christians massacred by Turkish irregular troops
1877		Russo-Turkish war breaks out in Balkans
1878	Peter Tchaikovsky produces *Eugene Onegin*	Zulu War begins
		Congress of Berlin meets to solve Balkans crisis
1879	Henrik Ibsen produces *A Doll's House*	
	Henry James publishes *Daisy Miller*	

Year	Age	Life
1880	30	19 May: marries Fanny Osbourne in San Francisco; Summer: in Silverado, Napa Valley, California; September: returns with new family to Edinburgh
1881	31	April: Davos, Switzerland. *Virginibus Puerisque*; Summer: France and Scotland
1882	32	February: *Familiar Studies of Men and Books*; April: moves to Davos, Switzerland; June: returns to Scotland; July: *New Arabian Nights*; Autumn: moves to France, Marseilles and Nice; December: first performance of *Deacon Brodie* in Bradford
1883	33	March: settles at Chalet La Solitude, Hyères, France; November: *Treasure Island*
1884	34	January: *The Silverado Squatters*. Further illness; Autumn: moves back to England following outbreak of cholera at Hyères.
1885	35	Spring: settles at Skerryvore, Bournemouth; Friendship with Henry James and Walter Besant; March: *A Child's Garden of Verses*; April: *More Arabian Nights* and *The Dynamiter*; November: *Prince Otto*
1886	36	January: *The Strange Case of Dr Jekyll and Mr Hyde*; July: *Kidnapped*
1887	37	February: *The Merry Men*; May: Thomas Stevenson dies in Edinburgh; July: *Underwoods*; August: sails for United States and settles at Saranac Lake; November: *Memories and Portraits*
1888	38	January: *Memoir of Fleeming Jenkin*; April: moves to New York and New Jersey. Meets Mark Twain. Quarrels with Henley; June: *The Black Arrow*. Sets out on first Pacific voyage to Marquesas on board the Casco
1889	39	January: stays in Hawaii; June: *The Wrong Box* (with Lloyd Osbourne) Second Pacific voyage to the Gilbert Islands on board the Equator; September: *The Master of Ballantrae*; December: visits Samoa and purchases land

CHRONOLOGY OF HIS TIMES

Year	Literary Context	Historical Events
1880	George Newnes starts *Tit-Bits* Guy de Maupassant publishes his first stories	William Ewart Gladstone becomes prime minister
1881	Death of Thomas Carlyle	Death of Disraeli First Boer War breaks out Alexander III becomes Tsar of Russia
1882	Publication begins of *Dictionary of National Biography*	Married Woman's Property Act passed Pretoria Convention ends Boer War Triple Alliance formed between Italy, Austria and Germany
1883	Compton Mackenzie born Death of Edward Fitzgerald, author of *The Rubáiyát of Omar Khayyám*	
1884	Publication begins of the *Oxford English Dictionary*	Fabian Society founded Third Reform Act passed
1885		Earl of Salisbury becomes prime minister Death of General Charles Gordon at Khartoum Death of General Ulysses S. Grant
1886	Thomas Hardy publishes *The Mayor of Casterbridge* Death of Emily Dickinson	First Irish Home Rule Bill fails
1887	Edwin Muir born Arthur Conan Doyle publishes the first Sherlock Holmes story, *A Study in Scarlet*	Queen Victoria's Golden Jubilee
1888	August Strindberg produces *Miss Julie*	Jack the Ripper murders six women in London John Boyd Dunlop produces pneumatic tyres William II becomes German emperor
1889	Death of Gerard Manley Hopkins W. B. Yeats publishes *The Wanderings of Oisin* J. M. Barrie publishes *A Window in Thrums*	First London dock strike

Year	Age	Life
1890	40	February: visits Sydney, Australia; April: Third voyage to Gilbert and Marshall islands on board the *Janet Nichol*; July: *Father Damien*; October: settles in Samoa and builds Vailima; December: *Ballads*
1891	41	Mother arrives in Samoa
1892	42	April: *Across the Plains*; June: *The Wrecker*; August: *A Footnote to History*
1893	43	January: Vailima completed; April: *Island Nights' Entertainments*; September: *Catriona*
1894	44	September: *The Ebb-Tide*; 3 December: Dies of cerebral haemorrhage at Vailima, Samoa
1895		January: *The Amateur Emigrant* (revised text of 1880 edition); October: *Vailima Letters*
1896		March: *Fables*; May: *Weir of Hermiston*; August: *Songs of Travel*; September: *In the South Seas*
1897		October: *St Ives*
1899		*Letters to His Family and Friends*, edited by Sidney Colvin

Year	Literary Context	Historical Events
1890		Bismarck is dismissed as chancellor
		Parnell/O'Shea divorce case
		Henri de Toulouse-Lautrec produces first Moulin Rouge paintings
1891	Birth of Neil Gunn	Elementary school fees abolished
		Paul Gauguin settles in Tahiti
1892	Oscar Wilde produces *Lady Windermere's Fan*	
	Birth of Hugh MacDiarmid	
1893	Sir Arthur Wing Pinero produces *The Second Mrs Tanqueray*	Matabele rising
		Second Irish Home Rule Bill fails
		Civil war breaks out in Samoa
1894	Rudyard Kipling publishes *The Jungle Book*	Death of Louis Kossuth
	John Buchan publishes his first book, *Essays and Apothegms of Francis Lord Bacon*	Earl of Rosebery becomes prime minister

INTRODUCTION

In an unsigned essay in the *Scottish Leader* of 14 April 1892 the
anonymous reviewer of *Across the Plains* (a collection of twelve
essays published originally in *Scribner's, Fraser's* and *Longman's
Magazines*) posed the question that had long teased Stevenson's
friends and critics. 'will Mr R. L. Stevenson take his definite and
final place in English literature as a writer of essays or of novels
... is it among the romancers, with Scott and Dumas that
Stevenson will stand, or among the essayists, the pleasant
prattlers and gossips of literature, with Montaigne and Addison
and Lamb?' The review, having praised his 'ingenious and
graceful' style in both forms, reached the cautious conclusion
that 'while his fiction is sound and brilliant beyond all question,
the best part of his work, nevertheless, and the most part, has
been done in the region of desultory imaginative prose.' It was a
judgment that would not have seemed out of place to the
contemporary men of letters who counted Stevenson as one of
their own, a stylist and literary craftsman whose work was a
model for any aspiring writer. That his novels were also highly
regarded was not doubted: but it was the view of fellow writers
and essayists like Richard Le Gallienne, William Archer and
Grant Allen that the acme of Stevenson's art was found in his
essays.

   During his own lifetime Stevenson suffered much from critical
over-enthusiasm and from an unrestrained hero-worship
brought about by his courageous fight against illness; yet within
half-a-dozen years after his death (1894) a critical reaction had
set in. Instead of general approbation for his output of verse,
essays and fiction, there was faint praise for his poetry, a
coolness towards his novels and short stories and a growing
belief that in his essays he was little more than a literary dabbler,
a poseur who refused to engage himself completely with the
subjects he chose to discuss. At best, argued his new critics, he
had found his true place in the nursery and the schoolroom, as

the creator of *The Child's Garden of Verses*, *Treasure Island* and *The Black Arrow*. Partly, the backlash was due to the aggrandisement of Stevenson as a lovable saint by family and close friends; he suffered, too, from literary association with Sidney Colvin, Edmund Gosse and Andrew Lang, whom a younger generation regarded as fin de siècle dilettanti; and attitudes towards his life swithered between contempt for his love affairs and quarrels with his father and glorification of his bohemian style of living in France, the United States of America and the South Seas. In recent years critical attention (J. C. Furnas, David Daiches, Robert Kiely, Edwin Eigner, Jenni Calder *et al*) has restored the balance and presented Stevenson as a complex writer who explored moral ambiguities in man's psychological make-up and who believed in the inevitable moral consequences of any action. For his novels he would now command without comment a place in nineteenth-century fiction (even though F. R. Leavis denied him that in his study *The Great Tradition*, 1948); but how then do we answer today the question posed by the anonymous reviewer of 1892? If his place as a novelist is now assured, what price his essays, those pleasant prattlings on which he founded his reputation?

From an early age Stevenson's sole ambition had been to become a writer, to lose himself in the web of words. 'In the future that Louis envisaged schooling, earning, loving had no major portions. He was committed to writing as fatally as a vendetta-haunted Corsican is to vengeance.'* At home there was much to fuel his youthful imagination. From Cummy – his nurse Alison Cunningham – he learned the stories of the Covenanting times when men died for their beliefs in moods of religious exaltation, and she also provided a diet of country lore and imperfectly related stories from the scriptures. From his father Thomas Stevenson there were tales at bedtime, and the house at 17 Heriot Row had the stimulus of a well stocked library: as Stevenson admitted in later life he played the 'sedulous ape' to a group of writers he listed as Hazlitt, Lamb, Wordsworth, Sir Thomas Browne, Defoe, Hawthorne, Montaigne and Baudelaire. But apart from *The Pentland Rising*, a gauche retelling of the Battle of Rullion Green of 1666 fought

---

* J. C. Furnas, *Voyage to Windward: The Life of Robert Louis Stevenson* (London, 1952), 43.

between Covenanters and a superior force of government troops which had been printed at his father's expense in 1866, it was not until he befriended Sidney Colvin in the summer of 1873, that he enjoyed his first literary successes. Through Colvin's prompting he contributed his first essay, 'Roads', to *Portfolio* and he soon became a regular contributor to Leslie Stephen's *Cornhill* magazine, a literary entrée that gave his work access to a small but important group of metropolitan critics. His election to the Savile Club in June 1874, then considered to be London's foremost literary club with its circle of clubmen and distinguished men of letters which included Colvin, Gosse, W. E. Henley and George Saintsbury was further proof to him and his admirers that he had become a young writer worthy of critical regard.

When he came to the subject matter of his first essays, Stevenson's fascination with travel provided ready material. His recurring bronchial illnesses meant that the cold and damp Edinburgh winters had to be fought against rather than simply endured and that travel abroad became first a physical necessity and then an abiding pleasure. In the company of his boyhood friend Walter Simpson he made his first forays into Europe and later his cousin R. A. M. 'Bob' Stevenson introduced him to France, a country that was to provide him with emancipation from Edinburgh's bleak winters and stern morality in the artists' colony at Fontainebleau.

> With Stevenson ... appreciation of the taste and the flavour of romance, which clings to the tradition of good wine, was as keen as his abhorrence of the intemperance that was common in Scotland. On the one hand, I remember his saying reflectively, over a final bottle of the Beaujolais-Fleury at Lavenues on the eve of one of his visits home, 'I wish that we could get this in Edinburgh, for you don't know how I dread returning there and adapting myself to the ration of drink usual in the land of my fathers.' On the other hand I remember his exclamation, 'Don't that make you just love France,' when I told him the legend that there was a standing order in the French Army that no detachment of troops should ever pass the narrow strip of land on which ripens the noble *cru* of Clos Vougeot without presenting arms.[*]

[*] Will Low, 'A Chronicle of Friendships', first published in 1908, and here quoted from J. Calder, ed., *The Robert Louis Stevenson Companion* (Edinburgh, 1980), 66.

If Will Low's description of Stevenson's fascination for France and things French is ripe enough, then Stevenson's own essay on Fontainebleau and neighbouring Grez, 'Forest Notes', was considered by Colvin to be 'too sweet and unwholesome'. (Low was an American member of the artists' colony and a friend of the Stevenson cousins). The over-writing in this essay owed as much to Stevenson's own inexperience as it did to the animal joy he felt at being considered a writer, a fellow artist in the somewhat self-consciously bohemian ambiance of his cousin's circle. France first seemed to be a fate, part of the scheme of things, then it became a vocation. In the summer of 1876, a year after he had been called to the Scottish Bar, he set off on a canoe trip from Antwerp to Pontoise in the company of his friend Simpson. On a walking trip along the Loire during the previous summer the two men had become fascinated by the slow rhythms of canal-boat life and had determined to emulate it by more modest means in two sail-powered canoes or skiffs called *Cigarette* and *Arethusa*.

As so often happened in Stevenson's life anticipation of the journey was sweeter than reality. Instead of languid waters and golden autumnal days they ran into squalls and dull rain, but it mattered not. *An Inland Voyage*, the story of their expedition, published two years later in 1878, made light of their difficulties and it is a deliberately picturesque account of the journey and the vagaries of their moods. It is also very much a young man's book, Stevenson giving a clue to his humour after meeting the strolling players at Précy: 'There is nobody, under thirty, so dead but his heart will stir a little at sight of a gypsies' camp' (p. 98). Earlier he had written to his mother that she had a tramp for a son and the modestly successful appearance of *An Inland Voyage* was proof to him that it might be possible to combine travel with writing. After all, he reasoned, other writers had managed to marry the two and at that time he was much influenced by George Borrow's tales of a wandering life. (Another fellow Scot with a similar predilection was William Gordon Stables whose *Cruise of the Land Yacht Wanderer*, 1886, evoked the joys of a Romany existence.) 'Charm' was the word most commonly used to describe the book when it first appeared and indeed there is much of that in Stevenson's account. But it is not for its author's amiability that *An Inland Voyage* stands out amongst Stevenson's early writing; rather it proved to him that he could write atmospherically, that he could delineate landscape and summon up the annoyance and the exhilaration of bad weather, a virtue that was to stand him in good stead when he came to write *The Master of Ballantrae* (1889) which contains some excellent descriptions of the vagaries of Scottish weather.

Before setting off on his voyage along the Scheldt and the Oise, he had visited Fontainebleau and Grez and there he had met Fanny Osbourne, the estranged wife of a Kentucky lawyer, Samuel Osbourne. Ten years older than Stevenson, she was living in some penury with her two daughters – but Fanny Osbourne exercised a good deal of magnetism for the members of the artists' colony. Although she was first attracted to Bob, it was with Louis that she fell in love. In 1877 he spent as much time as he could with her in Paris and Grez and she accompanied him to London where she stayed until August 1878 when she returned to California to attempt to disentangle her personal affairs. In her absence Stevenson's moods swung between the euphoria of his love for her and the anguish entailed by her absence. It was, perhaps, the combination of both emotions that persuaded him to embark on a walking tour through the Cévennes in September 1878, the journey that gave him the subject matter for *Travels with a Donkey*. During the course of the journey Stevenson kept a daily diary, writing usually first thing in the morning when he was refreshed, or at an inn at lunchtime: he had every intention of publishing his experiences when he returned to Britain. (*The Cévennes Journal*, the complete diary of the trip, was published in 1979.)*

As with the earlier book critics spotted its 'charm' and its author's attention to detail, even though some baulked at his exaggeratedly cruel treatment of his donkey, Modestine (in the diary Stevenson appeared to be more self-consciously unkind to the donkey than he was prepared to admit in the published *Travels*). The descriptions of the Camisards, those Protestant rebels who had held out against the French government in the early years of the eighteenth century, shows Stevenson at his best: no doubt because he was excited by their resemblance to the Covenanters he held in such high esteem. It was that

* J. Golding, ed., *The Cévennes Journal: Notes of a Journey through the French Highlands*, by Robert Louis Stevenson (Edinburgh, 1979).

underlying belief in the stern morality of the presbyterian tradition, too, that led him to react violently against the calm of the Trappist monastery at Vivarais. At its most facile his scanty treatment of the villages of Langogne and St Germain de Calberte show an impatience that is absent from his careful description of Monastier where it all began. Most surprisingly, there appears to be little remorse or anguish at Fanny's absence: Modestine becomes, though, a surrogate for life's ills, hence, perhaps, his less than gentle treatment of her. In that respect the book is so detached and the writing so carefully contrived that in some sections the reader could be forgiven for believing that Stevenson was not writing about himself but about another traveller he had met on the road.

In August 1879 a faintly hysterical telegram from Fanny sent Stevenson on a pell-mell journey from Scotland to New York by emigrant ship and thence by train across the continent to Monterey in California, an episode that found its expression in *The Amateur Emigrant* (1895). After a traumatic ten months, which included the first evidence of the haemorrhaging of the lungs that was to so disfigure his later life, Stevenson and Fanny were finally married in San Francisco on 19 May 1880. A few days later they left for a honeymoon in the Napa Valley where they set up temporary house in a shack at an old mining community called Silverado. Although the 'honeymoon', spent in the solitude of redwood forest and far enough removed from civilisation to be considered 'adventurous', only lasted some eight weeks the ambience of Silverado and the Napa Valley left an enduring impression on him. His account of the experience was begun the following winter in Switzerland (the Stevensons had returned to Britain in July and the greater part of their life together was to be spent in a search for a healthy environment for Louis).

The Silverado Squatters is a tender evocation of Stevenson's first days of married life and it also contains a vivid expression of their 'settler' existence in the old log cabin. There is a good deal of affected romance in those descriptions but some, such as his comparison of the fog in the valley with Noah's flood, are deftly drawn, and there is little doubt that he enjoyed the pose of a wild west rover. The book, though, is most notable for his new-found ability to make the characters he met in the valley spring into life. The vineyard owners, Schram and M'Eckron, the Jewish merchant, Kelmar, the poor white family, the Hansons, are all fully drawn characters. 'Quiet as he was,' he wrote of Rufe Hanson, 'there burned a deep, permanent excitement in his dark blue eyes; and when this grave man smiled, it was like sunshine in a shady place' (p. 261). Writing the book also helped him to put in proportion his love/hate for Scotland – his chapter 'The Scot Abroad' contains one of the finest descriptions of the pain of exile. Scotland might be a 'rainy sea-beat archipelago . . . and the wind squalls, and the salt showers fly and beat', but 'somehow life is warmer and closer; the hearth burns more redly; the lights of home shine softer on the rainy street; the very names, endeared in verse and music, cling nearer around our hearts' (p. 236). Earlier, he had flailed the city of his birth for its cold winters and equally austere morality:

> The weather is raw and boisterous in winter, shifty and ungenial in summer and downright meteorological purgatory in the spring. The delicate die early, and I, as a survivor, among bleak winds and plumping rain, have been sometimes tempted to envy them their fate.*

Now, six thousand miles away, he was able to place his feelings in greater perspective.

Of all Stevenson's travel books, *The Silverado Squatters* points the way to his later fiction. In the first two books he had learned his craft, an ability to describe landscape and atmosphere, and to view himself coolly and objectively. The California book taught him to characterise, in its pages he found his own voice, and it honed his style to the useful instrument with which he created his novels. It also, paradoxically, brought him home again to Scotland and cleared the way for those novels which are so rooted in Scottish atmosphere: *Kidnapped, The Master of Ballantrae, Weir of Hermiston* and *St Ives*.

It would be misleading, though, to see Stevenson's early travel books merely as harbingers for the later fiction. They stand in their own right as pieces of literature that have withstood the test of time and which offer us a highly personal insight into the life of a man with complicated and often contradictory swings of mood. Perhaps they do not aspire to the completeness of an essay by Montaigne or Addison, but they do underline

* *Edinburgh: Picturesque Notes*, 3.

Stevenson's abiding concern for language and style, and for the value of imaginative story-telling, the virtues which we associate with almost everything he wrote.

TREVOR ROYLE

NOTE ON THE TEXT

Texts taken from Tusitala Edition: *The Works of Robert Louis Stevenson*, 35 volumes (Heinemann, London, 1924)

An Inland Voyage

First published by C. Kegan Paul, London, 1878. Tusitala Edition 17.

Travels with a Donkey in the Cévennes

First published by C. Kegan Paul, London, 1879; with a frontispiece by Walter Crane. Tusitala Edition 17.

The Silverado Squatters

First published in *Century Magazine*, 7 November 1883; in book form by Chatto & Windus, London, 1884. Tusitala Edition 18.

AN INLAND
VOYAGE

Thus sang they in the English boat.

Marvell

TO
SIR WALTER GRINDLAY SIMPSON, Bart

My Dear 'Cigarette,'

It was enough that you should have shared so liberally in the rains and portages of our voyage; that you should have had so hard a paddle to recover the derelict *Arethusa* on the flooded Oise; and that you should thenceforth have piloted a mere wreck of mankind to Origny Sainte-Benoîte and a supper so eagerly desired. It was perhaps more than enough, as you once somewhat piteously complained, that I should have set down all the strong language to you, and kept the appropriate reflections for myself. I could not in decency expose you to share the disgrace of another and more public shipwreck. But now that this voyage of ours is going into a cheap edition, that peril, we shall hope, is at an end, and I may put your name on the burgee.

But I cannot pause till I have lamented the fate of our two ships. That, sir, was not a fortunate day when we projected the possession of a canal barge; it was not a fortunate day when we shared our day-dream with the most hopeful of day-dreamers. For a while, indeed, the world looked smilingly. The barge was procured and christened, and, as the *Eleven Thousand Virgins of Cologne*, lay for some months, the admired of all admirers, in a pleasant river and under the walls of an ancient town. M. Mattras, the accomplished carpenter of Moret, had made her a centre of emulous labour; and you will not have forgotten the amount of sweet champagne consumed in the inn at the bridge end, to give zeal to the workmen and speed to the work. On the financial aspect I would not willingly dwell. The *Eleven Thousand Virgins of Cologne* rotted in the stream where she was beautified. She felt not the impulse of the breeze; she was never harnessed to the patient track-horse. And when at length she was sold, by the indignant carpenter of Moret, there were sold along with her the *Arethusa* and the *Cigarette*, she of cedar, she, as we knew so keenly on a portage, of solid-hearted English oak. Now these historic vessels fly the tricolour and are known by new and alien names.

R.L.S.

PREFACE TO FIRST EDITION

To equip so small a book with a preface is, I am half afraid, to sin against proportion. But a preface is more than an author can resist, for it is the reward of his labours. When the foundation-stone is laid, the architect appears with his plans, and struts for an hour before the public eye. So with the writer in his preface: he may have never a word to say, but he must show himself for a moment in the portico, hat in hand, and with an urbane demeanour.

It is best, in such circumstances, to represent a delicate shade of manner between humility and superiority: as if the book had been written by some one else, and you had merely run over it and inserted what was good. But for my part I have not yet learned the trick to that perfection; I am not yet able to dissemble the warmth of my sentiments towards a reader; and if I meet him on the threshold, it is to invite him in with country cordiality.

To say truth, I had no sooner finished reading this little book in proof, than I was seized upon by a distressing apprehension. It occurred to me that I might not only be the first to read these pages, but the last as well; that I might have pioneered this very smiling tract of country all in vain, and find not a soul to follow in my steps. The more I thought, the more I disliked the notion; until the distaste grew into a sort of panic terror, and I rushed into this Preface, which is no more than an advertisement for readers.

What am I to say for my book? *Caleb* and *Joshua* brought back from *Palestine* a formidable bunch of grapes; alas! my book produces naught so nourishing; and for the matter of that, we live in an age when people prefer a definition to any quantity of fruit.

I wonder, would a negative be found enticing? for, from the negative point of view, I flatter myself this volume has a certain stamp. Although it runs to considerably upwards of two hundred pages, it contains not a single reference to the imbecility of *God's* universe, nor so much as a single hint that I could have made a better one myself. – I really do not know where my head can have been. I seem to have forgotten all that makes it glorious to be a man. – 'Tis an omission that renders the book philosophically unimportant; but I am in hopes the eccentricity may please in frivolous circles.

To the friend who accompanied me I owe many thanks already, indeed I wish I owed him nothing else; but at this moment I feel towards him an almost exaggerated tenderness. He, at least, will become my reader: – if it were only to follow his own travels alongside of mine

R.L.S.

CONTENTS

Antwerp to Boom

We made a great stir in *Antwerp Docks*. A stevedore and a lot
of dock porters took up the two canoes, and ran with them for
the slip. A crowd of children followed cheering. The *Cigarette*
went off in a splash and a bubble of small breaking water. Next
moment the *Arethusa* was after her. A steamer was coming
down, men on the paddle-box shouted hoarse warnings, the
stevedore and his porters were bawling from the quay. But in a
stroke or two the canoes were away out in the middle of the
Scheldt, and all steamers, and stevedores, and other 'long-shore
vanities were left behind.

The sun shone brightly; the tide was making – four jolly miles
an hour; the wind blew steadily, with occasional squalls. For
my part, I had never been in a canoe under sail in my life; and
my first experiment out in the middle of this big river was not
made without some trepidation. What would happen when the
wind first caught my little canvas? I suppose it was almost as
trying a venture into the regions of the unknown as to publish a
first book, or to marry. But my doubts were not of long
duration; and in five minutes you will not be surprised to learn
that I had tied my sheet.

I own I was a little struck by this circumstance myself; of
course, in company with the rest of my fellow-men, I had
always tied the sheet in a sailing-boat; but in so little and crank
a concern as a canoe, and with these charging squalls, I was
not prepared to find myself follow the same principle; and it
inspired me with some contemptuous views of our regard for
life. It is certainly easier to smoke with the sheet fastened; but I
had never before weighed a comfortable pipe of tobacco against
as obvious risk, and gravely elected for the comfortable pipe. It
is a commonplace, that we cannot answer for ourselves before
we have been tried. But it is not so common a reflection, and
surely more consoling, that we usually find ourselves a great
deal braver and better than we thought. I believe this is every

one's experience: but an apprehension that they may belie themselves in the future prevents mankind from trumpeting this cheerful sentiment abroad. I wish sincerely, for it would have saved me much trouble, there had been some one to put me in a good heart about life when I was younger; to tell me how dangers are most portentous on a distant sight; and how the good in a man's spirit will not suffer itself to be overlaid, and rarely or never deserts him in the hour of need. But we are all for tootling on the sentimental flute in literature; and not a man among us will go to the head of the march to sound the heady drums.

It was agreeable upon the river. A barge or two went past laden with hay. Reeds and willows bordered on the stream; and cattle and grey venerable horses came and hung their mild heads over the embankment. Here and there was a pleasant village among trees, with a noisy shipping yard; here and there a villa in a lawn. The wind served us well up the *Scheldt* and thereafter up the *Rupel*; and we were running pretty free when we began to sight the brickyards of *Boom*, lying for a long way on the right bank of the river. The left bank was still green and pastoral, with alleys of trees along the embankment, and here and there a flight of steps to serve a ferry, where perhaps there sat a woman with her elbows on her knees, or an old gentleman with a staff and silver spectacles. But *Boom* and its brickyards grew smokier and shabbier with every minute; until a great church with a clock, and a wooden bridge over the river, indicated the central quarters of the town.

Boom is not a nice place, and is only remarkable for one thing: that the majority of the inhabitants have a private opinion that they can speak English, which is not justified by fact. This gave a kind of haziness to our intercourse. As for the *Hôtel de la Navigation*, I think it is the worst feature of the place. It boasts of a sanded parlour, with a bar at one end, looking on the street; and another sanded parlour, darker and colder, with an empty birdcage and a tricolour subscription box by way of sole adornment, where we made shift to dine in the company of three uncommunicative engineer apprentices and a silent bagman. The food, as usual in *Belgium*, was of a nondescript occasional character; indeed I have never been able to detect anything in the nature of a meal among this pleasing people; they seem to peck and trifle with viands all day long in an amateur spirit: tentatively French, truly German, and somehow falling between the two.

The empty birdcage, swept and garnished, and with no trace of the old piping favourite, save where two wires had been pushed apart to hold its lump of sugar, carried with it a sort of graveyard cheer. The engineer apprentices would have nothing to say to us, nor indeed to the bagman; but talked low and sparingly to one another, or raked us in the gaslight with a gleam of spectacles. For though handsome lads, they were all (in the Scotch phrase) barnacled.

There was an English maid in the hotel, who had been long enough out of *England* to pick up all sorts of funny foreign idioms, and all sorts of curious foreign ways, which need not here be specified. She spoke to us very fluently in her jargon, asked us information as to the manners of the present day in *England*, and obligingly corrected us when we attempted to answer. But as we were dealing with a woman, perhaps our information was not so much thrown away as it appeared. The sex likes to pick up knowledge and yet preserve its superiority. It is good policy, and almost necessary in the circumstances. If a man finds a woman admire him, were it only for his acquaintance with geography, he will begin at once to build upon the admiration. It is only by unintermittent snubbing that the pretty ones can keep us in our place. Men, as Miss *Howe* or Miss *Harlowe* would have said, 'are such *encroachers*'. For my part, I am body and soul with the women; and after a well-married couple, there is nothing so beautiful in the world as the myth of the divine huntress. It is no use for a man to take to the woods; we know him; *Anthony* tried the same thing long ago, and had a pitiful time of it by all accounts. But there is this about some women, which overtops the best gymnosophist among men, that they suffice to themselves, and can walk in a high and cold zone without the countenance of any trousered being. I declare, although the reverse of a professed ascetic, I am more obliged to women for this ideal than I should be to the majority of them, or indeed to any but one, for a spontaneous kiss. There is nothing so encouraging as the spectable of self-sufficiency. And when I think of the slim and lovely maidens, running the woods all night to the note of *Diana's* horn; moving among the old oaks, as fancy-free as they; things of the forest and the starlight, not touched by the commotion of man's hot and turbid life –

although there are plenty other ideals that I should prefer – I find my heart beat at the thought of this one. 'Tis to fail in life, but to fail with what a grace! That is not lost which is not regretted. And where – here slips out the male – where would be much of the glory of inspiring love if there were no contempt to overcome?

On the Willebroek Canal

Next morning, when we set forth on the *Willebroek Canal*, the rain began heavy and chill. The water of the canal stood at about the drinking temperature of tea; and under this cold aspersion, the surface was covered with steam. The exhilaration of departure, and the easy motion of the boats under each stroke of the paddles, supported us through this misfortune while it lasted; and when the cloud passed and the sun came out again, our spirits went up above the range of stay-at-home humour. A good breeze rustled and shivered in the rows of trees that bordered the canal. The leaves flickered in and out of the light in tumultuous masses. It seemed sailing weather to eye and ear; but down between the banks, the wind reached us only in faint and desultory puffs. There was hardly enough to steer by. Progress was intermittent and unsatisfactory. A jocular person, of marine antecedents, hailed us from the towpath with a '*C'est vite, mais c'est long.*'

The canal was busy enough. Every now and then we met or overtook a long string of boats, with great green tillers; high sterns with a window on either side of the rudder, and perhaps a jug or a flower-pot in one of the windows; a dinghy following behind; a woman busied about the day's dinner, and a handful of children. These barges were all tied one behind the other with tow-ropes, to the number of twenty-five or thirty; and the line was headed and kept in motion by a steamer of strange construction. It had neither paddle-wheel nor screw; but by some gear not rightly comprehensible to the unmechanical mind, it fetched up over its bow a small bright chain which lay along the bottom of the canal, and paying it out again over the stern, dragged itself forward, link by link, with its whole retinue of loaded scows. Until one had found out the key to the enigma, there was something solemn and uncomfortable in the progress of one of these trains, as it moved gently along the water with nothing to mark its advance but an eddy alongside dying away into the wake.

Of all the creatures of commercial enterprise, a canal barge is by far the most delightful to consider. It may spread its sails, and then you see it sailing high above the tree-tops and the windmill, sailing on the aqueduct, sailing through the green corn-lands: the most picturesque of things amphibious. Or the horse plods along at a foot-pace as if there were no such thing as business in the world; and the man dreaming at the tiller sees the same spire on the horizon all day long. It is a mystery how things ever get to their destination at this rate; and to see the barges waiting their turn at a lock affords a fine lesson of how easily the world may be taken. There should be many contented spirits on board, for such a life is both to travel and to stay at home.

The chimney smokes for dinner as you go along; the banks of the canal slowly unroll their scenery to contemplative eyes; the barge floats by great forests and through great cities with their public buildings and their lamps at night; and for the bargee, in his floating home, 'travelling abed,' it is merely as if he were listening to another man's story or turning the leaves of a picture-book in which he had no concern. He may take his afternoon walk in some foreign country on the banks of the canal, and then come home to dinner at his own fire-side.

There is not enough in such a life for any high measure of health; but a high measure of health is only necessary for unhealthy people. The slug of a fellow, who is never ill nor well, has a quiet time of it in life, and dies all the easier.

I am sure I would rather be a bargee than occupy any position under Heaven that required attendance at an office. There are few callings, I should say, where a man gives up less of his liberty in return for regular meals. The bargee is on shipboard – he is master in his own ship – he can land whenever he will – he can never be kept beating off a lee-shore a whole frosty night when the sheets are as hard as iron; and so far as I can make out, time stands as nearly still with him as is compatible with the return of bed-time or the dinner-hour. It is not easy to see why a bargee should ever die.

Half-way between *Willebroek* and *Villevorde*, in a beautiful reach of canal like a squire's avenue, we went ashore to lunch. There were two eggs, a junk of bread, and a bottle of wine on

board the *Arethusa*; and two eggs and an Etna cooking appara-
tus on board the *Cigarette*. The master of the latter boat
smashed one of the eggs in the course of disembarkation; but
observing pleasantly that it might still be cooked *à la papier*, he
dropped it into the Etna, in its covering of Flemish newspaper.
We landed in a blink of fine weather; but we had not been two
minutes ashore before the wind freshened into half a gale, and
the rain began to patter on our shoulders. We sat as close about
the Etna as we could. The spirits burned with great ostentation;
the grass caught flame every minute or two, and had to be
trodden out; and before long there were several burnt fingers of
the party. But the solid quantity of cookery accomplished was
out of proportion with so much display; and when we desisted,
after two applications of the fire, the sound egg was little more
than loo-warm; and as for *à la papier*, it was a cold and sordid
fricassée of printer's ink and broken egg-shell. We made shift to
roast the other two, by putting them close to the burning spirits;
and that with better success. And then we uncorked the bottle
of wine, and sat down in a ditch with our canoe aprons over
our knees. It rained smartly. Discomfort, when it is honestly
uncomfortable and makes no nauseous pretensions to the contrary, is a vastly humorous business; and people well steeped
and stupefied in the open air are in a good vein for laughter.
From this point of view, even egg *à la papier* offered by way of
food may pass muster as a sort of accessory to the fun. But this
manner of jest, although it may be taken in good part, does not
invite repetition; and from that time forward, the Etna voyaged
like a gentleman in the locker of the *Cigarette*.

It is almost unnecessary to mention that when lunch was over
and we got aboard again and made sail, the wind promptly died
away. The rest of the journey to *Villevorde* we still spread our
canvas to the unfavouring air; and with now and then a puff,
and now and then a spell of paddling, drifted along from lock
to lock, between the orderly trees.

It was a fine, green, fat landscape; or rather a mere green
water-lane, going on from village to village. Things had a settled
look, as in places long lived in. Crop-headed children spat upon
us from the bridges as we went below, with a true conservative
feeling. But even more conservative were the fishermen, intent
upon their floats, who let us go by without one glance. They
perched upon starlings and buttresses and along the slope of the

embankment gently occupied. They were indifferent like pieces of dead nature. They did not move any more than if they had been fishing in an old Dutch print. The leaves fluttered, the water lapped, but they continued in one stay like so many churches established by law. You might have trepanned every one of their innocent heads, and found no more than so much coiled fishing line below their skulls. I do not care for your stalwart fellows in india-rubber stockings breasting up mountain torrents with a salmon rod; but I do dearly love the class of man who plies his unfruitful art, for ever and a day, by still and depopulated waters.

At the last lock just beyond *Villevorde* there was a lock mistress who spoke French comprehensibly, and told us we were still a couple of leagues from *Brussels*. At the same place, the rain began again. It fell in straight, parallel lines; and the surface of the canal was thrown up into an infinity of little crystal fountains. There were no beds to be had in the neighbourhood. Nothing for it but to lay the sails aside and address ourselves to steady paddling in the rain.

Beautiful country houses, with clocks and long lines of shuttered windows, and fine old trees standing in groves and avenues, gave a rich and sombre aspect in the rain and the deepening dusk to the shores of the canal. I seem to have seen something of the same effect in engravings; opulent landscapes, deserted and overhung with the passage of storm. And throughout we had the escort of a hooded cart, which trotted shabbily along the tow-path, and kept at an almost uniform distance in our wake.

The Royal Sport Nautique

The rain took off near *Laeken*. But the sun was already down; the air was chill; and we had scarcely a dry stitch between the pair of us. Nay, now we found ourselves near the end of the *Allée Verte*, and on the very threshold of *Brussels* we were confronted by a serious difficulty. The shores were closely lined by canal boats waiting their turn at the lock. Nowhere was there any convenient landing-place; nowhere so much as a stable-yard to leave the canoes in for the night. We scrambled ashore and entered an *estaminet* where some sorry fellows were drinking with the landlord. The landlord was pretty round with us; he knew of no coach-house or stable-yard, nothing of the sort; and seeing we had come with no mind to drink, he did not conceal his impatience to be rid of us. One of the sorry fellows came to the rescue. Somewhere in the corner of the basin there was a slip, he informed us, and something else besides, not very clearly defined by him, but hopefully construed by his hearers.

Sure enough there was the slip in the corner of the basin; and at the top of it two nice-looking lads in boating clothes. The *Arethusa* addressed himself to these. One of them said there would be no difficulty about a night's lodging for our boats; and the other, taking a cigarette from his lips, inquired if they were made by *Searle and Son*. The name was quite an introduction. Half a dozen other young men came out of a boat-house bearing the subscription ROYAL SPORT NAUTIQUE, and joined in the talk. They were all very polite, voluble and enthusiastic; and their discourse was interlarded with English boating terms, and the names of English boat-builders and English clubs. I do not know, to my shame, any spot in my native land where I should have been so warmly received by the same number of people. We were English boating-men, and the Belgian boating-men fell upon our necks. I wonder if French Huguenots were as cordially greeted by English Protestants when they came across the

Channel out of great tribulation. But after all, what religion knits people so closely as a common sport?

The canoes were carried into the boat-house; they were washed down for us by the Club servants, the sails were hung out to dry, and everything made as snug and tidy as a picture. And in the meanwhile we were led upstairs by our new-found brethren, for so more than one of them stated the relationship, and made free of their lavatory. This one lent us soap, that one a towel, a third and fourth helped us to undo our bags. And all the time such questions, such assurances of respect and sympathy! I declare I never knew what glory was before.

'Yes, yes, the *Royal Sport Nautique* is the oldest club in *Belgium*.'

'We number two hundred.'

'We' – this is not a substantive speech, but an abstract of many speeches, the impression left upon my mind after a great deal of talk; and very youthful, pleasant, natural and patriotic it seems to me to be – 'We have gained all races, except those where we were cheated by the *French*.'

'You must leave all your wet things to be dried.'

'O! *entre frères*! In any boat-house in *England* we should find the same.' (I cordially hope they might.)

'*En angleterre, vous employez des* sliding-seats, *n'est-ce pas*?'

'We are all employed in commerce during the day; but in the evening, *voyez vous, nous sommes sérieux*.'

These were the words. They were all employed over the frivolous mercantile concerns of *Belgium* during the day; but in the evening they found some hours for the serious concerns of life. I may have a wrong idea of wisdom, but I think that was a very wise remark. People connected with literature and philosophy are busy all their days in getting rid of second-hand notions and false standards. It is their profession, in the sweat of their brows, by dogged thinking, to recover their old fresh view of life, and distinguish what they really and originally like from what they have only learned to tolerate perforce. And these *Royal Nautical Sportsmen* had the distinction still quite legible in their hearts. They had still those clean perceptions of what is nice and nasty, what is interesting and what is dull, which envious old gentlemen refer to as illusions. The nightmare illusion of middle age, the bear's hug of custom gradually squeezing the life out of a man's soul, had not yet begun for these happy-star'd young *Belgians*. They still knew that the interest they took in their business was a trifling affair compared to their spontaneous, long-suffering affection for nautical sports. To know what you prefer, instead of humbly saying Amen to what the world tells you you ought to prefer, is to have kept your soul alive. Such a man may be generous! he may be honest in something more than the commercial sense; he may love his friends with an elective, personal sympathy, and not accept them as an adjunct of the station to which he has been called. He may be a man, in short, acting on his own instincts, keeping his own shape that *God* made him in; and not a mere crank in the social engine-house, welded on principles that he does not understand, and for purposes that he does not care for.

For will anyone dare to tell me that business is more entertaining than fooling among boats? He must have never seen a boat, or never seen an office, who says so. And for certain the one is a great deal better for the health. There should be nothing so much a man's business as his amusements. Nothing but money-grubbing can be put forward to the contrary; no one but

> Mammon, the least erected spirit that fell
> From Heaven,

durst risk a word in answer. It is but a lying cant that would represent the merchant and the banker as people disinterestedly toiling for mankind, and then most useful when they are more absorbed in their transaction; for the man is more important than his services. And when my *Royal Nautical Sportsman* shall have so far fallen from his hopeful youth that he cannot pluck up an enthusiasm over anything but his ledger, I venture to doubt whether he will be near so nice a fellow, and whether he would welcome, with so good a grace, a couple of drenched *Englishmen* paddling into *Brussels* in the dusk.

When we had changed our wet clothes and drunk a glass of pale ale to the Club's prosperity, one of their number escorted us to an hotel. He would not join us at our dinner, but he had no objection to a glass of wine. Enthusiasm is very wearing; and I begin to understand why prophets were unpopular in *Judæa*, where they were best known. For three stricken hours did this excellent young man sit beside us to dilate on boats and boat-races; and before he left he was kind enough to order our bedroom candles.

We endeavoured now and again to change the subject; but the diversion did not last a moment, the *Royal Nautical Sportsman* bridled, shied, answered the question, and then breasted once more into the swelling tide of his subject. I call it his subject; but I think it was he who was subjected. The *Arethusa*, who holds all racing as a creature of the devil, found himself in a pitiful dilemma. He durst not own his ignorance for the honour of Old *England*, and spoke away about English clubs and English oarsmen, whose fame had never before come to his ears. Several times, and, once above all, on the question of sliding-seats, he was within an ace of exposure. As for the *Cigarette*, who has rowed races in the heat of his blood, but now disowns these slips of his wanton youth, his case was still more desperate; for the *Royal Nautical* proposed that he should take an oar in one of their eights on the morrow, to compare the English with the Belgian stroke. I could see my friend perspiring in his chair whenever that particular topic came up. And there was yet another proposal which had the same effect on both of us. It appeared that the champion canoeist of *Europe* (as well as most other champions) was a *Royal Nautical Sportsman*. And if we would only wait until the *Sunday*, this infernal paddler would be so condescending as to accompany us on our next stage. Neither of us had the least desire to drive the coursers of the sun against *Apollo*.

When the young man was gone, we countermanded our candles, and ordered some brandy and water. The great billows had gone over our head. The *Royal Nautical Sportsmen* were as nice young fellows as a man would wish to see, but they were a trifle too young and a thought too nautical for us. We began to see that we were old and cynical; we liked ease and the agreeable rambling of the human mind about this and the other subject; we did not want to disgrace our native land by messing an eight, or toiling pitifully in the wake of the champion canoeist. In short, we had recourse to flight. It seemed ungrateful, but we tried to make that good on a card loaded with sincere compliments. And indeed it was no time for scruples; we seemed to feel the hot breath of the champion on our necks.

At Maubeuge

Partly from the terror we had of our good friends the *Royal Nauticals*, partly from the fact that there were no fewer than fifty-five locks between *Brussels* and *Charleroi*, we concluded that we should travel by train across the frontier, boats and all. Fifty-five locks in a day's journey was pretty well tantamount to trudging the whole distance on foot, with the canoes upon our shoulders, an object of astonishment to the trees on the canal side, and of honest derision to all right-thinking children.

To pass the frontier, even in a train, is a difficult matter for the *Arethusa*. He is somehow or other a marked man for the official eye. Wherever he journeys, there are the officers gathered together. Treaties are solemnly signed, foreign ministers, ambassadors, and consuls sit throned in state from *China* to *Peru*, and the Union Jack flutters on all the winds of heaven. Under these safeguards, portly clergymen, school-mistresses, gentlemen in grey tweed suits, and all the ruck and rabble of British touristry pour unhindered, *Murray* in hand, over the railways of the Continent, and yet the slim person of the *Arethusa* is taken in the meshes, while these great fish go on their way rejoicing. If he travels without a passport, he is cast, without any figure about the matter, into noisome dungeons: if his papers are in order, he is suffered to go his way indeed, but not until he has been humiliated by a general incredulity. He is a born British subject, yet he has never succeeded in persuading a single official of his nationality. He flatters himself he is indifferent honest; yet he is rarely taken for anything better than a spy, and there is no absurd and disreputable means of livelihood but has been attributed to him in some heat of official or popular distrust. . . .

For the life of me I cannot understand it. I too have been knolled to church, and sat at good men's feasts; but I bear no mark of it. I am as strange as a Jack Indian to their official spectacles. I might home from any part of the globe, it seems, except from where I do. My ancestors have laboured in vain, and the glorious Constitution cannot protect me in my walks abroad. It is a great thing, believe me, to present a good normal type of the nation you belong to.

Nobody else was asked for his papers on the way to *Maubeuge*; but I was; and although I clung to my rights, I had to choose at last between accepting the humiliation and being left behind by the train. I was sorry to give way; but I wanted to get to *Maubeuge*.

Maubeuge is a fortified town, with a very good inn, the *Grand Cerf*. It seemed to be inhabited principally by soldiers and bagmen; at least, these were all that we saw, except the hotel servants. We had to stay there some time, for the canoes were in no hurry to follow us, and at last stuck hopelessly in the custom-house until we went back to liberate them. There was nothing to do, nothing to see. We had good meals, which was a great matter; but that was all.

The *Cigarette* was nearly taken up upon a charge of drawing the fortifications: a feat of which he was hopelessly incapable. And besides, as I suppose each belligerent nation has a plan of the other's fortified places already, these precautions are of the nature of shutting the stable door after the steed is away. But I have no doubt they help to keep up a good spirit at home. It is a great thing if you can persuade people that they are somehow or other partakers in a mystery. It makes them feel bigger. Even the Freemasons, who have been shown up to satiety, preserve a kind of pride; and not a grocer among them, however honest, harmless and empty-headed he may feel himself to be at bottom, but comes home from one of their cœnacula with a portentous significance for himself.

It is an odd thing, how happily two people, if there are two, can live in a place where they have no acquaintance. I think the spectacle of a whole life in which you have no part paralyses personal desire. You are content to become a mere spectator. The baker stands in his door; the colonel with his three medals goes by to the *café* at night; the troops drum and trumpet and man the ramparts, as bold as so many lions. It would task language to say how placidly you behold all this. In a place where you have taken some root, you are provoked out of your indifference; you have a hand in the game; your friends are fighting with the army. But in a strange town, not small enough to grow too soon familiar, nor so large as to have laid itself out for travellers, you stand so far apart from the business, that you positively forget it would be possible to go nearer; you have so little human interest around you, that you do not remember yourself to be a man. Perhaps, in a very short time, you would be one no longer! Gymnosophists go into a wood, with all Nature seething around them, with romance on every side; it would be much more to the purpose if they took up their abode in a dull country town, where they should see just so much of humanity as to keep them from desiring more, and only the stale externals of man's life. These externals are as dead to us as so many formalities, and speak a dead language in our eyes and ears. They have no more meaning than an oath or a salutation. We are so much accustomed to see married couples going to church of a *Sunday* that we have clean forgotten what they represent; and novelists are driven to rehabilitate adultery, no less, when they wish to show us what a beautiful thing it is for a man and a woman to live for each other.

One person in *Maubeuge*, however, showed me something more than his outside. That was the driver of the hotel omnibus: a mean-enough looking little man, as well as I can remember; but with a spark of something human in his soul. He had heard of our little journey, and came to me at once in envious sympathy. How he longed to travel! he told me. How he longed to be somewhere else, and see the round world before he went into the grave! 'Here I am,' said he. 'I drive to the station. Well. And then I drive back again to the hotel. And so on every day and all the week round. My *God*, is that life?' I could not say I thought it was – for him. He pressed me to tell him where I had been, and where I hoped to go; and as he listened, I declare the fellow sighed. Might not this have been a brave African traveller, or gone to the *Indies* after *Drake*? But it is an evil age for the gypsily inclined among men. He who can sit squarest on a three-legged stool, he it is who has the wealth and glory.

I wonder if my friend is still driving the omnibus for the *Grand Cerf*? Not very likely, I believe; for I think he was on the eve of mutiny when we passed through, and perhaps our passage determined him for good. Better a thousand times that he should be a tramp, and mend pots and pans by the wayside, and sleep under trees, and see the dawn and the sunset every day above a new horizon. I think I hear you say that it is a respectable position to drive an omnibus? Very well. What right has he who likes it not to keep those who would like it dearly out of this respectable position? Suppose a dish were not to my taste, and you told me that it was a favourite among the rest of the company, what should I conclude from that? Not to finish the dish against my stomach, I suppose.

Respectability is a very good thing in its way, but it does not rise superior to all considerations. I would not for a moment venture to hint that it was a matter of taste; but I think I will go as far as this: that if a position is admittedly unkind, uncomfortable, unnecessary, and superfluously useless, although it were as respectable as the Church of *England*, the sooner a man is out of it, the better for himself and all concerned.

On the Sambre Canalised:
To Quartes

About three in the afternoon the whole establishment of the *Grand Cerf* accompanied us to the water's edge. The man of the omnibus was there with haggard eyes. Poor cagebird! Do I not remember the time when I myself haunted the station, to watch train after train carry its complement of freemen into the night, and read the names of distant places on the time-bills with indescribable longings?

We were not clear of the fortifications before the rain began. The wind was contrary, and blew in furious gusts; nor were the aspects of Nature any more clement than the doings of the sky. For we passed through a sketch of blighted country, sparsely covered with brush, but handsomely enough diversified with factory chimneys. We landed in a soiled meadow among some pollards, and there smoked a pipe in a flaw of fair weather. But the wind blew so hard, we could get little else to smoke. There were no natural objects in the neighbourhood, but some sordid workshops. A group of children headed by a tall girl stood and watched us from a little distance all the time we stayed. I heartily wonder what they thought of us.

At *Hautmont*, the lock was almost impassable! the landing-place being steep and high, and the launch at a long distance. Near a dozen grimy workmen lent us a hand. They refused any reward; and, what is much better, refused it handsomely, without conveying any sense of insult. 'It is a way we have in our countryside,' said they. And a very becoming way it is. In *Scotland*, where also you will get services for nothing, the good people reject your money as if you had been trying to corrupt a voter. When people take the trouble to do dignified acts, it is worth while to take a little more, and allow the dignity to be common to all concerned. But in our brave Saxon countries, where we plod threescore years and ten in the mud, and the wind keeps singing in our ears from birth to burial, we do our good and bad with a high hand and almost offensively; and

make even our alms a witness-bearing and an act of war against
the wrong.

After *Hautmont*, the sun came forth again and the wind went
down; and a little paddling took us beyond the iron-works and
through a delectable land. The river wound among low hills, so
that sometimes the sun was at our backs, and sometimes it stood
right ahead, and the river before us was one sheet of intolerable
glory. On either hand, meadows and orchards bordered, with a
margin of sedge and water flowers, upon the river. The hedges
were of great height, woven about the trunks of hedgerow elms;
and the fields, as they were often very small, looked like a series
of bowers along the stream. There was never any prospect;
sometimes a hill-top with its trees would look over the nearest
hedgerow, just to make a middle distance for the sky; but that
was all. The heaven was bare of clouds. The atmosphere, after
the rain, was of enchanting purity. The river doubled among the
hillocks, a shining strip of mirror glass; and the dip of the
paddles set the flowers shaking along the brink.

In the meadows wandered black and white cattle fantastically
marked. One beast, with a white head and the rest of the body
glossy black, came to the edge to drink, and stood gravely
twitching his ears at me as I went by, like some sort of
preposterous clergyman in a play. A moment after I heard a
loud plunge, and, turning my head, saw the clergyman struggling
to shore. The bank had given way under his feet.

Besides the cattle, we saw no living things except a few birds
and a great many fishermen. These sat along the edges of the
meadows, sometimes with one rod, sometimes with as many as
half a score. They seemed stupefied with contentment; and when
we induced them to exchange a few words with us about the
weather, their voices sounded quiet and far-away. There was a
strange diversity of opinion among them as to the kind of fish
for which they set their lures; although they were all agreed in
this, that the river was abundantly supplied. Where it was plain
that no two of them had ever caught the same kind of fish, we
could not help suspecting that perhaps not any one of them had
ever caught a fish at all. I hope, since the afternoon was so
lovely, that they were one and all rewarded; and that a silver
booty went home in every basket for the pot. Some of my
friends would cry shame on me for this; but I prefer a man,
were he only an angler, to the bravest pair of gills in all *God's*

waters. I do not affect fishes unless when cooked in sauce; whereas an angler is an important piece of river scenery, and hence deserves some recognition among canoeists. He can always tell you where you are after a mild fashion; and his quiet presence serves to accentuate the solitude and stillness, and remind you of the glittering citizens below your boat.

The *Sambre* turned so industriously to and fro among his little hills, that it was past six before we drew near the lock at *Quartes*. There were some children on the tow-path, with whom the *Cigarette* fell into a chaffing talk as they ran along beside us. It was in vain that I warned him. In vain I told him, in English, that boys were the most dangerous creatures; and if once you began with them, it was safe to end in a shower of stones. For my own part, whenever anything was addressed to me, I smiled gently and shook my head as though I were an inoffensive person inadequately acquainted with French. For indeed I have had such experience at home, that I would sooner meet many wild animals than a troop of healthy urchins.

But I was doing injusticee to these peaceable young *Hainaulters*. When the *Cigarette* went off to make inquiries, I got out upon the bank to smoke a pipe and superintend the boats, and became at once the centre of much amiable curiosity. The children had been joined by this time by a young woman and a mild lad who had lost an arm; and this gave me more security. When I let slip my first word or so in French, a little girl nodded her head with a comical grown-up air. 'Ah, you see,' she said, 'he understands well enough now; he was just making believe.' And the little group laughed together very good-naturedly.

They were much impressed when they heard we came from *England*; and the little girl proffered the information that *England* was an island 'and a far way from here – *bien loin d'ici.*'

'Ay, you may say that, a far way from here,' said the lad with one arm.

I was as nearly homesick as ever I was in my life; they seemed to make it such an incalculable distance to the place where I first saw the day.

They admired the canoes very much. And I observed one piece of delicacy in these children which is worthy of record. They had been deafening us for the last hundred yards with petitions for a sail; ay, and they deafened us to the same tune the next morning when we came to start; but then, when the canoes were lying empty, there was no word of any such petition. Delicacy? or perhaps a bit of fear for the water in so crank a vessel? I hate cynicism a great deal worse than I do the devil; unless perhaps the two were the same thing? And yet 'tis a good tonic; the cold tub and bath-towel of the sentiments; and positively necessary to life in cases of advanced sensibility.

From the boats they turned to my costume. They could not make enough of my red sash; and my knife filled them with awe.

'They make them like that in *England*,' said the boy with one arm. I was glad he did not know how badly we make them in *England* nowadays. 'They are for people who go away to sea,' he added, 'and to defend one's life against great fish.'

I felt I was becoming a more and more romantic figure to the little group at every word. And so I suppose I was. Even my pipe, although it was an ordinary French clay, pretty well 'trousered,' as they call it, would have been a rarity in their eyes, as a thing coming from so far away. And if my feathers were not very fine in themselves, they were all from overseas. One thing in my outfit, however, tickled them out of all politeness; and that was the bemired condition of my canvas shoes. I suppose they were sure the mud at any rate was a home product. The little girl (who was the genius of the party) displayed her own sabots in competition; and I wish you could have seen how gracefully and merrily she did it.

The young woman's milk can, a great amphora of hammered brass, stood some way off upon the sward. I was glad of an opportunity to divert public attention from myself, and return some of the compliments I had received. So I admired it cordially both for form and colour, telling them, and very truly, that it was as beautiful as gold. They were not surprised. The things were plainly the boast of the countryside. And the children expatiated on the coastlines of these amphoræ, which sell sometimes as high as thirty francs apiece; told me how they were carried on donkeys, one on either side of the saddle, a brave caparison in themselves; and how they were to be seen all over the district, and at the larger farms in great number and of great size.

Pont-sur-Sambre
We are Pedlars

The *Cigarette* returned with good news. There were beds to be had some ten minutes' walk from where we were, at a place called *Pont*. We stowed the canoes in a granary, and asked among the children for a guide. The circle at once widened round us, and our offers of reward were received in dispiriting silence. We were plainly a pair of *Bluebeards* to the children; they might speak to us in public places, and where they had the advantage of numbers; but it was another thing to venture off alone with two uncouth and legendary characters, who had dropped from the clouds upon their hamlet this quiet afternoon, sashed and beknived, and with a flavour of great voyages. The owner of the granary came to our assistance, singled out one little fellow and threatened him with corporalities; or I suspect we should have had to find the way for ourselves. As it was, he was more frightened at the granary man than the strangers, having perhaps had some experience of the former. But I fancy his little heart must have been going at a fine rate; for he kept trotting at a respectful distance in front, and looking back at us with scared eyes. Not otherwise may the children of the young world have guided *Jove* or one of his *Olympian* compeers on an adventure.

A miry lane led up from *Quartes* with its church and bickering windmill. The hinds were trudging homewards from the fields. A brisk little old woman passed us by. She was seated across a donkey between a pair of glittering milk cans; and, as she went, she kicked jauntily with her heels upon the donkey's side, and scattered shrill remarks among the wayfarers. It was notable that none of the tired men took the trouble of reply. Our conductor soon led us out of the lane and across country. The sun had gone down, but the west in front of us was one lake of level gold. The path wandered a while in the open, and then passed under a trellis like a bower indefinitely prolonged. On either hand were shadowy orchards; cottages lay low among the leaves and sent their smoke to heaven; every here and there, in an opening, appeared the great gold face of the west.

I never saw the *Cigarette* in such an idyllic frame of mind. He waxed positively lyrical in praise of country scenes. I was little less exhilarated myself; the mild air of the evening, the shadows, the rich lights and the silence, made a symphonious accompaniment about our walk; and we both determined to avoid towns for the future and sleep in hamlets.

At last the path went between two houses, and turned the party out into a wide muddy high-road, bordered, as far as the eye could reach on either hand, by an unsightly village. The houses stood well back, leaving a ribbon of waste land on either side of the road, where there were stacks of firewood, carts, barrows, rubbish heaps, and a little doubtful grass. Away on the left, a gaunt tower stood in the middle of the street. What it had been in past ages I know not: probably a hold in time of war; but nowadays it bore an illegible dial-plate in its upper parts, and near the bottom an iron letter-box.

The inn to which we had been recommended at *Quartes* was full, or else the landlady did not like our looks. I ought to say, that with our long, damp india-rubber bags we presented rather a doubtful type of civilisation; like rag and bone men, the *Cigarette* imagined. 'These gentlemen are pedlars? – *Ces messieurs sont des marchands*?' – asked the landlady. And then, without waiting for an answer, which I suppose she thought superfluous in so plain a case, recommended us to a butcher who lived hard by the tower and took in travellers to lodge.

Thither went we. But the butcher was flitting, and all his beds were taken down. Or else he didn't like our look. As a parting shot, we had 'These gentlemen are pedlars?'

It began to grow dark in earnest. We could no longer distinguish the faces of the people who passed us by with an inarticulate 'Good evening.' And the householders of *Pont* seemed very economical with their oil; for we saw not a single window lighted in all that long village. I believe it is the longest village in the world; but I daresay in our predicament every pace counted three times over. We were much cast down when we came to the last *auberge*; and looking in at the dark door, asked timidly if we could sleep there for the night. A female voice assented in no very friendly tones. We clapped the bags down and found our way to chairs.

The place was in total darkness, save a red glow in the chinks and ventilators of the stove. But now the landlady lit a lamp to see her new guests; I suppose the darkness was what saved us another expulsion; for I cannot say she looked gratified at our appearance. We were in a large bare apartment, adorned with two allegorical prints of *Music* and *Painting*, and a copy of the Law against Public Drunkenness. On one side there was a bit of a bar, with some half a dozen bottles. Two labourers sat waiting supper in attitudes of extreme weariness; a plain-looking lass bustled about with a sleepy child of two; and the landlady began to derange the pots upon the stove and set some beefsteak to grill.

'These gentlemen are pedlars?' she asked sharply. And that was all the conversation forthcoming. We began to think we might be pedlars after all. I never knew a population with so narrow a range of conjecture as the inn-keepers of *Pont-sur-Sambre*. But manners and bearing have not a wider currency than banknotes. You have only to get far enough out of your beat, and all your accomplished airs will go for nothing. These *Hainaulters* could see no difference between us and the average pedlar. Indeed we had some grounds for reflection while the steak was getting ready, to see how perfectly they accepted us at their own valuation, and how our best politeness and best efforts at entertainment seemed to fit quite suitably with the character of packmen. At least it seemed a good account of the profession in *France*, that even before such judges we could not beat them at our own weapons.

At last we were called to table. The two hinds (and one of them looked sadly worn and white in the face, as though sick with overwork and underfeeding) supped off a single plate of some sort of bread-berry, some potatoes in their jackets, a small cup of coffee sweetened with sugar candy, and one tumbler of swipes. The landlady, her son, and the lass aforesaid took the same. Our meal was quite a banquet by comparison. We had some beefsteak, not so tender as it might have been, some of the potatoes, some cheese, an extra glass of the swipes, and white sugar in our coffee.

You see what it is to be a gentleman – I beg your pardon, what it is to be a pedlar. It had not before occurred to me that a pedlar was a great man in a labourer's ale-house; but now that I had to enact that part for an evening, I found that so it was.

He has in his hedge quarters somewhat the same pre-eminency as the man who takes a private parlour in a hotel. The more you look into it, the more infinite are the class distinctions among men; and possibly, by a happy dispensation, there is no one at all at the bottom of the scale; no one but can find some superiority over somebody else, to keep up his pride withal.

We were pleased enough with our fare. Particularly the *Cigarette*; for I tried to make believe that I was amused with the adventure, tough beefsteak and all. According to the *Lucretian* maxim, our steak should have been flavoured by the look of the other people's bread-berry. But we did not find it so in practice. You may have a head knowledge that other people live more poorly than yourself, but it is not agreeable – I was going to say it is against the etiquette of the universe – to sit at the same table and pick your own superior diet from among their crusts. I had not seen such a thing done since the greedy boy at school with his birthday cake. It was odious enough to witness, I could remember; and I had never thought to play the part myself. But there again you see what it is to be a pedlar.

There is no doubt that the poorer classes in our country are much more charitably disposed than their superiors in wealth. And I fancy it must arise a great deal from the comparative indistinction of the easy and the not so easy in these ranks. A workman or a pedlar cannot shutter himself off from his less comfortable neighbours. If he treats himself to a luxury, he must do it in the face of a dozen who cannot. And what should more directly lead to charitable thoughts?... Thus the poor man, camping out in life, sees it as it is, and knows that every mouthful he puts in his belly has been wrenched out of the fingers of the hungry.

But at a certain stage of prosperity, as in a balloon ascent, the fortunate person passes through a zone of clouds, and sublunary matters are thenceforward hidden from his view. He sees nothing but the heavenly bodies, all in admirable order and positively as good as new. He finds himself surrounded in the most touching manner by the attentions of *Providence*, and compares himself involuntarily with the lilies and the skylarks. He does not precisely sing, of course; but then he looks so unassuming in his open *Landau*! If all the world dined at one table, this philosophy would meet with some rude knocks.

Pont-sur-Sambre
The Travelling Merchant

Like the lackeys in *Molière's* farce, when the true nobleman broke in on their high life below stairs, we were destined to be confronted with a real pedlar. To make the lesson still more poignant for fallen gentlemen like us, he was a pedlar of infinitely more consideration than the sort of scurvy fellows we were taken for: like a lion among mice, or a ship of war bearing down upon two cock-boats. Indeed, he did not deserve the name of pedlar at all: he was a travelling merchant.

I suppose it was about half-past eight when this worthy, Monsieur *Hector Gilliard of Maubeuge,* turned up at the ale-house door in a tilt-cart drawn by a donkey, and cried cheerily on the inhabitants. He was a lean, nervous flibbertigibbet of a man, with something the look of an actor, and something the look of a horse jockey. He had evidently prospered without any of the favours of education; for he adhered with stern simplicity to the masculine gender, and in the course of the evening passed off some fancy futures in a very florid style of architecture. With him came his wife, a comely young woman with her hair tied in a yellow kerchief, and their son, a little fellow of four, in a blouse and military *képi*. It was notable that the child was many degrees better dressed than either of the parents. We were informed he was already at a boarding school; but the holidays having just commenced, he was off to spend them with his parents on a cruise. An enchanting holiday occupation, was it not? to travel all day with father and mother in the tilt-cart full of countless treasures: the green country rattling by on either side, and the children in all the villages contemplating him with envy and wonder? It is better fun, during the holidays, to be the son of a travelling merchant, than son and heir of the greatest cotton spinner in creation. And as for being a reigning prince – indeed I never saw one if it was not master *Gilliard*!

While M. *Hector* and the son of the house were putting up the donkey, and getting all the valuables under lock and key, the landlady warmed up the remains of our beefsteak, and fried the cold potatoes in slices, and Madame *Gilliard* set herself to waken the boy, who had come far that day, and was peevish and dazzled by the light. He was no sooner awake than he began to prepare himself for supper by eating galette, unripe pears and cold potatoes – with, so far as I could judge, positive benefit to his appetite.

The landlady, fired with motherly emulation, awoke her own little girl; and the two children were confronted. Master *Gilliard* looked at her for a moment, very much as a dog looks at his own reflection in a mirror before he turns away. He was at that time absorbed in the galette. His mother seemed crestfallen that he should display so little inclination towards the other sex; and expressed her disappointment with some candour and a very proper reference to the influence of years.

Sure enough a time will come when he will pay more attention to the girls, and think a great deal less of his mother: let us hope she will like it as well as she seemed to fancy. But it is odd enough; the very women who profess most contempt for mankind as a sex, seem to find even its ugliest particulars rather lively and high-minded in their own sons.

The little girl looked longer and with more interest, probably because she was in her own house, while he was a traveller and accustomed to strange sights. And besides there was no galette in the case with her.

All the time of supper, there was nothing spoken of but my young lord. The two parents were both absurdly fond of their child. Monsieur kept insisting on his sagacity: how he knew all the children at school by name; and when this utterly failed on trial, how he was cautious and exact to a strange degree, and if asked anything, he would sit and think – and think, and if he did not know it, 'my faith, he wouldn't tell you at all – *ma foi, il ne vous le dira pas.*' Which is certainly a very high degree of caution. At intervals, M. *Hector* would appeal to his wife, with his mouth full of beefsteak, as to the little fellow's age at such or such a time when he had said or done something memorable; and I noticed that Madame usually pooh-poohed these inquiries. She herself was not boastful in her vein; but she never had her fill of caressing the child; and she seemed to take a gentle pleasure in recalling all that was fortunate in his little existence. No schoolboy could have talked more of the holidays which were just beginning and less of the black schooltime which must inevitably follow after. She showed, with a pride perhaps partly mercantile in origin, his pockets preposterously swollen with tops and whistles and string. When she called at a house in the way of business, it appeared he kept her company; and whenever a sale was made, received a sou out of the profit. Indeed they spoiled him vastly, these two good people. But they had an eye to his manners for all that, and reproved him for some little faults in breeding which occurred from time to time during supper.

On the whole, I was not much hurt at being taken for a pedlar. I might think that I ate with greater delicacy, or that my mistakes in French belonged to a different order; but it was plain that these distinctions would be thrown away upon the landlady and the two labourers. In all essential things, we and the *Gilliards* cut very much the same figure in the ale-house kitchen. M. *Hector* was more at home, indeed, and took a higher tone with the world; but that was explicable on the ground of his driving a donkey-cart, while we poor bodies tramped afoot. I daresay the rest of the company thought us dying with envy, though in no ill sense, to be as far up in the profession as the new arrival.

And of one thing I am sure: that everyone thawed and became more humanised and conversible as soon as these innocent people appeared upon the scene. I would not very readily trust the travelling merchant with any extravagant sum of money; but I am sure his heart was in the right place. In this mixed world, if you can find one or two sensible places in a man, above all, if you should find a whole family living together on such pleasant terms, you may surely be satisfied, and take the rest for granted; or, what is a great deal better, boldly make up your mind that you can do perfectly well without the rest; and that ten thousand bad traits cannot make a single good one any the less good.

It was getting late. M. *Hector* lit a stable lantern and went off to his cart for some arrangements; and my young gentleman proceeded to divest himself of the better part of his raiment, and play gymnastics on his mother's lap, and thence on to the floor, with accompaniment of laugher.

'Are you going to sleep alone?' asked the servant lass.

'There's a little fear of that,' says Master *Gilliard*.

'You sleep alone at school,' objected his mother. 'Come, come, you must be a man.'

But he protested that school was a different matter from the holidays; that there were dormitories at school; and silenced the discussion with kisses: his mother smiling, no one better pleased than she.

There certainly was, as he phrased it, very little fear that he should sleep alone, for there was but one bed for the trio. We, on our part, had firmly protested against one man's accommodation for two; and we had a double-bedded pen in the loft of the house, furnished, beside the beds, with exactly three hat pegs and one table. There was not so much as a glass of water. But the window would open, by good fortune.

Some time before I fell asleep the loft was full of the sound of mighty snoring: the *Gilliards*, and the labourers, and the people of the inn, all at it, I suppose, with one consent. The young moon outside shone very clearly over *Pont-sur-Sambre*, and down upon the ale-house where all we pedlars were abed.

On the Sambre Canalised:
To Landrecies

In the morning, when we came downstairs, the landlady pointed out to us two pails of water behind the street-door. '*Voilà de l'eau pour vous débarbouiller,*' says she. And so there we made shift to wash ourselves, while Madame *Gilliard* brushed the family boots on the outer doorstep, and M. *Hector*, whistling cheerily, arranged some small goods for the day's campaign in a portable chest of drawers, which formed a part of his baggage. Meanwhile the child was letting off *Waterloo* crackers all over the floor.

I wonder, by-the-by, what they call *Waterloo* crackers in *France*; perhaps *Austerlitz* crackers. There is a great deal in the point of view. Do you remember the *Frenchman* who, travelling by way of *Southampton*, was put down in *Waterloo* Station, and had to drive across *Waterloo* Bridge? He had a mind to go home again, it seems.

Pont itself is on the river, but whereas it is ten minutes' walk from *Quartes* by dry land, it is six weary kilometres by water. We left our bags at the inn, and walked to our canoes through the wet orchards unencumbered. Some of the children were there to see us off, but we were no longer the mysterious beings of the night before. A departure is much less romantic than an unexplained arrival in the golden evening. Although we might be greatly taken at a ghost's first appearance, we should behold him vanish with comparative equanimity.

The good folk of the inn at *Pont*, when we called there for the bags, were overcome with marvelling. At sight of these two dainty little boats, with a fluttering Union Jack on each, and all the varnish shining from the sponge, they began to perceive that they had entertained angels unawares. The landlady stood upon the bridge, probably lamenting she had charged so little; the son ran to and fro, and called out the neighbours to enjoy the sight; and we paddled away from quite a crowd of rapt

observers. These gentlemen pedlars, indeed! Now you see their
quality too late.

The whole day was showery, with occasional drenching
plumps. We were soaked to the skin, then partially dried in the
sun, then soaked once more. But there were some calm intervals,
and one notably, when we were skirting the forest of *Mormal*, a
sinister name to the ear, but a place most gratifying to sight and
smell. It looked solemn along the river-side, drooping its boughs
into the water, and piling them up aloft into a wall of leaves.
What is a forest but a city of Nature's own, full of hardy and
innocuous living things, where there is nothing dead and nothing
made with the hands, but the citizens themselves are the houses
and public monuments? There is nothing so much alive, and yet
so quiet, as a woodland; and a pair of people, swinging past in
canoes, feel very small and bustling by comparison.

And surely of all smells in the world, the smell of many trees
is the sweetest and most fortifying. The sea has a rude, pistolling
sort of odour, that takes you in the nostrils like snuff, and
carries with it a fine sentiment of open water and tall ships; but
the smell of a forest, which comes nearest to this in tonic quality,
surpasses it by many degrees in the quality of softness. Again,
the smell of the sea has little variety, but the smell of a forest is
infinitely changeful; it varies with the hour of the day not in
strength merely, but in character; and the different sorts of
trees, as you go from one zone of the wood to another, seem to
live among different kinds of atmosphere. Usually the resin of
the fir predominates. But some woods are more coquettish in
their habits; and the breath of the forest of *Mormal*, as it came
aboard upon us that showery afternoon, was perfumed with
nothing less delicate than sweetbriar.

I wish our way had always lain among woods. Trees are the
most civil society. An old oak that has been growing where he
stands since before the Reformation, taller than many spires,
more stately than the greater part of mountains, and yet a living
thing, liable to sicknesses and death, like you and me: is not
that in itself a speaking lesson in history? But acres on acres full
of such patriarchs contiguously rooted, their green tops billow-
ing in the wind, their stalwart younglings pushing up about their
knees: a whole forest, healthy and beautiful, giving colour to
the light, giving perfume to the air: what is this but the most
imposing piece in Nature's repertory? *Heine* wished to lie like

Merlin under the oaks of *Broceliande*. I should not be satisfied
with one tree; but if the wood grew together like a banyan
grove, I would be buried under the tap-root of the whole; my
parts should circulate from oak to oak; and my consciousness
should be diffused abroad in all the forest, and give a common
heart to that assembly of green spires, so that it also might
rejoice in its own loveliness and dignity. I think I feel a thousand
squirrels leaping from bough to bough in my vast mausoleum;
and the birds and the winds merrily coursing over its uneven
leafy surface.

Alas! the forest of *Mormal* is only a little bit of a wood, and
it was but for a little way that we skirted by its boundaries. And
the rest of the time the rain kept coming in squirts and the wind
in squalls, until one's heart grew weary of such fitful, scolding
weather. It was odd how the showers began when we had to
carry the boats over a lock, and must expose our legs. They
always did. This is a sort of thing that readily begets a personal
feeling against Nature. There seems no reason why the shower
should not come five minutes before or five minutes after, unless
you suppose an intention to affront you. The *Cigarette* had a
mackintosh which put him more or less above these contrarie-
ties. But I had to bear the brunt uncovered. I began to remember
that Nature was a woman. My companion, in a rosier temper,
listened with great satisfaction to my jeremiads, and ironically
concurred. He instanced, as a cognate matter, the action of the
tides, 'Which,' he said, 'was altogether designed for the confusion of canoeists, except in so far as it was calculated to minister
to a barren vanity on the part of the moon.'

At the last lock, some little way out of *Landreciens*, I refused
to go any further; and sat in a drift of rain by the side of the
bank, to have a reviving pipe. A vivacious old man, whom I take
to have been the devil, drew near and questioned me about our
journey. In the fulness of my heart, I laid bare our plans before
him. He said, it was the silliest enterprise that ever he heard of.
Why, did I not know, he asked me, that it was nothing but
locks, locks, locks, the whole way? not to mention that, at this
season of the year, we should find the *Oise* quite dry? 'Get into
a train, my little young man,' said he, 'and go you away home
to your parents.' I was so astounded at the man's malice, that I
could only stare at him in silence. A tree would never have
spoken to me like this. At last, I got out with some words. We

had come from *Antwerp* already, I told him, which was a good long way; and we should do the rest in spite of him. Yes, I said, if there were no other reason, I would do it now, just because he had dared to say we could not. The pleasant old gentleman looked at me sneeringly, made an allusion to my canoe, and marched off, wagging his head.

I was still inwardly fuming, when up came a pair of young fellows, who imagined I was the *Cigarette's* servant, on a comparison, I suppose, of my bare jersey with the other's mackintosh, and asked me many questions about my place and my master's character. I said he was a good enough fellow, but had this absurd voyage on the head. 'O no, no,' said one, 'you must not say that; it is not absurd; it is very courageous of him.' I believe these were a couple of angels sent to give me heart again. It was truly fortifying to reproduce all the old man's insinuations, as if they were original to me in my character of a malcontent footman, and have them brushed away like so many flies by these admirable young men.

When I recounted this affair to the *Cigarette*, 'They must have a curious idea of how English servants behave,' says he, dryly, 'for you treated me like a brute beast at the lock.'

I was a good deal mortified; but my temper had suffered, it is a fact.

At Landrecies

At *Landrecies* the rain still fell and the wind still blew; but we found a double-bedded room with plenty of furniture, real water-jugs with real water in them, and dinner: a real dinner, not innocent of real wine. After having been a pedlar for one night, and a butt for the elements during the whole of the next day, these comfortable circumstances fell on my heart like sunshine. There was an English fruiterer at dinner, travelling with a Belgian fruiterer; in the evening at the *café*, we watched our compatriot drop a good deal of money at corks; and I don't know why, but this pleased us.

It turned out that we were to see more of *Landrecies* than we expected; for the weather next day was simply bedlamite. It is not the place one would have chosen for a day's rest; for it consists almost entirely of fortifications. Within the ramparts, a few blocks of houses, a long row of barracks, and a church, figure, with what countenance they may, as the town. There seems to be no trade; and a shopkeeper from whom I bought a sixpenny flint and steel was so much affected, that he filled my pockets with spare flints into the bargain. The only public buildings that had any interest for us were the hotel and the *café*. But we visited the church. There lies Marshal *Clarke*. But as neither of us had ever heard of that military hero, we bore the associations of the spot with fortitude.

In all garrison towns, guard-calls, and *réveilles* and such like, make a fine romantic interlude in civic business. Bugles, and drums, and fifes, are of themselves most excellent things in nature; and when they carry the mind to marching armies, and the picturesque vicissitudes of war, they stir up something proud in the heart. But in a shadow of a town like *Landrecies*, with little else moving, these points of war made a proportionate commotion. Indeed, they were the only things to remember. It was just the place to hear the round going by at night in the darkness, with the solid tramp of men marching, and the startling reverberations of the drum. It reminded you that even this place was a point in the great warfaring system of *Europe*, and might on some future day be ringed about with cannon smoke and thunder, and make itself a name among strong towns.

The drum, at any rate, from its martial voice and notable physiological effect, nay even from its cumbrous and comical shape, stands alone among the instruments of noise. And if it be true, as I have heard it said, that drums are covered with asses' skin, what a picturesque irony is there in that! As if this long-suffering animal's hide had not been sufficiently belaboured during life, now by Lyonnese costermongers, now by presumptuous Hebrew prophets, it must be stripped from his poor hinder quarters after death, stretched on a drum, and beaten night after night round the streets of every garrison town in *Europe*. And up the heights of *Alma* and *Spicheren*, and whenever death has his red flag a-flying, and sounds his own potent tuck upon the cannons, there also must the drummer-boy, hurrying with white face over fallen comrades, batter and bemaul this slip of skin from the loins of peaceable donkeys.

Generally a man is never more uselessly employed than when he is at this trick of bastinadoing asses' hide. We know what effect it has in life, and how your dull ass will not mend his pace with beating. But in this state of mummy and melancholy survival of itself, when the hollow skin reverberates to the drummer's wrist, and each dub-a-dub goes direct to a man's heart, and puts madness there, and that disposition of the pulses which we, in our big way of talking, nickname Heroism: – is there not something in the nature of a revenge upon the donkey's persecutors? Of old, he might say, you drubbed me up hill and down dale, and I must endure; but now that I am dead, those dull thwacks that were scarcely audible in country lanes have become stirring music in front of the brigade; and for every blow that you lay on my old great-coat, you will see a comrade stumble and fall.

Not long after the drums had passed the *café*, the *Cigarette* and the *Arethusa* began to grow sleepy, and set out for the hotel which was only a door or two away. But although we had been somewhat indifferent to *Landrecies*, *Landrecies* had not been indifferent to us. All day, we learned, people had been running out between the squalls to visit our two boats. Hundreds of persons, so said report, although it fitted ill with our idea of the town – hundreds of persons had inspected them where they lay in a coal-shed. We were becoming lions in *Landrecies*, who had been only pedlars the night before in *Pont*.

And now, when we left the *café*, we were pursued and overtaken at the hotel door by no less a person than the *Juge de Paix*: a functionary, as far as I can make out, of the character of a Scotch *Sheriff Substitute*. He gave us his card and invited us to sup with him on the spot, very neatly, very gracefully, as *Frenchmen* can do these things. It was for the credit of *Landrecies*, said he; and although we knew very well how little credit we could do the place, we must have been churlish fellows to refuse an invitation so politely introduced.

The house of the Judge was close by; it was a well-appointed bachelor's establishment with a curious collection of old brass warming-pans upon the walls. Some of these were most elaborately carved. It seemed a picturesque idea for a collector. You could not help thinking how many nightcaps had wagged over these warming-pans in past generations; what jests may have been made, and kisses taken, while they were in service; and how often they had been uselessly paraded in the bed of death. If they could only speak, at what absurd, indecorous and tragical scenes had they not been present!

The wine was excellent. When we made the Judge our compliments upon a bottle, 'I do not give it you as my worst,' said he. I wonder when *Englishmen* will learn these hospitable graces. They are worth learning; they set off life, and make ordinary moments ornamental.

There were two other *Landreciens* present. One was the collector of something or other, I forget what; the other, we were told, was the principal notary of the place. So it happened that we all five more or less followed the law. At this rate, the talk was pretty certain to become technical. The *Cigarette* expounded the Poor Laws very magisterially. And a little later I found myself laying down the Scotch Law of Illegitimacy, of which I am glad to say I know nothing. The collector and the notary, who were both married men, accused the Judge, who was a bachelor, of having started the subject. He deprecated the charge, with a conscious, pleased air, just like all the men I have ever seen, be they French or English. How strange that we should all, in our unguarded moments, rather like to be thought a bit of a rogue with the women!

As the evening went on, the wine grew more to my taste; the spirits proved better than the wine; the company was genial. This was the highest water mark of popular favour on the whole cruise. After all, being in a Judge's house, was there not something semi-official in the tribute? And so, remembering what a great country *France* is, we did full justice to our entertainment. *Landrecies* had been a long while asleep before we returned to the hotel; and the sentries on the ramparts were already looking for daybreak.

Sambre and Oise Canal:
Canal Boats

Next day we made a late start in the rain. The Judge politely escorted us to the end of the lock under an umbrella. We had now brought ourselves to a pitch of humility in the matter of weather, not often attained except in the Scotch *Highlands*. A rag of blue sky or a glimpse of sunshine set our hearts singing; and when the rain was not heavy, we counted the day almost fair.

Long lines of barges lay one after another along the canal; many of them looking mighty spruce and ship-shape in their jerkin of *Archangel* tar picked out with white and green. Some carried gay iron railings, and quite a parterre of flower-pots. Children played on the decks, as heedless of the rain as if they had been brought up on *Loch Carron* side; men fished over the gunwale, some of them under umbrellas; women did their washing; and every barge boasted its mongrel cur by way of watch-dog. Each one barked furiously at the canoes, running alongside until he had got to the end of his own ship, and so passing on the word to the dog aboard the next. We must have seen something like a hundred of these embarkations in the course of that day's paddle, ranged one after another like the houses in a street; and from not one of them were we disappointed of this accompaniment. It was like visiting a menagerie, the *Cigarette* remarked.

These little cities by the canal side had a very odd effect upon the mind. They seemed, with their flower-pots and smoking chimneys, their washings and dinners, a rooted piece of Nature in the scene; and yet if only the canal below were to open, one junk after another would hoist sail or harness horses and swim away into all parts of *France*; and the impromptu hamlet would separate, house by house, to the four winds. The children who played together to-day by the *Sambre* and *Oise* Canal, each at his own father's threshold, when and where might they next meet?

For some time past the subject of barges had occupied a great deal of our talk, and we had projected an old age on the canals of *Europe*. It was to be the most leisurely of progresses, now on a swift river at the tail of a steamboat, now waiting horses for days together on some inconsiderable junction. We should be seen pottering on deck in all the dignity of years, our white beards falling into our laps. We were ever to be busied among paint-pots; so that there should be no white fresher, and no green more emerald than ours, in all the navy of the canals. There should be books in the cabin, and tobacco jars, and some old *Burgundy* as red as a *November* sunset and as odorous as a violet in *April*. There should be a flageolet whence the *Cigarette*, with cunning touch, should draw melting music under the stars; or perhaps, laying that aside, upraise his voice – somewhat thinner than of yore, and with here and there a quaver, or call it a natural grace note – in rich and solemn psalmody.

All this simmering in my mind, set me wishing to go aboard one of these ideal houses of lounging. I had plenty to choose from, as I coasted one after another, and the dogs bayed at me for a vagrant. At last I saw a nice old man and his wife looking at me with some interest, so I gave them good day and pulled up alongside. I began with a remark upon their dog, which had somewhat the look of a pointer; thence I slid into a compliment on Madame's flowers, and thence into a word in praise of their way of life.

If you ventured on such an experiment in *England* you would get a slap in the face at once. The life would be shown to be a vile one, not without a side shot at your better fortune. Now, what I like so much in *France* is the clear unflinching recognition by everybody of his own luck. They all know on which side their bread is buttered, and take a pleasure in showing it to others, which is surely the better part of religion. And they scorn to make a poor mouth over their poverty, which I take to be the better part of manliness. I have heard a woman in quite a better position at home, with a good bit of money in hand, refer to her own child with a horrid whine as 'a poor man's child.' I would not say such a thing to the Duke of *Westminster*. And the *French* are full of this spirit of independence. Perhaps it is the result of republican institutions, as they call them. Much more likely it is because there are so few people really poor that the whiners are not enough to keep each other in countenance.

The people on the barge were delighted to hear that I admired their state. They understood perfectly well, they told me, how Monsieur envied them. Without doubt Monsieur was rich; and in that case he might make a canal-boat as pretty as a villa – *joli comme un château*. And with that they invited me on board their own water villa. They apologised for their cabin; they had not been rich enough to make it as it ought to be.

'The fire should have been here, at this side,' explained the husband. 'Then one might have a writing-table in the middle – books – and' (comprehensively) 'all. It would be quite coquettish – *ça serait tout-à-fait coquet*.' And he looked about him as though the improvements were already made. It was plainly not the first time that he had thus beautified his cabin in imagination; and when next he makes a hit, I should expect to see the writing-table in the middle.

Madame had three birds in a cage. They were no great thing, she explained. Fine birds were so dear. They had sought to get a *Hollandais* last winter in *Rouen* (*Rouen*? thought I; and is this whole mansion, with its dogs and birds and smoking chimneys, so far a traveller as that? and as homely an object among the cliffs and orchards of the *Seine* as on the green plains of *Sambre*?) – they had sought to get a *Hollandais* last winter in *Rouen*; but these cost fifteen francs apiece – picture it – fifteen francs!

'*Pour un tout petit oiseau* – For quite a little bird,' added the husband.

As I continued to admire, the apologetics died away, and the good people began to brag of their barge, and their happy condition in life, as if they had been Emperor and Empress of the *Indies*. It was, in the Scotch phrase, a good hearing, and put me in good humour with the world. If people knew what an inspiriting thing it is to hear a man boasting, so long as he boasts of what he really has, I believe they would do it more freely and with a better grace.

They began to ask about our voyage. You should have seen how they sympathised. They seemed half ready to give up their barge and follow us. But these *canaletti* are only gypsies semi-domesticated. The semi-domestication came out in rather a pretty form. Suddenly Madame's brow darkened. '*Cependant*,' she began, and then stopped; and then began again by asking me if I were single?

'Yes,' said I.

'And your friend who went by just now ?'

He also was unmarried.

O then – all was well. She could not have wives left alone at home; but since there were no wives in the question, we were doing the best we could.

'To see about one in the world,' said the husband, '*il n'y a que ça* – there is nothing else worth while. A man, look you, who sticks in his own village like a bear,' he went on, – 'very well, he sees nothing. And then death is the end of all. And he has seen nothing.'

Madame reminded her husband of an *Englishman* who had come up this canal in a steamer.

'Perhaps Mr *Moens* in the *Ytene*,' I suggested.

'That's it,' assented the husband. 'He had his wife and family with him, and servants. He came ashore at all the locks and asked the name of the villages, whether from boatmen or lock-keepers; and then he wrote, wrote them down. O he wrote enormously ! I suppose it was a wager.'

A wager was a common enough explanation for our own exploits, but it seemed an original reason for taking notes.

The Oise in Flood

Before nine next morning the two canoes were installed on a light country cart at *Étreux*: and we were soon following them along the side of a pleasant valley full of hop-gardens and poplars. Agreeable villages lay here and there on the slope of the hill, notably *Tupigny*, with the hop-poles hanging their garlands in the very street, and the houses clustered with grapes. There was a faint enthusiasm on our passage; weavers put their heads to the windows; children cried out in ecstasy at sight of the two 'boaties – *barguettes*'; and bloused pedestrians, who were acquainted with our charioteer, jested with him on the nature of his freight.

We had a shower or two, but light and flying. The air was clean and sweet among all these green fields and green things growing. There was not a touch of autumn in the weather. And when, at *Vadencourt*, we launched from a little lawn opposite a mill, the sun broke forth and set all the leaves shining in the valley of the *Oise*.

The river was swollen with the long rains. From *Vadencourt* all the way to *Origny* it ran with ever-quickening speed, taking fresh heart at each mile, and racing as though it already smelt the sea. The water was yellow and turbulent, swung with an angry eddy among half-submerged willows, and made an angry clatter along stony shores. The course kept turning and turning in a narrow and well-timbered valley. Now, the river would approach the side, and run gliding along the chalky base of the hill, and show us a few open colza fields among the trees. Now, it would skirt the garden-walls of houses, where we might catch a glimpse through a doorway, and see a priest pacing in the chequered sunlight. Again, the foliage closed so thickly in front, that there seemed to be no issue; only a thicket of willows, overtopped by elms and poplars, under which the river ran flush and fleet, and where a kingfisher flew past like a piece of the blue sky. On these different manifestations the sun poured its clear and catholic looks. The shadows lay as solid on the swift surface of the stream as on the stable meadows. The light sparkled golden in the dancing poplar leaves, and brought the hills into communion with our eyes. And all the while the river never stopped running or took breath; and the reeds along the whole valley stood shivering from top to toe.

There should be some myth (but if there is, I know it not) founded on the shivering of the reeds. There are not many things in Nature more striking to man's eye. It is such an eloquent pantomime of terror; and to see such a number of terrified creatures taking sanctuary in every nook along the shore, is enough to infect a silly human with alarm. Perhaps they are only a-cold, and no wonder, standing waist deep in the stream. Or perhaps they have never got accustomed to the speed and fury of the river's flux, or the miracle of its continuous body. *Pan* once played upon their forefathers; and so, by the hands of his river, he still plays upon these later generations down all the valley of the *Oise*; and plays the same air, both sweet and shrill, to tell us of the beauty and the terror of the world.

The canoe was like a leaf in the current. It took it up and shook it, and carried it masterfully away, like a Centaur carrying off a nymph. To keep some command on our direction required hard and diligent plying of the paddle. The river was in such a hurry for the sea! Every drop of water ran in a panic, like as many people in a frightened crowd. But what crowd was ever so numerous, or so single-minded? All the objects of sight went by at a dance measure; the eyesight raced with the racing river; the exigencies of every moment kept the pegs screwed so tight, that our being quivered like a well-tuned instrument; and the blood shook off its lethargy, and trotted through all the highways and byways of the veins and arteries, and in and out of the heart, as if circulation were but a holiday journey, and not the daily moil of threescore years and ten. The reeds might nod their heads in warning, and with tremulous gestures tell how the river was as cruel as it was strong and cold, and how death lurked in the eddy underneath the willows. But the reeds had to stand where they were; and those who stand still are always timid advisers. As for us, we could have shouted aloud. If this lively and beautiful river were, indeed, a thing of death's contrivance, the old ashen rogue had famously outwitted himself with us. I was living three to the minute. I was scoring points against him every stroke of my paddle, every turn of the stream. I have rarely had better profit of my life.

For I think we may look upon our little private war with death somewhat in this light. If a man knows he will sooner or later be robbed upon a journey, he will have a bottle of the best in every inn, and look upon all his extravagances as so much gained upon the thieves. And above all, where instead of simply spending, he makes a profitable investment for some of his money, when it will be out of risk of loss. So every bit of brisk living, and above all when it is healthful, is just so much gained upon the wholesale filcher, death. We shall have the less in our pockets, the more in our stomach, when he cries stand and deliver. A swift stream is a favourable artifice of his, and one that brings him in a comfortable thing per annum; but when he and I come to settle our accounts, I shall whistle in his face for these hours upon the upper *Oise*.

Towards afternoon we got fairly drunken with the sunshine and the exhilaration of the pace. We could no longer contain ourselves and our content. The canoes were too small for us; we must be out and stretch ourselves on shore. And so in a green meadow we bestowed our limbs on the grass, and smoked deifying tobacco and proclaimed the world excellent. It was the last good hour of the day, and I dwell upon it with extreme complacency.

On one side of the valley, high upon the chalky summit of the hill, a ploughman with his team appeared and disappeared at regular intervals. At each revelation he stood still for a few seconds against the sky: for all the world (as the *Cigarette* declared) like a toy *Burns* who had just ploughed up the *Mountain Daisy*. He was the only living thing within view, unless we are to count the river.

On the other side of the valley a group of red roofs and a belfry showed among the foliage. Thence some inspired bell-ringer made the afternoon musical on a chime of bells. There was something very sweet and taking in the air he played; and we thought we had never heard bells speak so intelligibly, or sing so melodiously, as these. It must have been to some such measure that the spinners and the young maids sang, 'Come away, Death,' in the Shakespearean *Illyria*. There is so often a threatening note, something blatant and metallic, in the voice of bells, that I believe we have fully more pain than pleasure from hearing them; but these, as they sounded abroad, now high, now low, now with a plaintive cadence that caught the ear like the burthen of a popular song, were always moderate and tunable, and seemed to fall in with the spirit of still, rustic places, like the noise of a waterfall or the babble of a rookery in spring. I could have asked the bell-ringer for his blessing, good, sedate old man, who swung the rope so gently to the time of his meditations. I could have blessed the priest or the heritors, or whoever may be concerned with such affairs in *France*, who had left these sweet old bells to gladden the afternoon, and not held meetings, and made collections, and had their names repeatedly printed in the local paper, to rig up a peal of brand-new, brazen, *Birmingham*-hearted substitutes, who should bombard their sides to the provocation of a brand-new bell-ringer, and fill the echoes of the valley with terror and riot.

At last the bells ceased, and with their note the sun withdrew. The piece was at an end; shadow and silence possessed the valley of the *Oise*. We took to the paddle with glad hearts, like people who have sat out a noble performance and return to work. The river was more dangerous here; it ran swifter, the eddies were more sudden and violent. All the way down we had had our fill of difficulties. Sometimes it was a weir which could be shot, sometimes one so shallow and full of stakes that we must withdraw the boats from the water and carry them round. But the chief sort of obstacle was a consequence of the late high winds. Every two or three hundred yards a tree had fallen across the river and usually involved more than another in its fall. Often there was free water at the end, and we could steer round the leafy promontory and hear the water sucking and bubbling among the twigs. Often, again, when the tree reached from bank to bank, there was room, by lying close, to shoot through underneath, canoe and all. Sometimes it was necessary to get out upon the trunk itself and pull the boats across; and sometimes, where the stream was too impetuous for this, there was nothing for it but to land and 'carry over.' This made a fine series of accidents in the day's career, and kept us aware of ourselves.

Shortly after our re-embarkation, while I was leading by a long way, and still full of a noble, exulting spirit in honour of the sun, the swift pace, and the church bells, the river made one of its leonine pounces round a corner, and I was aware of another fallen tree within a stone-cast. I had my backboard down in a trice, and aimed for a place where the trunk seemed high enough above the water, and the branches not too thick to let me slip below. When a man has just vowed eternal brotherhood with the universe, he is not in a temper to take great determinations coolly, and this, which might have been a very important determination for me, had not been taken under a happy star. The tree caught me about the chest, and while I was yet struggling to make less of myself and get through, the river took the matter out of my hands and bereaved me of my boat. The *Arethusa* swung round broadside on, leaned over, ejected so much of me as still remained on board, and thus disencumbered, whipped under the tree, righted, and went merrily away down stream.

I do not know how long it was before I scrambled on to the tree to which I was left clinging, but it was longer than I cared about. My thoughts were of a grave and almost sombre character, but I still clung to my paddle. The stream ran away with my heels as fast as I could pull up my shoulders, and I seemed, by the weight, to have all the water of the *Oise* in my trouser pockets. You can never know, till you try it, what a dead pull a river makes against a man. Death himself had me by the heels, for this was his last ambuscade, and he must now join personally in the fray. And still I held to my paddle. At last I dragged myself on to my stomach on the trunk, and lay there a breathless sop, with a mingled sense of humour and injustice. A poor figure I must have presented to *Burns* upon the hilltop with his team. But there was the paddle in my hand. On my tomb, if ever I have one, I mean to get these words inscribed: 'He clung to his paddle.'

The *Cigarette* had gone past a while before; for, as I might have observed, if I had been a little less pleased with the universe at the moment, there was a clear way round the treetop at the farther side. He had offered his services to haul me out, but as I was then already on my elbows, I had declined, and sent him down-stream after the truant *Arethusa*. The stream was too rapid for a man to mount with one canoe, let alone two, upon his hands. So I crawled along the trunk to shore, and proceeded down the meadows by the river-side. I was so cold that my heart was sore. I had now an idea of my own, why the reeds so bitterly shivered. I could have given any of them a lesson. The

Cigarette remarked facetiously, that he thought I was 'taking exercise' as I drew near, until he made out for certain that I was only twittering with cold. I had a rub down with a towel, and donned a dry suit from the india-rubber bag. But I was not my own man again for the rest of the voyage. I had a queasy sense that I wore my last dry clothes upon my body. The struggle had tired me; and perhaps, whether I knew it or not, I was a little dashed in spirits. The devouring element in the universe had leaped out against me, in this green valley quickened by a running stream. The bells were all very pretty in their way, but I had heard some of the hollow notes of *Pan's* music. Would the wicked river drag me down by the heels, indeed? and look so beautiful all the time? Nature's good-humour was only skin-deep after all.

There was still a long way to go by the winding course of the stream, and darkness had fallen, and a late bell was ringing in *Origny Sainte-Benoîte*, when we arrived.

Origny Sainte-Benoîte
A By-day

The next day was *Sunday*, and the church bells had little rest; indeed I do not think I remember anywhere else so great a choice of services as were here offered to the devout. And while the bells made merry in the sunshine, all the world with his dog was out shooting among the beets and colza.

In the morning a hawker and his wife went down the street at a foot-pace, singing to a very slow, lamentable music. '*O France, mes amours.*' It brought everybody to the door; and when our landlady called in the man to buy the words, he had not a copy of them left. She was not the first nor the second who had been taken with the song. There is something very pathetic in the love of the French people, since the war, for dismal patriotic music-making. I have watched a forester from *Alsace* while someone was singing '*Les malheurs de la France*' at a baptismal party in the neighbourhood of *Fontainebleau*. He arose from the table and took his son aside, close by where I was standing. 'Listen, listen,' he said, bearing on the boy's shoulder, 'and remember this, my son.' A little after he went out into the garden suddenly, and I could hear him sobbing in the darkness.

The humiliation of their arms and the loss of *Alsace* and *Lorraine* made a sore pull on the endurance of this sensitive people; and their hearts are still hot, not so much against *Germany* as against the Empire. In what other country will you find a patriotic ditty bring all the world into the street? But affliction heightens love; and we shall never know we are *Englishmen* until we have lost *India*. Independent *America* is still the cross of my existence; I cannot think of *Farmer George* without abhorrence; and I never feel more warmly to my own land than when I see the stars and stripes, and remember what our empire might have been.

The hawker's little book, which I purchased, was a curious mixture. Side by side with the flippant, rowdy nonsense of the *Paris* music-halls, there were many pastoral pieces, not without a touch of poetry, I thought, and instinct with the brave independence of the poorer class in *France*. There you might read how the wood-cutter gloried in his axe, and the gardener scorned to be ashamed of his spade. It was not very well written, this poetry of labour, but the pluck of the sentiment redeemed what was weak or wordy in the expression. The martial and the patriotic pieces, on the other hand, were tearful, womanish productions one and all. The poet had passed under the *Caudine Forks*; he sang for an army visiting the tomb of its old renown, with arms reversed; and sang not of victory, but of death. There was a number in the hawker's collection called *Conscrits Française* which may rank amongst the most dissuasive war-lyrics on record. It would not be possible to fight at all in such a spirit. The bravest conscript would turn pale if such a ditty were struck up beside him on the morning of battle; and whole regiments would pile their arms to its tune.

If *Fletcher* of *Saltoun* is in the right about the influence of national songs, you would say *France* was come to a poor pass. But the thing will work its own cure, and a sound-hearted and courageous people weary at length of snivelling over their disasters. Already *Paul Déroulède* had written some manly military verses. There is not much of the trumpet note in them, perhaps, to stir a man's heart in his bosom; they lack the lyrical elation, and move slowly; but they are written in a grave, honourable, stoical spirit, which should carry soldiers far in a good cause. One feels as if one would like to trust *Déroulède* with something. It will be happy if he can so far inoculate his fellow-countrymen that they may be trusted with their own future. And in the meantime, here is an antidote to 'French Conscripts' and much other doleful versification.

We had left the boats over-night in the custody of one whom we shall call *Carnival*. I did not properly catch his name, and perhaps that was not unfortunate for him, as I am not in a position to hand him down with honour to posterity. To this person's premises we strolled in the course of the day, and found quite a little deputation inspecting the canoes. There was a stout gentleman with a knowledge of the river, which he seemed eager to impart. There was a very elegant young gentleman in a black coat, with a smattering of English, who led the talk at once to the *Oxford* and *Cambridge* boat race. And then there were three handsome girls from fifteen to twenty; and an old gentleman in a blouse, with no teeth to speak of, and a strong country accent. Quite the pick of *Origny*, I should suppose.

The *Cigarette* had some mysteries to perform with his rigging in the coach-house; so I was left to do the parade single-handed. I found myself very much of a hero whether I would or not. The girls were full of little shudderings over the dangers of our journey. And I thought it would be ungallant not to take my cue from the ladies. My mishap of yesterday, told in an off-hand way, produced a deep sensation. It was *Othello* over again, with no less than three *Desdemonas* and a sprinkling of sympathetic senators in the background. Never were the canoes more flattered, or flattered more adroitly.

'It is like a violin,' cried one of the girls in an ecstasy.

'I thank you for the world, mademoiselle,' said I. 'All the more since there are people who call out to me, that it is like a coffin.'

'O! but it is really like a violin. It is finished like a violin,' she went on.

'And polished like a violin,' added a senator.

'One has only to stretch the cords,' concluded another, 'and then tum-tumty-tum' – he imitated the result with spirit.

Was not this a graceful little ovation? Where this people finds the secret of its pretty speeches, I cannot imagine; unless the secret should be no other than a sincere desire to please? But then no disgrace is attached in *France* to saying a thing neatly; whereas in *England*, to talk like a book is to give in one's resignation to society.

The old gentleman in the blouse stole into the coach-house, and somewhat irrelevantly informed the *Cigarette* that he was the father of the three girls and four more; quite an exploit for a *Frenchman*.

'You are very fortunate,' answered the *Cigarette* politely.

And the old gentleman, having apparently gained his point, stole away again.

We all got very friendly together. The girls proposed to start with us on the morrow, if you please! And jesting apart, everyone was anxious to know the hour of our departure. Now, when you are going to crawl into your canoe from a bad launch, a crowd, however friendly, is undesirable; and so we told them not before twelve, and mentally determined to be off by ten at latest.

Towards evening, we went abroad again to post some letters. It was cool and pleasant; the long village was quite empty, except for one or two urchins who followed us as they might have followed a menagerie; the hills and the tree-tops looked in from all sides through the clear air; and the bells were chiming for yet another service.

Suddenly, we sighted the three girls standing, with a fourth sister, in front of a shop on the wide selvage of the roadway. We had been very merry with them a little while ago, to be sure. But what was the etiquette of *Origny*? Had it been a country road, of course we should have spoken to them, but here, under the eyes of all the gossips, ought we to do even as much as bow? I consulted the *Cigarette*.

'Look,' said he.

I looked. There were the four girls on the same spot; but now four backs were turned to us, very upright and conscious. Corporal Modesty had given the word of command, and the well-disciplined picket had gone right-about-face like a single person. They maintained this formation all the while we were in sight; but we heard them tittering among themselves, and the girl whom we had not met laughed with open mouth, and even looked over her shoulder at the enemy. I wonder was it altogether modesty after all? or in part a sort of country provocation?

As we were returning to the inn, we beheld something floating in the ample field of golden evening sky, above the chalk cliffs and the trees that grow along their summit. It was too high up, too large and too steady for a kite; and as it was dark, it could not be a star. For although a star were as black as ink and as rugged as a walnut, so amply does the sun bathe heaven with radiance that it would sparkle like a point of light for us. The village was dotted with people with their heads in the air; and the children were in a bustle all along the street and far up the straight road that climbs the hills, where we could still see them running in loose knots. It was a balloon, we learned, which had left *Saint Quentin* at half-past five that evening. Mighty composedly the majority of the grown people took it. But we were English, and were soon running up the hill with the best. Being travellers ourselves in a small way, we would fain have seen these other travellers alight.

The spectacle was over by the time we gained the top of the

hill. All the gold had withered out of the sky, and the balloon had disappeared. Whither? I ask myself; caught up into the seventh heaven? or come safely to land somewhere in that blue uneven distance into which the roadway dipped and melted before our eyes? Probably the aeronauts were already warming themselves at a farm chimney, for they say it is cold in these unhomely regions of the air. The night fell swiftly. Roadside trees and disappointed sightseers, returning through the meadows, stood out in black against a margin of low red sunset. It was cheerfuller to face the other way, and so down the hill we went, with a full moon, the colour of a melon, swinging high above the wooded valley, and the white cliffs behind us faintly reddened by the fire of the chalk kilns.

The lamps were lighted, and the salads were being made in *Origny Sainte-Benoîte* by the river.

Origny Sainte-Benoîte
The Company at Table

Although we came late for dinner, the company at table treated us to sparkling wine. 'That is how we are in *France*,' said one. 'Those who sit down with us are friends.' And the rest applauded.

They were three altogether, and an odd trio to pass the *Sunday* with.

Two of them were guests like ourselves, both men of the north. One ruddy, and of a full habit of body, with copious black hair and beard, the intrepid hunter of *France*, who thought nothing so small, not even a lark or a minnow, but he might vindicate his prowess by its capture. For such a great, healthy man, his hair flourishing like *Samson's*, his arteries running buckets of red blood, to boast of these infinitesimal exploits produced a feeling of disproportion in the world, as when a steam-hammer is set to cracking nuts. The other was a quiet, subdued person, blond and lymphatic and sad, with something the look of a Dane: '*Tristes têtes de Danois!*' as *Gaston Lafenestre* used to say.

I must not let that name go by without a word for the best of all good fellows now gone down into the dust. We shall never again see *Gaston* in his forest costume – he was *Gaston* with all the world, in affection, not in disrespect – nor hear him wake the echoes of *Fontainebleau* with the woodland horn. Never again shall his kind smile put peace among all races of artistic men, and make the *Englishman* at home in *France*. Never more shall the sheep, who were not more innocent at heart than he, sit all unconsciously for his industrious pencil. He died too early, at the very moment when he was beginning to put forth fresh sprouts, and blossom into something worthy of himself; and yet none who knew him will think he lived in vain. I never knew a man so little, for whom yet I had so much affection; and I find it a good test of others, how much they had learned to understand and value him. His was indeed a good influence in life while he was still among us; he had a fresh laugh, it did you good to see him; and however sad he may have been at heart, he always bore a bold and cheerful countenance, and took fortune's worst as it were the showers of spring. But now his mother sits alone by the side of *Fontainebleau* woods, where he gathered mushrooms in his hardy and penurious youth.

Many of his pictures found their way across the Channel: besides those which were stolen, when a dastardly *Yankee* left him alone in *London* with two English pence, and perhaps twice as many words of English. If anyone who reads these lines should have a scene of sheep, in the manner of *Jacques*, with this fine creature's signature, let him tell himself that one of the kindest and bravest of men has lent a hand to decorate his lodging. There may be better pictures in the *National Gallery*; but not a painter among the generations had a better heart. Precious in the sight of the *Lord* of humanity, the *Psalms* tell us, is the death of His saints. It had need to be precious; for it is very costly, when by the stroke a mother is left desolate, and the peacemaker, and *peace-looker*, of a whole society is laid in the ground with *Cæsar* and the *Twelve Apostles*.

There is something lacking among the oaks of *Fontainebleau*; and when the dessert comes in at *Barbizon*, people look to the door for a figure that is gone.

The third of our companions at *Origny* was no less a person than the landlady's husband: not properly the landlord, since he worked himself in a factory during the day, and came to his own house at evening as a guest: a man worn to skin and bone by perpetual excitement, with baldish head, sharp features, and swift, shining eyes. On *Saturday*, describing some paltry adventure at a duck-hunt, he broke a plate into a score of fragments. Whenever he made a remark, he would look all round the table, with his chin raised, and a spark of green light in either eye, seeking approval. His wife appeared now and again in the doorway of the room, where she was superintending dinner, with a '*Henri*, you forget yourself,' or a '*Henri*, you can surely talk without making such a noise.' Indeed, that was what the honest fellow could not do. On the most trifling matter, his eyes kindled, his fist visited the table, and his voice rolled abroad in changeful thunder. I never saw such a petard of a man; I think the devil was in him. He had two favourite expressions: 'it is logical,' or illogical as the case might be: and this other, thrown out with a certain bravado, as a man might unfurl a banner, at the beginning of many a long and sonorous story: 'I am a proletarian, you see.' Indeed, we saw it very well. *God* forbid that ever I should find him handling a gun in *Paris* streets. That will not be a good moment for the general public.

I thought his two phrases very much represented the good and evil of his class, and to some extent of his country. It is a strong thing to say what one is, and not be ashamed of it, even although it be in doubtful taste to repeat the statement too often in one evening. I should not admire it in a duke, of course; but as times go, the trait is honourable in a workman. On the other hand, it is not at all a strong thing to put one's reliance upon logic; and our own logic particularly, for it is generally wrong. We never know where we are to end, if once we begin following words or doctors. There is an upright stock in a man's own heart, that is trustier than any syllogism; and the eyes, and the sympathies and appetites, know a thing or two that have never yet been stated in controversy. Reasons are as plentiful as blackberries; and like fisticuffs, they serve impartially with all sides. Doctrines do not stand or fall by their proofs, and are only logical in so far as they are cleverly put. An able controversialist no more than an able general demonstrates the justice of his cause. But *France* is all gone wandering after one or two big words; it will take some time before they can be satisfied that they are no more than words, however big; and when once that is done, they will perhaps find logic less diverting.

The conversation opened with details of the day's shooting. When all the sportsmen of a village shoot over the village territory *pro indiviso*, it is plain that many questions of etiquette and priority must arise.

'Here now,' cried the landlord, brandishing a plate, 'here is a field of beetroot. Well. Here am I then. I advance, do I not? *Eh bien*! *sacristi*,' and the statement, waxing louder, rolls off into a reverberation of oaths, the speaker glaring about for sympathy, and everybody nodding his head to him in the name of peace.

The ruddy *Northman* told some tales of his own prowess in keeping order: notably one of a Marquis.

'Marquis,' I said, 'if you take another step I fire upon you. You have committed a dirtiness, Marquis.'

Whereupon, it appeared, the Marquis touched his cap and withdrew.

The landlord applauded noisily. 'It was well done,' he said. 'He did all that he could. He admitted he was wrong.' And then oath upon oath. He was no marquis-lover either, but he had a sense of justicee in him, this proletarian host of ours.

From the matter of hunting, the talk veered into a general comparison of *Paris* and the country. The proletarian beat the table like a drum in praise of *Paris*. 'What is *Paris*? *Paris* is the cream of *France*. There are no Parisians: it is you and I and everybody who are Parisians. A man has eighty chances per cent. to get on in the world in *Paris*.' And he drew a vivid sketch of the workman in a den no bigger than a dog-hutch, making articles that were to go all over the world. '*Eh bien, quoi, c'est magnifigue, ça*!' cried he.

The sad *Northman* interfered in praise of a peasant's life; he thought *Paris* bad for men and women; 'Centralisation,' said he –

But the landlord was at his throat in a moment. It was all logical, he showed him; and all magnificent. 'What a spectacle! What a glance for an eye!' And the dishes reeled upon the table under a cannonade of blows.

Seeking to make peace, I threw in a word in praise of the liberty of opinion in *France*. I could hardly have shot more amiss. There was an instant silence, and a great wagging of significant heads. They did not fancy the subject, it was plain; but they gave me to understand that the sad *Northman* was a martyr on account of his views. 'Ask him a bit,' said they. 'Just ask him.'

'Yes, sir,' said he in his quiet way, answering me, although I had not spoken. 'I am afraid there is less liberty of opinion in *France* than you may imagine.' And with that he dropped his eyes, and seemed to consider the subject at an end.

Our curiosity was mightily excited at this. How, or why, or when, was this lymphatic bagman martyred? We concluded at once it was on some religious question, and brushed up our memories of the *Inquisition*, which were principally drawn from *Poe's* horrid story, and the sermon in *Tristram Shandy*, I believe.

On the morrow we had an opportunity of going further into the question; for when we rose very early to avoid a sympathising deputation at our departure, we found the hero up before us. He was breaking his fast on white wine and raw onions, in order to keep up the character of martyr, I conclude. We had a long conversation, and made out what we wanted in spite of his reserve. But here was a truly curious circumstance. It seems possible for two *Scotchmen* and a *Frenchman* to discuss during a long half-hour, and each nationality have a different idea in view throughout. It was not till the very end that we discovered his heresy had been political, or that he suspected our mistake. The terms and spirit in which he spoke of his political beliefs were, in our eyes, suited to religious beliefs. And *vice versa*.

Nothing could be more characteristic of the two countries. Politics are the religion of *France*; as *Nanty Ewart* would have said, 'A d – d bad religion'; while we, at home, keep most of our bitterness for little differences about a hymn-book, or a Hebrew word which, perhaps, neither of the parties can translate. And perhaps the misconception is typical of many others that may never be cleared up: not only between people of different race, but between those of different sex.

As for our friend's martyrdom, he was a Communist, or perhaps only a Communard, which is a very different thing; and had lost one or more situations in consequence. I think he had also been rejected in marriage; but perhaps he had a sentimental way of considering business which deceived me. He was a mild, gentle creature, anyway; and I hope he has got a better situation, and married a more suitable wife since then.

Down the Oise : To Moy

Carnival notoriously cheated us at first. Finding us easy in our ways, he regretted having let us off so cheaply; and taking me aside, told me a cock-and-bull story with the moral of another five francs for the narrator. The thing was palpably absurd; but I paid up, and at once dropped all friendliness of manner, and kept him in his place as an inferior with freezing British dignity. He saw in a moment that he had gone too far, and killed a willing horse; his face fell; I am sure he would have refunded if he could only have thought of a decent pretext. He wished me to drink with him, but I would none of his drinks. He grew pathetically tender in his professions; but I walked beside him in silence or answered him in stately courtesies; and when we got to the landing-place, passed the word in English slang to the *Cigarette*.

In spite of the false scent we had thrown out the day before, there must have been fifty people about the bridge. We were as pleasant as we could be with all but *Carnival*. We said good-bye, shaking hands with the old gentleman who knew the river and the young gentleman who had a smattering of English; but never a word for *Carnival*. Poor *Carnival*, here was a humili-ation. He who had been so much identified with the canoes, who had given orders in our name, who had shown off the boats and even the boatmen like a private exhibition of his own, to be now so publicly shamed by the lions of his caravan! I never saw anybody look more crestfallen than he. He hung in the background, coming timidly forward ever and again as he thought he saw some symptom of a relenting humour, and falling hurriedly back when he encountered a cold stare. Let us hope it will be a lesson to him.

I would not have mentioned *Carnival's* peccadillo had not the thing been so uncommon in *France*. This, for instance, was the only case of dishonesty or even sharp practice in our whole voyage. We talk very much about our honesty in *England*. It is a good rule to be on your guard wherever you hear great professions about a very little piece of virtue. If the English could only hear how they are spoken of abroad, they might confine themselves for a while to remedying the fact; and perhaps even when that was done, give us fewer of their airs.

The young ladies, the graces of *Origny*, were not present at our start, but when we got round to the second bridge, behold it was black with sightseers! We were loudly cheered, and for a good way below young lads and lasses ran along the bank still cheering. What with current and paddling, we were flashing along like swallows. It was no joke to keep up with us upon the woody shore. But the girls picked up their skirts, as if they were sure they had good ankles, and followed until their breath was out. The last to weary were the three graces and a couple of companions; and just as they too had had enough, the foremost of the three leaped upon a tree stump and kissed her hand to the canoeists. Not *Diana* herself, although this was more of a *Venus* after all, could have done a graceful thing more gracefully. 'Come back again!' she cried, and all the others echoed her; and the hills about *Origny* repeated the words, 'Come back.' But the river had us round an angle in a twinkling, and we were alone with the green trees and running water.

Come back? There is no coming back, young ladies, on the impetuous stream of life.

> The merchant bows unto the seaman's star,
> The ploughman from the sun his season takes.

And we must all set out pocket watches by the clock of fate. There is a headlong, forthright tide, that bears away man with his fancies like a straw, and runs fast in time and space. It is full of curves like this, your winding river of the *Oise*; and lingers and returns in pleasant pastorals; and yet, rightly thought upon, never returns at all. For though it should revisit the same acre of meadow in the same hour, it will have made an ample sweep between whiles; many little streams will have fallen in; many exhalations risen towards the sun; and even although it were the same acre, it will no more be the same river of *Oise*. And thus, O graces of *Origny*, although the wandering fortune of my life should carry me back again to where you await death's whistle by the river, that will not be the old I who walks the street; and those wives and mothers, say, will those be you?

There was never any mistake about the *Oise*, as a matter of fact. In these upper reaches, it was still in a prodigious hurry for the sea. It ran so fast and merrily, through all the windings of its channel, that I strained my thumb fighting with the rapids, and had to paddle all the rest of the way with one hand turned up. Sometimes, it had to serve mills; and being still a little river, ran very dry and shallow in the meanwhile. We had to put our legs out of the boat, and shove ourselves off the sand of the bottom with our feet. And still it went on its way singing among the poplars, and making a green valley in the world. After a good woman, and a good book, and tobacco, there is nothing so agreeable on earth as a river. I forgave it its attempt on my life; which was after all one part owing to the unruly winds of heaven that had blown down the tree, one part to my own mismanagement, and only a third part to the river itself, and that not out of malice, but from its great pre-occupation over its business of getting to the sea. A difficult business, too; for the detours it had to make are not to be counted. The geographers seem to have given up the attempt; for I found no map represent the infinite contortion of its course. A fact will say more than any of them. After we had been some hours, three if I mistake not, flitting by the trees at this smooth, breakneck gallop, when we came upon a hamlet and asked where we were, we had got no farther than four kilometres (say two miles and a half) from *Origny*. If it were not for the honour of the thing (in the Scotch saying), we might almost as well have been standing still.

We lunched on a meadow inside a parallelogram of poplars. The leaves danced and prattled in the wind all round about us. The river hurried on meanwhile, and seemed to chide at our delay. Little we cared. The river knew where it was going; not so we; the less our hurry, where we found good quarters and a pleasant theatre for a pipe. At that hour, stockbrokers were shouting in the *Paris* Bourse for two or three per cent.; but we minded them as little as the sliding stream, and sacrificed a hecatomb of minutes to the gods of tobacco and digestion. Hurry is the resource of the faithless. Where a man can trust his own heart, and those of his friends, to-morrow is as good as to-day. And if he die in the meanwhile, why then, there he dies, and the question is solved.

We had to take to the canal in the course of the afternoon; because, where it crossed the river, there was not a bridge, but a siphon. If it had not been for an excited fellow on the bank, we should have paddled right into the siphon, and thenceforward not paddled any more. We met a man, a gentleman, on the tow-path, who was much interested in our cruise. And I was witness to a strange seizure of lying suffered by the *Cigarette*; who, because his knife came from *Norway*, narrated all sorts of adventures in that country, where he has never been. He was quite feverish at the end, and pleaded demoniacal possession.

Moy (pronounce Moÿ) was a pleasant little village, gathered round a *château* in a moat. The air was perfumed with hemp from neighbouring fields. At the *Golden Sheep* we found excellent entertainment. German shells from the siege of *La Fère*, *Nürnberg* figures, gold fish in a bowl, and all manner of knick-knacks, embellished the public room. The landlady was a stout, plain, short-sighted, motherly body, with something not far short of a genius for cookery. She had a guess of her excellence herself. After every dish was sent in, she would come and look on at the dinner for a while, with puckered, blinking eyes. '*C'est bon, n'est-ce pas?*' she would say; and when she had received a proper answer, she disappeared into the kitchen. That common French dish, partridge and cabbages, became a new thing in my eyes at the *Golden Sheep*; and many subsequent dinners have bitterly disappointed me in consequence. Sweet was our rest in the *Golden Sheep* at *Moy*.

La Fère of Cursed Memory

We lingered in *Moy* a good part of the day, for we were fond of being philosophical, and scorned long journeys and early starts on principle. The place, moreover, invited to repose. People in elaborate shooting costumes sallied from the *château* with guns and game-bags; and this was a pleasure in itself to remain behind while these elegant pleasure-seekers took the first of the morning. In this way, all the world may be an aristocrat, and play the duke among marquises, and the reigning monarch among dukes, if he will only outvie them in tranquillity. An imperturbable demeanour comes from perfect patience. Quiet minds cannot be perplexed or frightened, but go on in fortune or misfortune at their own private pace, like a clock during a thunderstorm.

We made a very short day of it to *La Fère*; but the dusk was falling, and a small rain had begun before we stowed the boats. *La Fère* is a fortified town in a plain, and has two belts of rampart. Between the first and the second extends a region of waste land and cultivated patches. Here and there along the wayside were posters forbidding trespass in the name of military engineering. At last, a second gateway admitted us to the town itself. Lighted windows looked gladsome, whiffs of comfortable cookery came abroad upon the air. The town was full of the military reserve, out for the French *Autumn* manœuvres, and the reservists walked speedily and wore their formidable greatcoats. It was a fine night to be within doors over dinner, and hear the rain upon the windows.

The *Cigarette* and I could not sufficiently congratulate each other on the prospect, for we had been told there was a capital inn at *La Fère*. Such a dinner as we were going to eat! such beds as we were to sleep in! – and all the while the rain raining on houseless folk over all the poplared country-side! It made our mouths water. The inn bore the name of some woodland animal, stag, or hart, or hind, I forget which. But I shall never forget how spacious and how eminently habitable it looked as we drew near. The carriage entry was lighted up, not by intention, but from the mere superfluity of fire and candle in the house. A rattle of many dishes came to our ears; we sighted a great field of tablecloth; the kitchen glowed like a forge and smelt like a garden of things to eat.

Into this, the inmost shrine, the physiological heart, of a hostelry, with all its furnaces in action, and all its dressers charged with viands, you are now to suppose us making our triumphal entry, a pair of damp rag-and-bone men, each with a limp india-rubber bag upon his arm. I do not believe I have a sound view of that kitchen; I saw it through a sort of glory: but it seemed to me crowded with the snowy caps of cookmen, who all turned round from their saucepans and looked at us with surprise. There was no doubt about the landlady, however: there she was, heading her army, a flushed, angry woman, full of affairs. Her I asked politely – too politely, thinks the *Cigarette* – if we could have beds: she surveying us coldly from head to foot.

'You will find beds in the suburb,' she remarked. 'We are too busy for the like of you.'

If we could make an entrance, change our clothes, and order a bottle of wine, I felt sure we could put things right; so said I: 'If we cannot sleep, we may at least dine,' – and was for depositing my bag.

What a terrible convulsion of nature was that which followed in the landlady's face! She made a run at us, and stamped her foot.

'Out with you – out of the door!' she screeched. '*Sortez! sortez! sortez par la porte!*'

I do not know how it happened, but next moment we were out in the rain and darkness, and I was cursing before the carriage entry like a disappointed mendicant. Where were the boating men of *Belgium*? where the Judge and his good wines? and where the graces of *Origny*? Black, black was the night after the firelit kitchen; but was that to the blackness in our heart? This was not the first time that I have been refused a lodging. Often and often have I planned what I should do if such a misadventure happened to me again. And nothing is easier to plan. But to put in execution, with the heart boiling at the indignity? Try it; try it only once; and tell me what you did.

It is all very fine to talk about tramps and morality. Six hours of police surveillance (such as I have had), or one brutal rejection from an inn door, change your views upon the subject like a course of lectures. As long as you keep in the upper regions, with all the world bowing to you as you go, social arrangements have a very handsome air; but once get under the wheels, and you wish society were at the devil. I will give most respectable men a fortnight of such a life, and then I will offer them twopence for what remains of their morality.

For my part, when I was turned out of the *Stag*, or the *Hind*, or whatever it was, I would have set the temple of *Diana* on fire, if it had been handy. There was no crime complete enough to express my disapproval of human institutions. As for the *Cigarette*, I never knew a man so altered. 'We have been taken for pedlars again,' said he. 'Good *God*, what it must be to be a pedlar in reality!' He particularised a complaint for every joint in the landlady's body. *Timon* was a philanthropist alongside of him. And then, when he was at the top of his maledictory bent, he would suddenly break away and begin whimperingly to commiserate the poor. 'I hope to *God*,' he said – and I trust the prayer was answered, – 'that I shall never be uncivil to a pedlar.' Was this the imperturbable *Cigarette*? This, this was he. O change beyond report, thought, or belief!

Meantime the heaven wept upon our heads; and the windows grew brighter as the night increased in darkness. We trudged in and out of *La Fère* streets; we saw shops, and private houses where people were copiously dining; we saw stables where carters' nags had plenty of fodder and clean straw; we saw no end of reservists, who were very sorry for themselves this wet night, I doubt not, and yearned for their country homes; but had they not each man his place in *La Fère* barracks? And we, what had we?

There seemed to be no other inn in the whole town. People gave us directions, which we followed as best we could, generally with the effect of bringing us out again upon the scene of our disgrace. We were very sad people indeed by the time we had gone all over *La Fère*; and the *Cigarette* had already made up his mind to lie under a poplar and sup off a loaf of bread. But right at the other end, the house next the towngate was full of light and bustle. '*Bazin, aubergiste, loge à pied*', was the sign. '*A la Croix de Malte*'. There were we received.

The room was full of noisy reservists drinking and smoking; and we were very glad indeed when the drums and bugles began to go about the streets, and one and all had to snatch shakoes and be off for the barracks.

Bazin was a tall man, running to fat: soft-spoken, with a delicate, gentle face. We asked him to share our wine; but he excused himself, having pledged reservists all day long. This was a very different type of the workman-innkeeper from the bawling disputatious fellow at *Origny*. He also loved *Paris*, where he had worked as a decorative painter in his youth. There were such opportunities for self-instruction there, he said. And if anyone had read *Zola's* description of the workman's marriage party visiting the *Louvre*, they would do well to have heard *Bazin* by way of antidote. He had delighted in the museums in his youth. 'One sees there little miracles of work,' he said; 'that is what makes a good workman; it kindles a spark.' We asked him how he managed in *La Fère*. 'I am married,' he said, 'and I have my pretty children. But frankly, it is no life at all. From morning to night, I pledge a pack of good enough fellows who know nothing.'

It faired as the night went on, and the moon came out of the clouds. We sat in front of the door, talking softly with *Bazin*. At the guard-house opposite, the guard was being for ever turned out, as trains of field artillery kept clanking in out of the night, or patrols of horsemen trotted by in their cloaks. Madame *Bazin* came out after a while; she was tired with her day's work, I suppose; and she nestled up to her husband and laid her head upon his breast. He had his arm about her and kept gently patting her on the shoulder. I think *Bazin* was right and he was really married. Of how few people can the same be said!

Little did the *Bazins* know how much they served us. We were charged for candles, for food and drink, and for the beds we slept in. But there was nothing in the bill for the husband's pleasant talk; nor for the pretty spectacle of their married life. And there was yet another item uncharged. For these people's politeness really set us up again in our own esteem. We had a thirst for consideration; the sense of insult was still hot in our spirits; and civil usage seemed to restore us to our position in the world.

How little we pay our way in life! Although we have our purses continually in our hand, the better part of service goes still unrewarded. But I like to fancy that a grateful spirit gives as good as it gets. Perhaps the *Bazins* knew how much I liked them? perhaps they, also, were healed of some slights by the thanks that I gave them in my manner?

Down the Oise:
Through the Golden Valley

Below *La Fère* the river runs through a piece of open pastoral country; green, opulent, loved by breeders; called the *Golden Valley*. In wide sweeps, and with a swift and equable gallop, the ceaseless stream of water visits and makes green the fields. Kine, and horses, and little humorous donkeys, browse together in the meadows, and come down in troops to the riverside to drink. They make a strange feature in the landscape; above all when startled, and you see them galloping to and fro, with their incongruous forms and faces. It gives a feeling as of great, unfenced pampas, and the herds of wandering nations. There were hills in the distance upon either hand; and on one side, the river sometimes bordered on the wooded spurs of *Coucy* and *St Gobain*.

The artillery were practising at *La Fère*; and soon the cannon of heaven joined in that loud play. Two continents of cloud met and exchanged salvos overhead; while all round the horizon we could see sunshine and clear air upon the hills. What with the guns and the thunder, the herds were all frighted in the *Golden Valley*. We could see them tossing their heads, and running to and fro in timorous indecision; and when they had made up their minds, and the donkey followed the horse, and the cow was after the donkey, we could hear their hooves thundering abroad over the meadows. It had a martial sound, like cavalry charges. And altogether, as far as the ears are concerned, we had a very rousing battle-piece performed for our amusement.

At last, the guns and the thunder dropped off; the sun shone on the wet meadows; the air was scented with the breath of rejoicing trees and grass; and the river kept unweariedly carrying us on at its best pace. There was a manufacturing district about *Chauny*; and after that the banks grew so high that they hid the adjacent country, and we could see nothing but clay sides, and one willow after another. Only, here and there, we passed by a village or a ferry, and some wondering child upon the bank would stare after us until we turned the corner. I daresay we continued to paddle in that child's dreams for many a night after.

Sun and shower alternated like day and night, making the hours longer by their variety. When the showers were heavy I could feel each drop striking through my jersey to my warm skin; and the accumulation of small shocks put me nearly beside myself. I decided I should buy a mackintosh at *Noyon*. It is nothing to get wet; but the misery of these individual pricks of cold all over my body at the same instant of time made me flail the water with my paddle like a madman. The *Cigarette* was greatly amused by these ebullitions. It gave him something else to look at, besides clay banks and willows.

All the time, the river stole away like a thief in straight places, or swung round corners with an eddy; the willows nodded and were undermined all day long; the clay banks tumbled in; the *Oise*, which had been so many centuries making the *Golden Valley*, seemed to have changed its fancy, and be bent upon undoing its performance. What a number of things a river does, by simply following Gravity in the innocence of its heart!

Noyon Cathedral

Noyon stands about a mile from the river, in a little plain surrounded by wooded hills, and entirely covers an eminence with its tile roofs, surmounted by a long, straight-backed cathedral with two stiff towers. As we got into the town, the tile roofs seemed to tumble uphill one upon another, in the oddest disorder; but for all their scrambling, they did not attain above the knees of the cathedral, which stood, upright and solemn, over all. As the streets drew near to this presiding genius, through the market-place under the *Hôtel de Ville*, they grew emptier and more composed. Blank walls and shuttered windows were turned to the great edifice, and grass grew on the white causeway. 'Put off thy shoes from off thy feet, for the place whereon thou standest is holy ground.' The *Hôtel du Nord*, nevertheless, lights its secular tapers within a stone-cast of the church; and we had the superb east end before our eyes all morning from the window of our bedroom. I have seldom looked on the east end of a church with more complete sympathy. As it flanges out in three wide terraces, and settles down broadly on the earth, it looks like the poop of some great old battleship. Hollow-backed buttresses carry vases, which figure for the stern lanterns. There is a roll in the ground, and the towers just appear above the pitch of the roof, as though the good ship were bowling lazily over an *Atlantic* swell. At any moment if might be a hundred feet away from you, climbing the next billow. At any moment a window might open, and some old admiral thrust forth a cocked hat, and proceed to take an observation. The old admirals sail the sea no longer; the old ships of battle are all broken up, and live only in pictures; but this that was a church before ever they were thought upon, is still a church, and makes as brave an appearance by the *Oise*. The cathedral and the river are probably the two oldest things for miles around; and certainly they have both a grand old age.

The *Sacristan* took us to the top of one of the towers, and showed us the five bells hanging in their loft. From above, the town was a tessellated pavement of roofs and gardens; the old line of rampart was plainly traceable; and the *Sacristan* pointed out to us, far across the plain, in a bit of gleaming sky between two clouds, the towers of *Château Coucy*.

I find I never weary of great churches. It is my favourite kind of mountain scenery. Mankind was never so happily inspired as when it made a cathedral: a thing as single and specious as a statue to the first glance, and yet, on examination, as lively and interesting as a forest in detail. The height of spires cannot be taken by trigonometry; they measure absurdly short, but how tall they are to the admiring eye! And where we have so many elegant proportions, growing one out of the other, and all together into one, it seems as if proportion transcended itself and became something different and more imposing. I could never fathom how a man dares to lift up his voice to preach in a cathedral. What is he to say that will not be an anti-climax? For though I have heard a considerable variety of sermons, I never yet heard one that was so expressive as a cathedral. 'Tis the best preacher itself, and preaches day and night; not only telling you of man's art and aspirations in the past, but convicting your own soul of ardent sympathies; or rather, like all good preachers, it sets you preaching to yourself; – and every man is his own doctor of divinity in the last resort.

As I sat outside of the hotel in the course of the afternoon, the sweet groaning thunder of the organ floated out of the church like a summons. I was not averse, liking the theatre so well, to sit out an act or two of the play, but I could never rightly make out the nature of the service I beheld. Four or five priests and as many choristers were singing *Miserere* before the high altar when I went in. There was no congregation but a few old women on chairs and old men kneeling on the pavement. After a while a long train of young girls, walking two and two, each with a lighted taper in her hand, and all dressed in black with a white veil, came from behind the altar and began to descend the nave; the four first carrying a Virgin and Child upon a table. The priests and choristers arose from their knees and followed after, singing 'Ave Mary' as they went. In this order, they made the circuit of the cathedral, passing twice before me where I leaned against a pillar. The priest who seemed of most consequence was a strange, down-looking old man. He kept mumbling prayers with his lips; but as he looked upon me darkling, it did not seem as if prayer were uppermost in his heart. Two others, who bore the burthen of the chaunt, were stout, brutal, military-looking men of forty, with bold, overfed eyes; they sang with some lustiness, and trolled forth 'Ave Mary' like a garrison catch. The little girls were timid and grave. As they footed slowly up the aisle, each one took a moment's glance at the *Englishman*; and the big nun who played marshal fairly stared him out of countenance. As for the choristers, from first to last they misbehaved as only boys can misbehave; and cruelly marred the performance with their antics.

I understood a great deal of the spirit of what went on. Indeed it would be difficult not to understand the *Miserere*, which I take to be the composition of an atheist. If it ever be a good thing to take such despondency to heart, the *Miserere* is the right music and a cathedral a fit scene. So far I am at one with the Catholics: – an odd name for them, after all! But why, in *God's* name, these holiday choristers? Why these priests who steal wandering looks about the congregation while they feign to be at prayer? Why this fat nun, who rudely arranges her procession and shakes delinquent virgins by the elbows? Why this spitting, and snuffing, and forgetting of keys, and the thousand and one little misadventures that disturb a frame of mind, laboriously edified with chaunts and organings? In any play-house reverend fathers may see what can be done with a little art, and how, to move high sentiments, it is necessary to drill the supernumeraries and have every stool in its proper place.

One other circumstance distressed me. I could bear a *Miserere* myself, having had a good deal of open-air exercise of late; but I wished the old people somewhere else. It was neither the right sort of music nor the right sort of divinity for men and women who have come through most accidents by this time, and probably have an opinion of their own upon the tragic element in life. A person up in years can generally do his own *Miserere* for himself; although I notice that such an one often prefers *Jubilate Deo* for his ordinary singing. On the whole, the most religious exercise for the aged is probably to recall their own experience; so many friends dead, so many hopes disappointed, so many slips and stumbles, and withal so many bright days and smiling providences; there is surely the matter of a very eloquent sermon in all this.

On the whole, I was greatly solemnised. In the little pictorial map of our whole *Inland Voyage*, which my fancy still preserves, and sometimes unrolls for the amusement of odd moments, *Noyon* cathedral figures on a most preposterous scale, and must be nearly as large as a department. I can still see the faces of the priests as if they were at my elbow, and hear *Ave Maria, ora pro nobis* sounding through the church. All *Noyon* is blotted out for me by these superior memories; and I do not care to say more about the place. It was but a stack of brown roofs at the best, where I believe people live very reputably in a quiet way; but the shadow of the church falls upon it when the sun is low, and the five bells are heard in all quarters, telling that the organ has begun. If ever I join the church of *Rome*, I shall stipulate to be Bishop of *Noyon* on the *Oise*.

Down the Oise: to Compiègne

The most patient people grow weary at last with being continually wetted with rain; except of course in the Scotch *Highlands*, where there are not enough fine intervals to point the difference. That was like to be our case the day we left *Noyon*. I remember nothing of the voyage; it was nothing but clay banks and willows, and rain; incessant, pitiless, beating rain: until we stopped to lunch at a little inn at *Pimprez*, where the canal ran very near the river. We were so sadly drenched that the landlady lit a few sticks in the chimney for our comfort; there we sat in a steam of vapour, lamenting our concerns. The husband donned a game bag and strode out to shoot; the wife sat in a far corner watching us. I think we were worth looking at. We grumbled over the misfortune of *La Fère*; we forecast other *La Fères* in the future; – although things went better with the *Cigarette* for spokesman; he had more aplomb altogether than I; and a dull, positive way of approaching a landlady that carried off the india-rubber bags. Talking of *La Fère* put us talking of the reservists.

'Reservery,' said he, 'seems a pretty mean way to spend one's autumn holiday.'

'About as mean,' returned I dejectedly, 'as canoeing.'

'These gentlemen travel for their pleasure?' asked the landlady, with unconscious irony.

It was too much. The scales fell from our eyes. Another wet day, it was determined, and we put the boats into the train.

The weather took the hint. That was our last wetting. The afternoon faired up: grand clouds still voyaged in the sky, but now singly, and with a depth of blue around their path; and a sunset, in the daintiest rose and gold, inaugurated a thick night of stars and a month of unbroken weather. At the same time, the river began to give us a better outlook into the country. The banks were not so high, the willows disappeared from along the margin, and pleasant hills stood all along its course and marked their profile on the sky.

In a little while the canal, coming to its last lock, began to discharge its water-houses on the *Oise*; so that we had no lack of company to fear. Here were all our old friends; the *Deo Gratias* of *Condé* and the *Four Sons of Aymon* journeyed cheerily down-stream along with us; we exchanged waterside pleasantries with the steersman perched among the lumber, or the driver hoarse with bawling to his horses; and the children came and looked over the side as we paddled by. We had never known all this while how much we missed them; but it gave us a fillip to see the smoke from their chimneys.

A little below this junction, we made another meeting of yet more account. For there we were joined by the *Aisne*, already a far-travelled river and fresh out of *Champagne*. Here ended the adolescence of the *Oise*; this was his marriage day; thenceforward he had a stately, brimming march, conscious of his own dignity and sundry dams. He became a tranquil feature in the scene. The trees and towns saw themselves in him, as in a mirror. He carried the canoes lightly on his broad breast; there was no need to work hard against an eddy; but idleness became the order of the day, and mere straightforward dipping of the paddle, now on this side, now on that, without intelligence or effort. Truly we were coming into halcyon weather upon all accounts, and were floated towards the sea like gentlemen.

We made *Compiègne* as the sun was going down: a fine profile of a town above the river. Over the bridge, a regiment was parading to the drum. People loitered on the quay, some fishing, some looking idly at the stream. And as the two boats shot in along the water, we could see them pointing them out and speaking one to another. We landed at a floating lavatory, where the washerwomen were still beating the clothes.

At Compiègne

We put up at a big, bustling hotel in *Compiègne*, where nobody observed our presence.

Reservery and general militarismus (as the Germans call it) were rampant. A camp of conical white tents without the town looked like a leaf out of a picture Bible; sword-belts decorated the walls of the *cafés*; and the streets kept sounding all day long with military music. It was not possible to be an *Englishman* and avoid a feeling of elation; for the men who followed the drums were small, and walked shabbily. Each man inclined at his own angle, and jolted to his own convenience, as he went. There was nothing of the superb gait with which a regiment of tall Highlanders moves behind its music, solemn and inevitable, like a natural phenomenon. Who, that has seen it, can forget the drum-major pacing in front, the drummers' tiger-skins, the pipers swinging plaids, the strange elastic rhythm of the whole regiment footing it in time – and the bang of the drum, when the brasses cease, and the shrill pipes take up the martial story in their place?

A girl, at school in *France*, began to describe one of our regiments on parade, to her French schoolmates; and as she went on, she told me, the recollection grew so vivid, she became so proud to be the countrywoman of such soldiers, and so sorry to be in another country, that her voice failed her and she burst into tears. I have never forgotten that girl; and I think she very nearly deserves a statue. To call her a young lady, with all its niminy associations, would be to offer her an insult. She may rest assured of one thing; although she never should marry a heroic general, never see any great or immediate result of her life, she will not have lived in vain for her native land.

But though French soldiers show to ill-advantage on parade, on the march they are gay, alert, and willing like a troop of fox-hunters. I remember once seeing a company pass through the forest of *Fontainebleau*, on the *Chailly* road, between the *Bas*

Bréau and the *Reine Blanche*. One fellow walked a little before the rest and sang a loud, audacious marching song. The rest bestirred their feet, and even swung their muskets in time. A young officer on horseback had hard ado to keep his countenance at the words. You never saw anything so cheerful and spontaneous as their gait; schoolboys do not look more eagerly at hare and hounds; and you would have thought it impossible to tire such willing marchers.

My great delight in *Compiègne* was the town-hall. I doted upon the town-hall. It is a monument of Gothic insecurity, all turreted, and gargoyled, and slashed, and bedizened with half a score of architectural fancies. Some of the niches are gilt and painted; and in a great square panel in the centre, in black relief on a gilt ground, *Louis XII* rides upon a pacing horse, with hand on hip, and head thrown back. There is royal arrogance in every line of him; the stirruped foot projects insolently from the frame; the eye is hard and proud; the very horse seems to be treading with gratification over prostrate serfs, and to have the breath of the trumpet in his nostrils. So rides for ever, on the front of the town-hall, the good king *Louis XII*, the father of his people.

Over the king's head, in the tall centre turret, appears the dial of a clock; and high above that, three little mechanical figures, each one with a hammer in his hand, whose business it is to chime out the hours and halves and quarters for the burgesses of *Compiègne*. The centre figure has a gilt breastplate; the two others wear gilt trunk-hose; and they all three have elegant, flapping hats like cavaliers. As the quarter approaches, they turn their heads and look knowingly one to the other; and then *kling* go the three hammers on three little bells below. The hour follows, deep and sonorous, from the interior of the tower; and the gilded gentlemen rest from their labours with contentment.

I had a great deal of healthy pleasure from their manœuvres, and took good care to miss as few performances as possible; and I found that even the *Cigarette*, while he pretended to despite my enthusiasm, was more or less a devotee himself. There is something highly absurd in the exposition of such toys to the outrages of winter on a housetop. They would be more in keeping in a glass case before a *Nürnberg* clock. Above all, at night, when the children are abed, and even grown people are snoring under quilts, does it not seem impertinent to leave these gingerbread figures winking and tinkling to the stars and the rolling moon? The gargoyles may fitly enough twist their ape-like heads; fitly enough may the potentate bestride his charger, like centurion in an old German print of the *Via Dolorosa*; but the toys should be put away in a box among some cotton, until the sun rises, and the children are abroad again to be amused.

In *Compiègne* post-office a great packet of letters awaited us; and the authorities were, for this occasion only, so polite as to hand them over upon application.

In some ways, our journey may be said to end with this letter-bag at *Compiègne*. The spell was broken. We had partly come home from that moment.

No one should have any correspondence on a journey; it is bad enough to have to write, but the receipt of letters is the death of all holiday feeling.

'Out of my country and myself I go.' I wish to take a dive among new conditions for awhile, as into another element. I have nothing to do with my friends or my affections for the time; when I came away, I left my heart at home in a desk, or sent it forward with my portmanteau to await me at my destination. After my journey is over, I shall not fail to read your admirable letters with the attention they deserve. But I have paid all this money, look you, and paddled all these strokes, for no other purpose than to be abroad; and yet you keep me at home with your perpetual communications. You tug the string, and I feel that I am a tethered bird. You pursue me all over *Europe* with the little vexations that I came away to avoid. There is no discharge in the war of life, I am well aware; but shall there not be so much as a week's furlough?

We were up by six the day we were to leave. They had taken so little note of us that I hardly thought they would have condescended on a bill. But they did, with some smart particulars too; and we paid in a civilised manner to an uninterested clerk, and went out of that hotel, with the india-rubber bags, unremarked. No one cared to know about us. It is not possible to rise before a village; but *Compiègne* was so grown a town that it took its ease in the morning; and we were up and away while it was still in dressing-gown and slippers. The streets were left to people washing door-steps; nobody was in full dress but the cavaliers upon the town-hall; they were all washed with dew, spruce in their gilding, and full of intelligence and a sense of professional responsibility. *Kling* went they on the bells for the half-past six, as we went by. I took it kind of them to make me this parting compliment; they never were in better form, not even at noon upon a *Sunday*.

There was no one to see us off but the early washerwomen – early and late – who were already beating the linen in their floating lavatory on the river. They were very merry and matutinal in their ways; plunged their arms boldly in, and seemed not to feel the shock. It would be dispiriting to me, this early beginning and first cold dabble of a most dispiriting day's work. But I believe they would have been as unwilling to change days with us, as we could be to change with them. They crowded to the door to watch us paddle away into the thin sunny mists upon the river and shouted heartily after us till we were through the bridge.

Changed Times

There is a sense in which those mists never rose from off our journey; and from that time forth they lie very densely in my note-book. As long as the *Oise* was a small, rural river, it took us near by people's doors, and we could hold a conversation with natives in the riparian fields. But now that it had grown so wide, the life along shore passed us by at a distance. It was the same difference as between a great public highway and a country bypath that wanders in and out of cottage gardens. We now lay in towns, where nobody troubled us with questions; we had floated into civilised life, where people pass without salutation. In sparsely inhabited places, we make all we can of each encounter; but when it comes to a city, we keep to ourselves, and never speak unless we have trodden on a man's toes. In these waters we were no longer strange birds, and nobody supposed we had travelled farther than from the last town. I remember, when we came into *L'Isle Adam*, for instance, how we met dozens of pleasure-boats outing it for the afternoon, and there was nothing to distinguish the true voyager from the amateur, except, perhaps, the filthy condition of my sail. The company in one boat actually thought they recognised me for a neighbour. Was there ever anything more wounding? All the romance had come down to that. Now, on the upper *Oise*, where nothing sailed as a general thing but fish, a pair of canoeists could not be thus vulgarly explained away; we were strange and picturesque intruders; and out of people's wonder sprang a sort of light and passing intimacy all along our route. There is nothing but tit for tat in this world, though sometimes it be a little difficult to trace: for the scores are older than we ourselves, and there has never yet been a settling-day since things were. You get entertainment pretty much in proportion as you give. As long as we were a sort of odd wanderers, to be stared at and followed like a quack doctor or a caravan, we had no want of amusement in return; but as soon as we sank into

commonplace ourselves, all whom we met were similarly disen-
chanted. And here is one reason of a dozen why the world is
dull to dull persons.

In our earlier adventures there was generally something to do,
and that quickened us. Even the showers of rain had a revivify-
ing effect, and shook up the brain from torpor. But now, when
the river no longer ran in a proper sense, only glided seaward
with an even, outright, but imperceptible speed, and when the
sky smiled upon us day after day without variety, we began to
slip into that golden doze of the mind which follows upon much
exercise in the open air. I have stupefied myself in this way more
than once; indeed, I dearly love the feeling; but I never had it to
the same degree as when paddling down the *Oise*. It was the
apotheosis of stupidity.

We ceased reading entirely. Sometimes when I found a new
paper, I took a particular pleasure in reading a single number of
the current novel; but I never could bear more than three
instalments; and even the second was a disappointment. As
soon as the tale became in any way perspicuous, it lost all merit
in my eyes; only a single scene, or, as is the way with these
feuilletons, half a scene, without antecedent or consequence, like
a piece of a dream, had the knack of fixing my interest. The less
I saw of the novel, the better I liked it: a pregnant reflection.
But for the most part, as I said, we neither of us read anything
in the world, and employed the very little while we were awake
between bed and dinner in poring upon maps. I have always
been fond of maps, and can voyage in an atlas with the greatest
enjoyment. The names of places are singularly inviting; the
contour of coasts and rivers is enthralling to the eye, and to hit,
in a map, upon some place you have heard of before, makes
history a new possession. But we thumbed our charts, on these
evenings, with the blankest unconcern. We cared not a fraction
for this place or that. We stared at the sheet as children listen to
their rattle; and read the names of towns or villages to forget
them again at once. We had no romance in the matter; there
was nobody so fancy-free. If you had taken the maps away
while we were studying them most intently, it is a fair bet
whether we might not have continued to study the table with
the same delight.

About one thing we were mightily taken up, and that was
eating. I think I made a god of my belly. I remember dwelling in

imagination upon this or that dish till my mouth watered, and long before we got in for the night my appetite was a clamant, instant annoyance. Sometimes we paddled alongside for awhile and whetted each other with gastronomical fancies as we went. Cake and sherry, a homely reflection, but not within reach upon the *Oise*, trotted through my head for many a mile; and once as we were approaching *Verberie*, the *Cigarette* brought my heart into my mouth by the suggestion of oyster patties and *Sauternes*.

I suppose none of us recognise the great part that is played in life by eating and drinking. The appetite is so imperious, that we can stomach the least interesting viands, and pass off a dinner hour thankfully enough on bread and water; just as there are men who must read something, if it were only *Bradshaw's Guide*. But there is a romance about the matter after all. Probably the table has more devotees than love; and I am sure that food is much more generally entertaining than scenery. Do you give in, as *Walt Whitman* would say, that you are any the less immortal for that? The true materialism is to be ashamed of what we are. To detect the flavour of an olive is no less a piece of human perfection than to find beauty in the colours of the sunset.

Canoeing was easy work. To dip the paddle at the proper inclination, now right, now left; to keep the head down-stream; to empty the little pool that gathered in the lap of the apron; to screw up the eyes against the glittering sparkles of sun upon the water; or now and again to pass below the whistling tow-rope of the *Deo Gratias* of *Condé*, or the *Four Sons of Aymon* – there was not much art in that; certain silly muscles managed it between sleep and waking; and meanwhile the brain had a whole holiday, and went to sleep. We took in, at a glance, the larger features of the scene, and beheld, with half an eye, bloused fishers and dabbling washerwomen on the bank. Now and again we might be half wakened by some church spire, by a leaping fish, or by a trail of river grass that clung about the paddle and had to be plucked off and thrown away. But these luminous intervals were only partially luminous. A little more of us was called into action, but never the whole. The central bureau of nerves, what in some moods we call *Ourselves*, enjoyed its holiday without disturbance like a Government Office. The great wheels of intelligence turned idly in the head, like fly-wheels, grinding no grist. I have gone on for half an hour at a time, counting my strokes and forgetting the hundreds. I flatter myself the beasts that perish could not underbid that, as a low form of consciousness. And what a pleasure it was! What a hearty, tolerant temper did it bring about! There is nothing captious about a man who has attained to this, the one possible apotheosis in life, the Apotheosis of Stupidity; and he begins to feel dignified and longœvous like a tree.

There was one odd piece of practical metaphysics which accompanied what I may call the depth, if I must not call it the intensity, of my abstraction. What philosophers call *me* and *not me*, *ego* and *non ego*, preoccupied me whether I would or no. There was less *me* and more *not me* than I was accustomed to expect. I looked on upon somebody else, who managed the paddling; I was aware of somebody else's feet against the stretcher; my own body seemed to have no more intimate relation to me than the canoe, or the river, or the river banks. Nor this alone: something inside my mind, a part of my brain, a province of my proper being, had thrown off allegiance and set up for itself, or perhaps for the somebody else who did the paddling. I had dwindled into quite a little thing in a corner of myself. I was isolated in my own skull. Thoughts presented themselves unbidden; they were not my thoughts, they were plainly someone else's; and I considered them like a part of the landscape. I take it, in short, that I was about as near *Nirvana* as would be convenient in practical life; and if this be so, I make the Buddhists my sincere compliments; 'tis an agreeable state, not very consistent with mental brilliancy, not exactly profitable in a money point of view, but very calm, golden and incurious, and one that sets a man superior to alarms. It may be best figured by supposing yourself to get dead drunk, and yet keep sober to enjoy it. I have a notion that open-air labourers must spend a large portion of their days in this ecstatic stupor, which explains their high composure and endurance. A pity to go to the expense of laudanum, when here is a better paradise for nothing!

This frame of mind was the great exploit of our voyage, take it all in all. It was the farthest piece of travel accomplished. Indeed, it lies so far from the beaten paths of language, that I despair of getting the reader into sympathy with the smiling, complacent idiocy of my condition; when ideas came and went like motes in a sunbeam; when trees and church spires along the bank surged up from time to time into my notice, like solid objects through a rolling cloudland; when the rhythmical swish of boat and paddle in the water became a cradle-song to lull my thoughts asleep; when a piece of mud on the deck was some-times an intolerable eyesore, and sometimes quite a companion for me, and the object of pleased consideration: – and all the time, with the river running and the shores changing upon either hand, I kept counting my strokes and forgetting the hundreds, the happiest animal in *France*.

Down the Oise : Church Interiors

We made our first stage below *Compiègne* to *Pont Sainte Maxence*. I was abroad a little after six the next morning. The air was biting and smelt of frost. In an open place, a score of women wrangled together over the day's market; and the noise of their negotiation sounded thin and querulous like that of sparrows on a winter's morning. The rare passengers blew into their hands, and shuffled in their wooden shoes to set the blood agog. The streets were full of icy shadow, although the chimneys were smoking overhead in golden sunshine. If you wake early enough at this season of the year, you may get up in *December* to break your fast in *June*.

I found my way to the church; for there is always something to see about a church, whether living worshippers or dead men's tombs; you find there the deadliest earnest, and the hollowest deceit; and even where it is not a piece of history, it will be certain to leak out some contemporary gossip. It was scarcely so cold in the church as it was without, but it looked colder. The white nave was positively arctic to the eye; and the tawdriness of a continental altar looked more forlorn than usual in the solitude and the bleak air. Two priests sat in the chancel, reading and waiting penitents; and out in the nave, one very old woman was engaged in her devotions. It was a wonder how she was able to pass her beads when healthy young people were breathing in their palms and slapping their chests; but though this concerned me, I was yet more dispirited by the nature of her exercises. She went from chair to chair, from altar to altar, circumnavigating the church. To each shrine she dedicated an equal number of beads and an equal length of time. Like a prudent capitalist with a somewhat cynical view of the commercial prospect, she desired to place her supplications in a great variety of heavenly securities. She would risk nothing on the credit of any single intercessor. Out of the whole company of saints and angels, not one but was to suppose himself her

champion elect against the Great Assizes! I could only think of
it as a dull, transparent jugglery, based upon unconscious
unbelief.

She was as dead an old woman as ever I saw; no more than
bone and parchment, curiously put together. Her eyes, with
which she interrogated mine, were vacant of sense. It depends
on what you call seeing, whether you might not call her blind.
Perhaps she had known love; perhaps borne children, suckled
them and given them pet names. But now that was all gone by,
and had left her neither happier nor wiser; and the best she
could do with her mornings was to come up here into the cold
church and juggle for a slice of heaven. It was not without a
gulp that I escaped into the streets and the keen morning air.
Morning? why, how tired of it she would be before night! and
if she did not sleep, how then? It is fortunate that not many of
us are brought up publicly to justify our lives at the bar of
threescore years and ten; fortunate that such a number are
knocked opportunely on the head in what they call the flower
of their years, and go away to suffer for their follies in private
somewhere else. Otherwise, between sick children and discon-
tented old folk, we might be put out of all conceit of life.

I had need of all my cerebral hygiene during that day's
paddle: the old devotee stuck in my throat sorely. But I was
soon in the seventh heaven of stupidity; and knew nothing but
that somebody was paddling a canoe, while I was counting his
strokes and forgetting the hundreds. I used sometimes to be
afraid I should remember the hundreds; which would have
made a toil of a pleasure; but the terror was chimerical, they
went out of my mind by enchantment, and I knew no more than
the man in the moon about my only occupation.

At *Creil*, where we stopped to lunch, we left the canoes in
another floating lavatory, which as it was high noon was packed
with washerwomen, red-handed and loud-voiced; and they and
their broad jokes are about all I remember of the place. I could
look up my history books, if you were very anxious, and tell
you a date or two; for it figured rather largely in the English
wars. But I prefer to mention a girls' boarding-school, which
had an interest for us because it was a girls' boarding-school,
and because we imagined we had rather an interest for it. At
least – there were the girls about the garden; and here were we
on the river; and there was more than one handkerchief waved

as we went by. It caused quite a stir in my heart; and yet how we should have wearied and despised each other, these girls and I, if we had been introduced at a croquet party! But this is a fashion I love: to kiss the hand or wave a handkerchief to people I shall never see again, to play with possibility, and knock in a peg for fancy to hang upon. It gives the traveller a jog, reminds him that he is not a traveller everywhere, and that his journey is no more than a siesta by the way on the real march of life.

The church at *Creil* was a nondescript place in the inside, splashed with gaudy lights from the windows, and picked out with medallions of the *Dolorous Way*. But there was one oddity, in the way of an *ex voto*, which pleased me hugely; a faithful model of a canal boat swung from the vault, with a written aspiration that *God* should conduct the *Saint Nicolas* of *Creil* to a good haven. The thing was neatly executed, and would have made the delight of a party of boys on the waterside. But what tickled me was the gravity of the peril to be conjured. You might hang up the model of a sea-going ship, and welcome: one that is to plough a furrow round the world, and visit the tropic or the frosty poles, runs dangers that are well worth a candle and a mass. But the *Saint Nicolas* of *Creil*, which was to be tugged for some ten years by patient draught-horses, in a weedy canal, with the poplars chattering overhead, and the skipper whistling at the tiller; which was to do all its errands in green, inland places, and never got out of sight of a village belfry in all its cruising; why, you would have thought if anything could be done without the intervention of Providence, it would be that! But perhaps the skipper was a humorist: or perhaps a prophet, reminding people of the seriousness of life by this preposterous token.

At *Creil*, as at *Noyon*, Saint *Joseph* seemed a favourite saint on the score of punctuality. Day and hour can be specified; and grateful people do not fail to specify them on a votive tablet, when prayers have been punctually and neatly answered. Whenever time is a consideration, Saint *Joseph* is the proper intermediary. I took a sort of pleasure in observing the vogue he had in *France*, for the good man plays a very small part in my religion at home. Yet I could not help fearing that, where the Saint is so much commended for exactitude, he will be expected to be very grateful for his tablet.

This is foolishness to us Protestants; and not of great importance anyway. Whether people's gratitude for the good gifts that come to them be wisely conceived or dutifully expressed, is a secondary matter, after all, so long as they feel gratitude. The true ignorance is when a man does not know that he has received a good gift, or begins to imagine that he has got it for himself. The self-made man is the funniest windbag after all! There is a marked difference between decreeing light in chaos, and lighting the gas in a metropolitan back-parlour with a box of patent matches; and do what we will, there is always something made to our hand, if it were only our fingers.

But there was something worse than foolishness placarded in *Creil* Church. *The Association of the Living Rosary* (of which I had never previously heard) is responsible for that. This association was founded, according to the printed advertisement, by a brief of Pope *Gregory* Sixteenth, on the 17th of *January*, 1832: according to a coloured bas-relief, it seems to have been founded, sometime or other, by the *Virgin* giving one rosary to Saint *Dominic* and the Infant *Saviour* giving another to Saint *Catherine* of *Siena*. Pope *Gregory* is not so imposing, but he is nearer hand. I could not distinctly make out whether the association was entirely devotional, or had an eye to good works; at least it is highly organised: the names of fourteen matrons and misses were filled in for each week of the month as associates, with one other, generally a married woman, at the top for *Zélatrice*: the choragus of the band. Indulgences, plenary and partial, follow on the performance of the duties of the association. 'The partial indulgences are attached to the recitation of the rosary.' On 'the recitation of the required *dizaine*', a partial indulgence promptly follows. When people serve the kingdom of Heaven with a pass-book in their hands, I should always be afraid lest they should carry the same commercial spirit into their dealings with their fellow-men, which would make a sad and sordid business of this life.

There is one more article, however, of happier import. 'All these indulgences,' it appeared, 'are applicable to souls in purgatory.' For *God's* sake, ye ladies of *Creil*, apply them all to the souls in purgatory without delay! *Burns* would take no hire for his last songs, preferring to serve his country out of unmixed love. Suppose you were to imitate the exciseman, mesdames, and even if the souls in purgatory were not greatly bettered, some souls in *Creil* upon the *Oise* would find themselves none the worse either here or hereafter.

I cannot help wondering, as I transcribe these notes, whether a Protestant born and bred is in a fit state to understand these signs, and do them what justice they deserve; and I cannot help answering that he is not. They cannot look so merely ugly and mean to the faithful as they do to me. I see that as clearly as a proposition in *Euclid*. For these believers are neither weak nor wicked. They can put up their tablet commending Saint *Joseph* for his despatch, as if he were still a village carpenter; they can 'recite the required *dizaine*,' and metaphorically pocket the indulgence, as if they had done a job for heaven; and then they can go out and look down unabashed upon this wonderful river flowing by, and up without confusion at the pin-point stars, which are themselves great worlds full of flowing rivers greater than the *Oise*. I see it as plainly, I say, as a proposition in *Euclid*, that my Protestant mind has missed the point, and that there goes with these deformities some higher and more religious spirit than I dream.

I wonder if other people would make the same allowances for me? Like the ladies of *Creil*, having recited my rosary of toleration, I look for my indulgence on the spot.

Précy and the Marionettes

We made *Précy* about sundown. The plain is rich with tufts of poplar. In a wide, luminous curve, the *Oise* lay under the hillside. A faint mist began to rise and confound the different distances together. There was not a sound audible but that of the sheep-bells in some meadows by the river, and the creaking of a cart down the long road that descends the hill. The villas in their gardens, the shops along the street, all seemed to have been deserted the day before; and I felt inclined to walk discreetly as one feels in a silent forest. All of a sudden, we came round a corner, and there, in a little green round the church, was a bevy of girls in Parisian costumes playing croquet. Their laughter and the hollow sound of ball and mallet made a cheery stir in the neighbourhood; and the look of these slim figures, all corseted and ribboned, produced an answerable disturbance in our hearts. We were within sniff of *Paris*, it seemed. And here were females of our own species playing croquet, just as if *Précy* had been a place in real life, instead of a stage in a fairy land of travel. For, to be frank, the peasant woman is scarcely to be counted as a woman at all, and after having passed by such a succession of people in petticoats digging and hoeing and making dinner, this company of coquettes under arms made quite a surprising feature in the landscape, and convinced us at once of being fallible males.

The inn at *Précy* is the worst inn in *France*. Not even in *Scotland* have I found worse fare. It was kept by a brother and sister, neither of whom was out of their teens. The sister, so to speak, prepared a meal for us; and the brother, who had been tippling, came in and brought with him a tipsy butcher, to entertain us as we ate. We found pieces of loo-warm pork among the salad, and pieces of unknown yielding substance in the *ragoût*. The butcher entertained us with pictures of Parisian life, with which he professed himself well acquainted; the brother sitting the while on the edge of the billiard table, toppling precariously, and sucking the stump of a cigar. In the midst of these diversions, bang went a drum past the house, and a hoarse voice began issuing a proclamation. It was a man with marionettes announcing a performance for that evening.

He had set up his caravan and lighted his candles on another part of the girls' croquet green, under one of those open sheds which are so common in *France* to shelter markets; and he and his wife, by the time we strolled up there, were trying to keep order with the audience.

It was the most absurd contention. The show-people had set out a certain number of benches; and all who sat upon them were to pay a couple of *sous* for the accommodation. They were always quite full – a bumper house – as long as nothing was going forward; but let the show-woman appear with an eye to a collection, and at the first rattle of her tambourine, the audience slipped off the seats, and stood round on the outside with their hands in their pockets. It certainly would have tried an angel's temper. The showman roared from the proscenium; he had been all over *France*, and nowhere, nowhere, 'not even on the borders of *Germany*', had he met with such misconduct. Such thieves and rogues and rascals, as he called them! And every now and again, the wife issued on another round, and added her shrill quota to the tirade. I remarked here, as elsewhere, how far more copious is the female mind in the material of insult. The audience laughed in high good humour over the man's declamations; but they bridled and cried aloud under the woman's pungent sallies. She picked out the sore points. She had the honour of the village at her mercy. Voices answered her angrily out of the crowd, and received a smarting retort for their trouble. A couple of old ladies beside me, who had duly paid for their seats, waxed very red and indignant, and discoursed to each other audibly about the impudence of these mountebanks; but as soon as the show-woman caught a whisper of this, she was down upon them with a swoop: if mesdames could persuade their neighbours to act with common honesty, the mountebanks, she assured them, would be polite enough: mesdames had probably had their bowl of soup, and perhaps a glass of wine that evening; the mountebanks also had a taste for soup and did not choose to have their little earnings stolen from them before their eyes. Once, things came as far as a brief personal encounter between the showman and some lads, in which the former went down as readily as one of his own marionettes to a peal of jeering laughter.

I was a good deal astonished at this scene because I am pretty well acquainted with the ways of French strollers, more or less artistic; and have always found them singularly pleasing. Any stroller must be dear to the right-thinking heart; if it were only as a living protest against offices and the mercantile spirit, and as something to remind us that life is not by necessity the kind of thing we generally make it. Even a German band, if you see it leaving town in the early morning for a campaign in country places, among trees and meadows, has a romantic flavour for the imagination. There is nobody, under thirty, so dead but his heart will stir a little at sight of a gypsies' camp. 'We are not cotton-spinners all'; or, at least, not all through. There is some life in humanity yet; and youth will now and again find a brave word to say in dispraise of riches, and throw up a situation to go strolling with a knapsack.

An Englishman has always special facilities for intercourse with French gymnasts; for *England* is the natural home of gymnasts. This or that fellow, in his tights and spangles, is sure to know a word or two of English, to have drunk English *aff-'n-aff*, and perhaps performed in an English music-hall. He is a countryman of mine by profession. He leaps, like the Belgian boating men, to the notion that I must be an athlete myself.

But the gymnast is only my favourite; he has little or no tincture of the artist in his composition; his soul is small and pedestrian, for the most part, since his profession makes no call upon it, and does not accustom him to high ideas. But if a man is only so much of an actor that he can stumble through a farce, he is made free of a new order of thoughts. He has something else to think about beside the money-box. He has a pride of his own, and, what is of far more importance, he has an aim before him that he can never quite attain. He has gone upon a pilgrimage that will last him his life long, because there is no end to it short of perfection. He will better upon himself a little day by day; or even if he has given up the attempt, he will always remember that once upon a time he had conceived this high ideal, that once upon a time he had fallen in love with a star. ''Tis better to have loved and lost.' Although the moon should have nothing to say to *Endymion*, although he should settle down with *Audrey* and feed pigs, do you not think he would move with a better grace, and cherish higher thoughts to the end? The louts he meets at church never had a fancy above *Audrey's* snood, but there is a reminiscence in *Endymion's* heart that, like a spice, keeps it fresh and haughty.

To be even one of the outskirters of art leaves a fine stamp on a man's countenance. I remember once dining with a party in the inn at *Château Landon*. Most of them were unmistakable bagmen; others well-to-do peasantry; but there was one young fellow in a blouse whose face stood out from among the rest surprisingly. It looked more finished; more of the spirit looked out through it; it had a living, expressive air, and you could see that his eyes took things in. My companion and I wondered greatly who and what he could be. It was fair time in *Château Landon*, and when we went along to the booths, we had our question answered; for there was our friend busily fiddling for the peasants to caper to. He was a wandering violinist.

A troop of strollers once came to the inn where I was staying, in the department of *Seine et Marne*. There was a father and mother; two daughters, brazen, blowsy huzzies who sang and acted, without an idea of how to set about either; and a dark young man, like a tutor, a recalcitrant house-painter, who sang and acted not amiss. The mother was the genius of the party, so far as genius can be spoken of with regard to such a pack of incompetent humbugs; and her husband could not find words to express his admiration for her comic countryman. 'You should see my old woman,' said he, and nodded his beery countenance. One night they performed in the stable-yard, with flaring lamps: a wretched exhibition, coldly looked upon by a village audience. Next night, as soon as the lamps were lighted, there came a plump of rain, and they had to sweep away their baggage as fast as possible, and make off to the barn where they harboured, cold, wet, and supperless. In the morning, a dear friend of mine, who has as warm a heart for strollers as I have myself, made a little collection and sent it by my hands to comfort them for their disappointment. I gave it to the father; he thanked me cordially, and we drank a cup together in the kitchen, talking of roads, and audiences, and hard times.

When I was going, up got my old stroller, and off with his hat. 'I am afraid,' said he, 'that Monsieur will think me altogether a beggar; but I have another demand to make upon him.' I began to hate him on the spot. 'We play again to-night,' he went on. 'Of course, I shall refuse to accept any more money from Monsieur and his friends, who have been already so liberal. But our programme of to-night is something truly creditable; and I cling to the idea that Monsieur will honour us with his presence.' And then, with a shrug and a smile: 'Monsieur understands – the vanity of an artist!' Save the mark! The vanity of an artist! That is the kind of thing that reconciles me to life: a ragged, tippling, incompetent old rogue, with the manners of a gentleman and the vanity of an artist, to keep up his self-respect!

But the man after my own heart is M. de *Vauversin*. It is nearly two years since I saw him first, and indeed I hope I may see him often again. Here is his first programme, as I found it on the breakfast table, and have kept it ever since as a relic of bright days:

Mesdames et Messieurs,
Mademoiselle Ferrario et M. de Vauversin auront l'honneur de chanter ce soir les morceaux suivants:
  Mademoiselle Ferrario chantera – Mignon – Oiseaux Légers – France – Des Français dorment là – Le château bleu – Où voulez-vous aller?
  M. de Vauversin – Madame Fontaine et M. Robinet – Les plongeurs à cheval – Le Mari mécontent – Tais-toi, gamin – Mon voisin l'original – Heureux comme ça – Comme on est trompé.

They made a stage at one end of the *salle-à-manger*. And what a sight it was to see M. de *Vauversin*, with a cigarette in his mouth, twanging a guitar, and following Mademoiselle *Ferrario's* eyes with the obedient, kindly look of a dog! The entertainment wound up with a tombola, or auction of lottery tickets: an admirable amusement, with all the excitement of gambling, and no hope of gain to make you ashamed of your eagerness; for there, all is loss; you make haste to be out of pocket; it is a competition who shall lose most money for the benefit of M. de *Vauversin* and Mademoiselle *Ferrario*.

M. de *Vauversin* is a small man, with a great head of black hair, a vivacious and engaging air, and a smile that would be delightful if he had better teeth. He was once an actor in the *Châtelet*; but he contracted a nervous affection from the heat and glare of the footlights, which unfitted him for the stage. At this crisis Mademoiselle *Ferrario*, otherwise Mademoiselle *Rita* of the *Alcazar*, agreed to share his wandering fortunes. 'I could never forget the generosity of that lady,' said he. He wears trousers so tight that it has long been a problem to all who knew him how he manages to get in and out of them. He sketches a little in water-colours; he writes verses; he is the most patient of fishermen, and spent long days at the bottom of the inn-garden fruitlessly dabbling a line in the clear river.

You should hear him recounting his experiences over a bottle of wine; such a pleasant vein of talk as he has, with a ready smile at his own mishaps and every now and then a sudden gravity, like a man who should hear the surf roar while he was telling the perils of the deep. For it was no longer ago than last night, perhaps, that the receipts only amounted to a franc and a half, to cover three francs of railway fare and two of board and lodging. The *Maire*, a man worth a million of money, sat in the front seat, repeatedly applauding Mdlle. *Ferrario*, and yet gave no more than three *sous* the whole evening. Local authorities look with such an evil eye upon the strolling artist. Alas! I know it well, who have been myself taken for one, and pitilessly incarcerated on the strength of the misapprehension. Once, M. de *Vauversin* visited a commissary of police for permission to sing. The commissary, who was smoking at his ease, politely doffed his hat upon the singer's entrance. 'Mr. Commissary,' he began, 'I am an artist.' And on went the commissary's hat again. No courtesy for the companions of *Apollo*! 'They are as degraded as that,' said M. de *Vauversin*, with a sweep of his cigarette.

But what pleased me most was one outbreak of his, when we had been talking all the evening of the rubs, indignities, and pinchings of his wandering life. Someone said it would be better to have a million of money down, and Mdlle. *Ferrario* admitted that she would prefer that mightily. '*Eh bien, moi non*; – not I,' cried De *Vauversin*, striking the table with his hand. 'If anyone is a failure in the world, is it not I? I had an art, in which I have done things well – as well as some – better perhaps than others; and now it is closed against me. I must go about the country gathering coppers and singing nonsense. Do you think I regret my life? Do you think I would rather be a fat burgess, like a calf? Not I! I have had moments when I have been applauded on the boards: I think nothing of that; but I have known in my own mind, sometimes, when I had not a clap from the whole house, that I had found a true intonation, or an exact and speaking gesture; and then, messieurs, I have known what pleasure was, what it was to do a thing well, what it was to be an artist. And to know what art is, is to have an interest for ever, such as no burgess can find in his petty concerns. *Tenez, messieurs, je vais vous le dire* – it is like a religion.'

Such, making some allowance for the tricks of memory and the inaccuracies of translation, was the profession of faith of M. de *Vauversin*. I have given him his own name, lest any other wanderer should come across him, with his guitar and cigarette, and Mademoiselle *Ferrario*; for should not all the world delight to honour this unfortunate and loyal follower of the Muses? May *Apollo* send him rimes hitherto undreamed of; may the river be no longer scanty of her silver fishes to his lure; may the cold not pinch him on long winter rides, nor the village jack-in-office affront him with unseemly manners; and may he never miss Mademoiselle *Ferrario* from his side, to follow with his dutiful eyes and accompany on the guitar!

The marionettes made a very dismal entertainment. They performed a piece, called *Pyramus and Thisbe*, in five moral acts, and all written in Alexandrines fully as long as the performers. One marionette was the king; another the wicked counsellor; a third, credited with exceptional beauty, represented *Thisbe*; and then there were guards, and obdurate fathers, and walking gentlemen. Nothing particular took place during the two or three acts that I sat out; but you will be pleased to learn that the unities were properly respected, and the whole piece, with one exception, moved in harmony with classical rules. That exception was the comic countryman, a lean marionette in wooden shoes, who spoke in prose and in a broad *patois* much appreciated by the audience. He took unconstitutional liberties with the person of his sovereign; kicked his fellow-marionettes in the mouth with his wooden shoes, and whenever none of the versifying suitors were about, made love to *Thisbe* on his own account in comic prose.

This fellow's evolutions, and the little prologue, in which the showman made a humorous eulogium of his troop, praising their indifference to applause and hisses, and their single devotion to their art, were the only circumstances in the whole affair that you could fancy would so much as raise a smile. But the villagers of *Précy* seemed delighted. Indeed, so long as a thing is an exhibition, and you pay to see it, it is nearly certain to amuse. If we were charged so much a head for sunsets, or if *God* sent round a drum before the hawthorns came in flower, what a work should we not make about their beauty! But these things, like good companions, stupid people early cease to observe: and the Abstract Bagman tittups past in his spring gig, and is positively not aware of the flowers along the lane, or the scenery of the weather overhead.

Back to the World

Of the next two days' sail little remains in my mind, and nothing whatever in my note-book. The river streamed on steadily through pleasant riverside landscapes. Washerwomen in blue dresses, fishers in blue blouses, diversified the green banks; and the relation of the two colours was like that of the flower and the leaf in the *forget-me-not*. A symphony in *forget-me-not*; I think *Théophile Gautier* might thus have characterised that two days' panorama. The sky was blue and cloudless; and the sliding surface of the river held up, in smooth places, a mirror to the heaven and the shores. The washerwomen hailed us laughingly; and the noise of trees and water made an accompaniment of our dozing thoughts, as we fleeted down the stream.

The great volume, the indefatigable purpose of the river, held the mind in chain. It seemed now so sure of its end, so strong and easy in its gait, like a grown man full of determination. The surf was roaring for it on the sands of *Havre*.

For my own part, slipping along this moving thoroughfare in my fiddle-case of a canoe, I also was beginning to grow aweary for my ocean. To the civilised man there must come, sooner or later, a desire for civilisation. I was weary of dipping the paddle; I was weary of living on the skirts of life; I wished to be in the thick of it once more; I wished to get to work; I wished to meet people who understand my own speech, and could meet with me on equal terms, as a man, and no longer as a curiosity.

And so a letter at *Pontoise* decided us, and we drew up our keels for the last time out of that river of *Oise* that had faithfully piloted them, through rain and sunshine, for so long. For so many miles had this fleet and footless beast of burthen charioted our fortunes, that we turned our back upon it with a sense of separation. We had made a long detour out of the world, but now we were back in the familiar places, where life itself makes all the running, and we are carried to meet adventure without a stroke of the paddle. Now we were to return, like the voyager in the play, and see what rearrangements fortune had perfected the while in our surroundings; what surprises stood ready made for us at home; and whither and how far the world had voyaged in our absence. You may paddle all day long; but it is when you come back at nightfall, and look in at the familiar room, that you find Love or Death awaiting you beside the stove; and the most beautiful adventures are not those we go to seek.

The End

TRAVELS WITH A DONKEY
IN THE CÉVENNES

My Dear Sidney Colvin,

The journey which this little book is to describe was very agreeable and fortunate for me. After an uncouth beginning, I had the best of luck to the end. But we are all travellers in what John Bunyan calls the wilderness of this world – all, too, travellers with a donkey; and the best that we find in our travels is an honest friend. He is a fortunate voyager who finds many. We travel, indeed, to find them. They are the end and the reward of life. They keep us worthy of ourselves; and, when we are alone, we are only nearer to the absent.

Every book is, in an intimate sense, a circular letter to the friends of him who writes it. They alone take his meaning; they find private messages, assurances of love, and expressions of gratitude dropped for them in every corner. The public is but a generous patron who defrays the postage. Yet though the letter is directed to all, we have an old and kindly custom of addressing it on the outside to one. Of what shall a man be proud, if he is not proud of his friends? And so, my dear Sidney Colvin, it is with pride that I sign myself affectionately yours,

R.L.S.

CONTENTS

Note

No. VI in *Essays of Travel* is a pleasant short paper which Stevenson wrote in 1879, though it did not appear in print till after his death. It is called 'A Mountain Town in France', and was originally intended to serve as the opening chapter of 'Travels with a Donkey in the Cévennes'. In it Stevenson describes the town in which he bought his donkey and whence he started his travels, the country round it, and his relations with its inhabitants. One or two brief extracts (*see* below) make an apposite prelude to the book, and it will be noticed that the first sentence explains, as the book itself does not, the significance of the title of the first three chapters of the book ('Velay').   M.R.R.

Le Monastier is the chief place of a hilly canton in Haute Loire, the ancient Velay. As the name betokens, the town is of monastic origin; and it still contains a towered bulk of monastery and a church of some architectural pretensions, the seat of an arch-priest and several vicars. . . . As far as the eye can reach, one swelling line of hill top rises and falls behind another, and if you climb an eminence, it is only to see new and farther ranges behind these. . . . On the whole, this is a Scottish landscape, although not so noble as the best in Scotland; and by an odd coincidence, the population is, in its way, as Scottish as the country. They have abrupt, uncouth, Fifeshire manners, and accost you, as if you were trespassing, with an '*Où'st-ce que vous allez?*' only translatable into the Lowland 'Whaur ye gaun?' . . .

I soon became a popular figure, and was known for miles in the country. *Où'st-ce que vous allez?* was changed for me into *Quoi, vous rentrez au Monastier ce soir?* and in the town itself every urchin seemed to know my name, although no living creature could pronounce it. There was one particular group of lace-makers who brought out a chair for me whenever I went by, and detained me from my walk to gossip. They were filled with curiosity about England, its language, its religion, the dress of the women, and were never weary of seeing the Queen's head on English postage-stamps, or seeking for French words in English Journals. The language, in particular, filled them with surprise.

'Do they speak *patois* in England?' I was once asked; and when I told them not, 'Ah, then, French?' said they.

'No, no,' I said, 'not French.'

'Then,' they concluded, 'they speak *patois*.'

You must obviously either speak French or *patois*. Talk of the force of logic – here it was in all its weakness. I gave up the point, but proceeding to give illustrations of my native jargon, I was met with a new mortification. Of all *patois* they declared that mine was the most preposterous and the most jocose in sound. At each new word there was a new explosion of laughter, and some of the younger ones were glad to rise from their chairs and stamp about the street in ecstasy; and I looked on upon their mirth in a faint and slightly disagreeable bewilderment. 'Bread,' which sounds a commonplace, plain-sailing monosyllable in England, was the word that most delighted these good ladies in Monastier; it seemed to them frolicsome and racy, like a page of Pickwick; and they all got it carefully by heart, as a stand-by, I presume, for winter evenings. I have tried it since then with every sort of accent and inflection, but I seem to lack the sense of humour.

Velay

Many are the mighty things, and naught is more mighty than man. . . .
He masters by his devices the tenant of the fields. – *Sophocles*

Who hath loosed the bands of the wild ass? – *Job*

The Donkey, the Pack,
and the Pack-Saddle

In a little place called Le Monastier, in a pleasant highland valley fifteen miles from Le Puy, I spent about a month of fine days. Monastier is notable for the making of lace, for drunkenness, for freedom of language, and for unparalleled political dissension. There are adherents of each of the four French parties – Legitimists, Orleanists, Imperialists, and Republicans – in this little mountain-town; and they all hate, loathe, decry, and calumniate each other. Except for business purposes, or to give each other the lie in a tavern brawl, they have laid aside even the civility of speech. 'Tis a mere mountain Poland. In the midst of this Babylon I found myself a rallying point; everyone was anxious to be kind and helpful to the stranger. This was not merely from the natural hospitality of mountain people, nor even from the surprise with which I was regarded as a man living of his own free will in Le Monastier, when he might just as well have lived anywhere else in this big world; it arose a good deal from my projected excursion southward through the Cévennes. A traveller of my sort was a thing hitherto unheard of in that district. I was looked upon with contempt, like a man who should project a journey to the moon, but yet with a respectful interest, like one setting forth for the inclement Pole. All were ready to help in my preparations; a crowd of sympathisers supported me at the critical moment of a bargain; not a step was taken but was heralded by glasses round and celebrated by a dinner or a breakfast.

It was already hard upon October before I was ready to set forth, and at the high altitudes over which my road lay there was no Indian summer to be looked for. I was determined, if not to camp out, at least to have the means of camping out in my possession; for there is nothing more harassing to an easy mind than the necessity of reaching shelter by dusk, and the hospitality of a village inn is not always to be reckoned sure by those who trudge on foot. A tent, above all for a solitary traveller, is troublesome to pitch, and troublesome to strike again; and even on the march it forms a conspicuous feature in your baggage. A sleeping-sack, on the other hand, is always ready – you have only to get into it; it serves a double purpose – a bed by night, a portmanteau by day; and it does not advertise your intention of camping out to every curious passer-by. This is a huge point. If the camp is not secret, it is but a troubled resting-place; you become a public character; the convivial rustic visits your bedside after an early supper; and you must sleep with one eye open, and be up before the day. I decided on a sleeping-sack; and after repeated visits to Le Puy, and a deal of high living for myself and my advisers, a sleeping-sack was designed, constructed, and triumphantly brought home.

This child of my invention was nearly six feet square, exclusive of two triangular flaps to serve as a pillow by night and as the top and bottom of the sack by day. I call it 'the sack,' but it was never a sack by more than courtesy; only a sort of long roll or sausage, green waterproof cart-cloth without and blue sheep's fur within. It was commodious as a valise, warm and dry for a bed. There was luxurious turning room for one; and at a pinch the thing might serve for two. I could bury myself in it up to the neck; for my head I trusted to a fur cap, with a hood to fold down over my ears and a band to pass under my nose like a respirator; and in case of heavy rain I proposed to make myself a little tent, or tentlet, with my waterproof coat, three stones, and a bent branch.

It will readily be conceived that I could not carry this huge package on my own, merely human, shoulders. It remained to choose a beast of burden. Now, a horse is a fine lady among animals, flighty, timid, delicate in eating, of tender health; he is too valuable and too restive to be left alone, so that you are chained to your brute as to a fellow galley-slave; a dangerous road puts him out of his wits; in short, he's an uncertain and exacting ally, and adds thirty-fold to the troubles of the voyager. What I required was something cheap and small and hardy, and of a stolid and peaceful temper; and all these requisites pointed to a donkey.

There dwelt an old man in Monastier, of rather unsound intellect according to some, much followed by street-boys, and known to fame as Father Adam. Father Adam had a cart, and to draw the cart a diminutive she-ass, not much bigger than a dog, the colour of a mouse, with a kindly eye and a determined under-jaw. There was something neat and high-bred, a quaker-ish elegance, about the rogue that hit my fancy on the spot. Our first interview was in Monastier market-place. To prove her good temper, one child after another was set upon her back to ride, and one after another went head over heels into the air; until a want of confidence began to reign in youthful bosoms, and the experiment was discontinued from a dearth of subjects. I was already backed by a deputation of my friends; but as if this were not enough, all the buyers and sellers came round and helped me in the bargain; and the ass and I and Father Adam were the centre of a hubbub for near half an hour. At length she passed into my service for the consideration of sixty-five francs and a glass of brandy. The sack had already cost eighty francs and two glasses of beer; so that Modestine, as I instantly baptised her, was upon all accounts the cheaper article. Indeed, that was as it should be; for she was only an appurtenance of my mattress, or self-acting bedstead on four castors.

I had a last interview with Father Adam in a billiard-room at the witching hour of dawn, when I administered the brandy. He professed himself greatly touched by the separation, and declared he had often bought white bread for the donkey when he had been content with black bread for himself; but this, according to the best authorities, must have been a flight of fancy. He had a name in the village for brutally misusing the ass; yet it is certain that he shed a tear, and the tear made a clean mark down one cheek.

By the advice of a fallacious local saddler, a leather pad was made for me with rings to fasten on my bundle; and I thought-fully completed my kit and arranged my toilette. By way of armoury and utensils, I took a revolver, a little spirit-lamp and pan, a lantern and some half-penny candles, a jack-knife and a large leather flask. The main cargo consisted of two entire changes of warm clothing – besides my travelling wear of country velveteen, pilot-coat, and knitted spencer – some books, and my railway rug, which, being also in the form of a bag, made me a double castle for cold nights. The permanent larder was represented by cakes of chocolate and tins of Bologna sausage. All this, except what I carried about my person, was easily stowed into the sheepskin bag; and by good fortune I threw in my empty knapsack, rather for convenience of carriage than from any thought that I should want it on my journey. For more immediate needs I took a leg of cold mutton, a bottle of Beaujolais, an empty bottle to carry milk, an egg-beater, and a considerable quantity of black bread and white, like Father Adam, for myself and the donkey, only in my scheme of things the destinations were reversed.

Monastrians, of all shades of thought in politics, had agreed in threatening me with many ludicrous misadventures, and with sudden death in many surprising forms. Cold, wolves, robbers, above all the nocturnal practical joker, were daily and eloquently forced on my attention. Yet in these vaticinations, the true, patent danger was left out. Like Christian, it was from my pack I suffered by the way. Before telling my own mishaps, let me in two words relate the lesson of my experience. If the pack is well strapped at the ends, and hung at full length – not doubled, for your life – across the pack-saddle, the traveller is safe. The saddle will certainly not fit, such is the imperfection of our transitory life; it will assuredly topple and tend to overset; but there are stones on every roadside, and a man soon learns the art of correcting any tendency to overbalance with a well-adjusted stone.

On the day of my departure I was up a little after five; by six, we began to load the donkey; and ten minutes after, my hopes were in the dust. The pad would not stay on Modestine's back for half a moment. I returned it to its maker, with whom I had so contumelious a passage that the street outside was crowded from wall to wall with gossips looking on and listening. The pad changed hands with much vivacity; perhaps it would be more descriptive to say that we threw it at each other's heads; and, at any rate, we were very warm and unfriendly, and spoke with a deal of freedom.

I had a common donkey pack-saddle – a *barde*, as they call it – fitted upon Modestine; and once more loaded her with my effects. The doubled sack, my pilot-coat (for it was warm, and I was to walk in my waistcoat), a great bar of black bread, and an open basket containing the white bread, the mutton, and the bottles, were all corded together in a very elaborate system of knots, and I looked on the result with fatuous content. In such a monstrous deck-cargo, all poised above the donkey's shoulders, with nothing below to balance, on a brand-new pack-saddle that had not yet been worn to fit the animal, and fastened with brand-new girths that might be expected to stretch and slacken by the way, even a very careless traveller should have seen disaster brewing. That elaborate system of knots, again, was the work of too many sympathisers to be very artfully designed. It is true they tightened the cords with a will; as many as three at a time would have a foot against Modestine's quarters, and be hauling with clenched teeth; but I learned afterwards that one thoughtful person, without any exercise of force, can make a more solid job than half-a-dozen heated and enthusiastic grooms. I was then but a novice; even after the misadventure of the pad nothing could disturb my security, and I went forth from the stable-door as an ox goeth to the slaughter.

The Green Donkey-Driver

The bell of Monastier was just striking nine as I got quit of these preliminary troubles and descended the hill through the common. As long as I was within sight of the windows, a secret shame and the fear of some laughable defeat withheld me from tampering with Modestine. She tripped along upon her four small hoofs with a sober daintiness of gait; from time to time she shook her ears or her tail; and she looked so small under the bundle that my mind misgave me. We got across the ford without difficulty – there was no doubt about the matter, she was docility itself – and once on the other bank, where the road begins to mount through pine-woods, I took in my right hand the unhallowed staff, and with a quaking spirit applied it to the donkey. Modestine brisked up her pace for perhaps three steps, and then relapsed into her former minuet. Another application had the same effect, and so with the third. I am worthy the name of an Englishman, and it goes against my conscience to lay my hand rudely on a female. I desisted, and looked her all over from head to foot; the poor brute's knees were trembling and her breathing was distressed; it was plain that she could go no faster on a hill. God forbid, thought I, that I should brutalise this innocent creature; let her go at her own pace, and let me patiently follow.

What that pace was, there is no word mean enough to describe; it was something as much slower than a walk as a walk is slower than a run; it kept me hanging on each foot for an incredible length of time; in five minutes it exhausted the spirit and set up a fever in all the muscles of the leg. And yet I had to keep close at hand and measure my advance exactly upon hers; for if I dropped a few yards into the rear, or went on a few yards ahead, Modestine came instantly to a halt and began to browse. The thought that this was to last from here to Alais nearly broke my heart. Of all conceivable journeys, this promised to be the most tedious. I tried to tell myself it was a lovely day; I tried to charm my foreboding spirit with tobacco; but I had a vision ever present to me of the long, long roads, up hill and down dale, and a pair of figures ever infinitesimally moving, foot by foot, a yard to the minute, and, like things enchanted in a nightmare, approaching no nearer to the goal.

In the meantime there came up behind us a tall peasant, perhaps forty years of age, of an ironical snuffy countenance, and arrayed in the green tail-coat of the country. He overtook us hand over hand, and stopped to consider our pitiful advance.

'Your donkey,' says he, 'is very old?'

I told him, I believed not.

Then, he supposed, we had come far.

I told him, we had but newly left Monastier.

'*Et vous marchez comme ça!*' cried he; and, throwing back his head, he laughed long and heartily. I watched him, half prepared to feel offended, until he had satisfied his mirth; and then, 'You must have no pity on these animals,' said he; and, plucking a switch out of a thicket, he began to lace Modestine about the stern-works, uttering a cry. The rogue pricked up her ears and broke into a good round pace, which she kept up without flagging, and without exhibiting the least symptom of distress, as long as the peasant kept beside us. Her former panting and shaking had been, I regret to say, a piece of comedy.

My *deus ex machina*, before he left me, supplied some excellent, if inhumane, advice; presented me with the switch, which he declared she would feel more tenderly than my cane; and finally taught me the true cry or masonic word of donkey-drivers, 'Proot!' All the time, he regarded me with a comical, incredulous air, which was embarrassing to confront; and smiled over my donkey-driving, as I might have smiled over his orthography, or his green tail-coat. But it was not my turn for the moment.

I was proud of my new lore, and thought I had learned the art to perfection. And certainly Modestine did wonders for the rest of the forenoon, and I had a breathing space to look about me. It was Sabbath; the mountain-fields were all vacant in the sunshine; and as we came down through St Martin de Frugères, the church was crowded to the door, there were people kneeling without upon the steps, and the sound of the priest's chanting came forth out of the dim interior. It gave me a home feeling on the spot; for I am a countryman of the Sabbath, so to speak,

and all Sabbath observances, like a Scottish accent, strike in me
mixed feelings, grateful and the reverse. It is only a traveller,
hurrying by like a person from another planet, who can rightly
enjoy the peace and beauty of the great ascetic feast. The sight
of the resting country does his spirit good. There is something
better than music in the wide unusual silence; and it disposes
him to amiable thoughts, like the sound of a little river or the
warmth of sunlight.

In this pleasant humour I came down the hill to where Goudet
stands in a green end of a valley, with Château Beaufort opposite
upon a rocky steep, and the stream, as clear as crystal, lying in
a deep pool between them. Above and below, you may hear it
wimpling over the stones, an amiable stripling of a river, which
it seems absurd to call the Loire. On all sides, Goudet is shut in
by mountains; rocky footpaths, practicable at best for donkeys,
join it to the outer world of France; and the men and women
drink and swear, in their green corner, or look up at the snow-
clad peaks in winter from the threshold of their homes, in an
isolation, you would think, like that of Homer's Cyclops. But it
is not so; the postman reaches Goudet with the letter-bag; the
aspiring youth of Goudet are within a day's walk of the railway
at Le Puy; and here in the inn you may find an engraved portrait
of the host's nephew, Régis Senac, 'Professor of Fencing and
Champion of the two Americas', a distinction gained by him,
along with the sum of five hundred dollars, at Tammany Hall,
New York, on the 10th April, 1876.

I hurried over my mid-day meal, and was early forth again.
But, alas, as we climbed the interminable hill upon the other
side, 'Proot!' seemed to have lost its virtue. I prooted like a lion,
I prooted mellifluously like a sucking-dove; but Modestine
would be neither softened nor intimidated. She held doggedly to
her pace; nothing but a blow would move her, and that only for
a second. I must follow at her heels, incessantly belabouring. A
moment's pause in this ignoble toil, and she relapsed into her
own private gait. I think I never heard of anyone in as mean a
situation. I must reach the lake of Bouchet, where I meant to
camp, before sun-down, and, to have even a hope of this, I must
instantly maltreat this uncomplaining animal. The sound of my
own blows sickened me. Once, when I looked at her, she had a
faint resemblance to a lady of my acquaintance who formerly

loaded me with kindness; and this increased my horror of my cruelty.

To make matters worse, we encountered another donkey ranging at will upon the roadside; and this other donkey chanced to be a gentleman. He and Modestine met nickering for joy, and I had to separate the pair and beat down their young romance with a renewed and feverish bastinado. If the other donkey had had the heart of a male under his hide, he would have fallen upon me tooth and hoof; and this was a kind of consolation – he was plainly unworthy of Modestine's affection. But the incident saddened me, as did everything that spoke of my donkey's sex.

It was blazing hot up the valley, windless, with vehement sun upon my shoulders; and I had to labour so consistently with my stick that the sweat ran into my eyes. Every five minutes, too, the pack, the basket, and the pilot-coat would take an ugly slew to one side or the other; and I had to stop Modestine, just when I had got her to a tolerable pace of about two miles an hour, to tug, push, shoulder, and readjust the load. And at last, in the village of Ussel, saddle and all, the whole hypothec turned round and grovelled in the dust below the donkey's belly. She, none better pleased, incontinently drew up and seemed to smile; and a party of one man, two women, and two children came up, and, standing round me in a half-circle, encouraged her by their example.

I had the devil's own trouble to get the thing righted; and the instant I had done so, without hesitation, it toppled and fell down upon the other side. Judge if I was hot! And yet not a hand was offered to assist me. The man, indeed, told me I ought to have a package of a different shape. I suggested if he knew nothing better to the point in my predicament, he might hold his tongue. And the good-natured dog agreed with me smilingly. It was the most despicable fix. I must plainly content myself with the pack for Modestine, and take the following items for my own share of the portage; a cane, a quart flask, a pilot-jacket heavily weighted in the pockets, two pounds of black bread, and an open basket full of meats and bottles. I believe I may say I am not devoid of greatness of soul; for I did not recoil from this infamous burden. I disposed it, Heaven knows how, so as to be mildly portable, and then proceeded to steer Modestine through the village. She tried, as was indeed her invariable habit, to enter every house and every courtyard in the whole length; and, encumbered as I was, without a hand to help myself, no words can render an idea of my difficulties. A priest, with six or seven others, was examining a church in process of repair, and he and his acolytes laughed loudly as they saw my plight. I remembered having laughed myself when I had seen good men struggling with adversity in the person of a jackass, and the recollection filled me with penitence. That was in my old light days, before this trouble came upon me. God knows at least that I shall never laugh again, thought I. But oh, what a cruel thing is a farce to those engaged in it!

A little out of the village, Modestine, filled with the demon, set her heart upon a by-road, and positively refused to leave it. I dropped all my bundles, and, I am ashamed to say, struck the poor sinner twice across the face. It was pitiful to see her lift up her head with shut eyes, as if waiting for another blow. I came very near crying; but I did a wiser thing than that, and sat squarely down by the roadside to consider my situation under the cheerful influence of tobacco and a nip of brandy. Modestine, in the meanwhile, munched some black bread with a contrite hypocritical air. It was plain that I must make a sacrifice to the gods of shipwreck. I threw away the empty bottle destined to carry milk; I threw away my own white bread, and, disdaining to act by general average, kept the black bread for Modestine; lastly, I threw away the cold leg of mutton and the egg-whisk, although this last was dear to my heart. Thus I found room for everything in the basket, and even stowed the boating-coat on the top. By means of an end of cord I slung it under one arm; and although the cord cut my shoulder, and the jacket hung almost to the ground, it was with a heart greatly lightened that I set forth again.

I had now an arm free to thrash Modestine, and cruelly I chastised her. If I were to reach the lakeside before dark, she must bestir her little shanks to some tune. Already the sun had gone down into a windy-looking mist; and although there were still a few streaks of gold far off to the east on the hills and the black fir-woods, all was cold and grey about our onward path. An infinity of little country by-roads led hither and thither among the fields. It was the most pointless labyrinth. I could see my destination overhead, or rather the peak that dominates it; but choose as I pleased, the roads always ended by turning away from it, and sneaking back towards the valley, or northward along the margin of the hills. The failing light, the waning colour, the naked, unhomely, stony country through which I was travelling, threw me into some despondency. I promise you, the stick was not idle; I think every decent step that Modestine took must have cost me at least two emphatic blows. There was not another sound in the neighbourhood but that of my unwearying bastinado.

Suddenly, in the midst of my toils, the load once more hit the dust, and, as by enchantment, all the cords were simultaneously loosened, and the road scattered with my dear possessions. The packing was to begin again from the beginning; and as I had to invent a new and better system, I do not doubt but I lost half an hour. It began to be dusk in earnest as I reached a wilderness of turf and stones. It had the air of being a road which should lead everywhere at the same time; and I was falling into something not unlike despair when I saw two figures stalking towards me over the stones. They walked one behind the other like tramps, but their pace was remarkable. The son led the way, a tall, ill-made, sombre, Scottish-looking man; the mother followed, all in her Sunday's best, with an elegantly embroidered ribbon to her cap, and a new felt hat atop, and proffering, as she strode along with kilted petticoats, a string of obscene and blasphemous oaths.

I hailed the son, and asked him my direction. He pointed loosely west and north-west, muttered an inaudible comment, and, without slackening his pace for an instant, stalked on, as he was going, right athwart my path. The mother followed without so much as raising her head. I shouted and shouted after them, but they continued to scale the hillside, and turned a deaf ear to my outcries. At last, leaving Modestine by herself, I was constrained to run after them, hailing the while. They stopped as I drew near, the mother still cursing; and I could see she was a handsome, motherly, respectable-looking woman. The son once more answered me roughly and inaudibly, and was for setting out again. But this time I simply collared the mother, who was nearest me, and, apologising for my violence, declared that I could not let them go until they had put me on my road. They were neither of them offended – rather mollified than otherwise; told me I had only to follow them; and then the mother asked me what I wanted by the lake at such an hour. I replied, in the Scottish manner, by inquiring if she had far to go herself. She told me, with another oath, that she had an hour and a half's road before her. And then, without salutation, the pair strode forward again up the hillside in the gathering dusk.

I returned to Modestine, pushed her briskly forward, and, after a sharp ascent of twenty minutes, reached the edge of a plateau. The view, looking back on my day's journey, was both wild and sad. Mount Mézenc and the peaks beyond St Julien stood out in trenchant gloom against a cold glitter in the east; and the intervening field of hills had fallen together into one broad wash of shadow, except here and there the outline of a wooded sugar-loaf in black, here and there a white irregular patch to represent a cultivated farm; and here and there a blot where the Loire, the Gazeille, or the Laussonne wandered in a gorge.

Soon we were on a high-road, and surprise seized on my mind as I beheld a village of some magnitude close at hand; for I had been told that the neighbourhood of the lake was uninhabited except by trout. The road smoked in the twilight with children driving home cattle from the fields; and a pair of mounted stride-legged women, hat and cap and all, dashed past me at a hammering trot from the canton where they had been to church and market. I asked one of the children where I was. At Bouchet St Nicolas, he told me. Thither, about a mile south of my destination, and on the other side of a respectable summit, had these confused roads and treacherous peasantry conducted me. My shoulder was cut, so that it hurt sharply; my arm ached like toothache from perpetual beating; I gave up the lake and my design to camp, and asked for the *auberge*.

I Have a Goad

The *auberge* of Bouchet St Nicolas was among the least pretentious I have ever visited; but I saw many more of the like upon my journey. Indeed, it was typical of these French highlands. Imagine a cottage of two stories, with a bench before the door; the stable and kitchen in a suite, so that Modestine and I could hear each other dining; furniture of the plainest, earthen floors, a single bedchamber for travellers, and that without any convenience but beds. In the kitchen cooking and eating go forward side by side, and the family sleep at night. Anyone who has a fancy to wash must do so in public at the common table. The food is sometimes spare; hard fish and omelette have been my portion more than once; the wine is of the smallest, the brandy abominable to man; and the visit of a fat sow, grouting under the table and rubbing against your legs, is no impossible accompaniment to dinner.

But the people of the inn, in nine cases out of ten, show themselves friendly and considerate. As soon as you cross the doors you cease to be a stranger; and although these peasantry are rude and forbidding on the highway, they show a tincture of kind breeding when you share their hearth. At Bouchet, for instance, I uncorked my bottle of Beaujolais, and asked the host to join me. He would take but little.

'I am an amateur of such wine, do you see,' he said, 'and I am capable of leaving you not enough.'

In these hedge-inns the traveller is expected to eat with his own knife; unless he ask, no other will be supplied: with a glass, a whang of bread, and an iron fork, the table is completely laid. My knife was cordially admired by the landlord of Bouchet, and the spring filled him with wonder.

'I should never have guessed that,' he said. 'I would bet,' he added, weighing it in his hand, 'that this cost you not less than five francs.'

When I told him it had cost me twenty, his jaw dropped.

He was a mild, handsome, sensible, friendly old man, astonishingly ignorant. His wife, who was not so pleasant in her manners, knew how to read, although I do not suppose she ever did so. She had a share of brains and spoke with a cutting emphasis, like one who ruled the roost.

'My man knows nothing,' she said, with an angry nod; 'he is like the beasts.'

And the old gentleman signified acquiescence with his head. There was no contempt on her part, and no shame on his; the facts were accepted loyally, and no more about the matter.

I was tightly cross-examined about my journey; and the lady understood in a moment, and sketched out what I should put into my book when I got home. 'Whether people harvest or not in such or such a place; if there were forests; studies of manners; what, for example, I and the master of the house say to you; the beauties of Nature, and all that.' And she interrogated me with a look.

'It is just that,' said I.

'You see,' she added to her husband, 'I understood that.'

They were both much interested by the story of my misadventures.

'In the morning,' said the husband, 'I will make you something better than your cane. Such a beast as that feels nothing; it is in the proverb – *dur comme un âne*; you might beat her insensible with a cudgel, and yet you would arrive nowhere.'

Something better! I little knew what he was offering.

The sleeping-room was furnished with two beds. I had one; and I will own I was a little abashed to find a young man and his wife and child in the act of mounting into the other. This was my first experience of that sort; and, if I am always to feel equally silly and extraneous, I pray God it be my last as well. I kept my eyes to myself, and know nothing of the woman except that she had beautiful arms, and seemed no whit embarrassed by my appearance. As a matter of fact, the situation was more trying to me than to the pair. A pair keep each other in countenance; it is the single gentleman who has to blush. But I could not help attributing my sentiments to the husband, and sought to conciliate his tolerance with a cup of brandy from my flask. He told me that he was a cooper of Alais travelling to St Étienne in search of work, and that in his spare moments he followed the fatal calling of a maker of matches. Me he readily enough divined to be a brandy merchant.

I was up first in the morning (Monday, September 23rd), and hastened my toilette guiltily, so as to leave a clear field for madam, the cooper's wife. I drank a bowl of milk, and set off to explore the neighbourhood of Bouchet. It was perishing cold, a grey, windy, wintry morning; misty clouds flew fast and low; the wind piped over the naked platform; and the only speck of colour was away behind Mount Mézenc and the eastern hills, where the sky still wore the orange of the dawn.

It was five in the morning, and four thousand feet above the sea; and I had to bury my hands in my pockets and trot. People were trooping out to the labours of the field by twos and threes, and all turned round to stare upon the stranger. I had seen them coming back last night, I saw them going afield again; and there was the life of Bouchet in a nutshell.

When I came back to the inn for a bit of breakfast, the landlady was in the kitchen combing out her daughter's hair; and I made her my compliments upon its beauty.

'Oh no,' said the mother; 'it is not so beautiful as it ought to be. Look, it is too fine.'

Thus does a wise peasantry console itself under adverse physical circumstances, and by a startling democratic process the defects of the majority decide the type of beauty.

'And where,' said I, 'is monsieur?'

'The master of the house is upstairs,' she answered, 'making you a goad.'

Blessed be the man who invented goads! Blessed the innkeeper of Bouchet St Nicolas, who introduced me to their use! This plain wand, with an eighth of an inch of pin, was indeed a sceptre when he put it in my hands. Thenceforward Modestine was my slave. A prick, and she passed the most inviting stable door. A prick, and she broke forth into a gallant little trotlet that devoured the miles. It was not a remarkable speed, when all was said; and we took four hours to cover ten miles at the best of it. But what a heavenly change since yesterday! No more wielding of the ugly cudgel; no more flailing with an aching arm; no more broadsword exercise, but a discreet and gentlemanly fence. And what although now and then a drop of blood should appear on Modestine's mouse-coloured wedge-like rump? I should have preferred it otherwise, indeed; but yesterday's exploits had purged my heart of all humanity. The perverse little devil, since she would not be taken with kindness, must even go with pricking.

It was bleak and bitter cold, and, except a cavalcade of stride-legged ladies and a pair of post-runners, the road was dead solitary all the way to Pradelles. I scarce remember an incident but one. A handsome foal with a bell about his neck came charging up to us upon a stretch of common, sniffed the air martially as one about to do great deeds, and suddenly thinking otherwise in his green young heart, put about and galloped off as he had come, the bell tinkling in the wind. For a long while afterwards I saw his noble attitude as he drew up, and heard the note of his bell; and when I struck the high-road, the song of the telegraph-wires seemed to continue the same music.

Pradelles stands on a hillside, high above the Allier, sur-rounded by rich meadows. They were cutting aftermath on all sides, which gave the neighbourhood, this gusty autumn morn-ing, an untimely smell of hay. On the opposite bank of the Allier the land kept mounting for miles to the horizon: a tanned and sallow autumn landscape, with black blots of fir-wood and white roads wandering through the hills. Over all this the clouds shed a uniform and purplish shadow, sad and somewhat men-acing, exaggerating height and distance, and throwing into still higher relief the twisted ribbons of the highway. It was a cheerless prospect, but one stimulating to a traveller. For I was now upon the limit of Velay, and all that I beheld lay in another county – wild Gévaudan, mountainous, uncultivated, and but recently disforested from terror of the wolves.

Wolves, alas, like bandits, seem to flee the traveller's advance; and you may trudge through all our comfortable Europe, and not meet with an adventure worth the name. But here, if anywhere, a man was on the frontiers of hope. For this was the land of the ever-memorable BEAST, the Napoleon Bonaparte of wolves. What a career was his! He lived ten months at free quarters in Gévaudan and Vivarais; he ate women and children and 'shepherdesses celebrated for their beauty'; he pursued armed horsemen; he had been seen at broad noonday chasing a postchaise and outrider along the king's high-road, and chaise and outrider fleeing before him at the gallop. He was placarded like a political offender, and ten thousand francs were offered for his head. And yet, when he was shot and sent to Versailles, behold! a common wolf, and even small for that. 'Though I could reach from pole to pole,' sang Alexander Pope; the Little Corporal shook Europe; and if all wolves had been as this wolf, they would have changed the history of man. M. Élie Berthet has made him the hero of a novel, which I have read, and do not wish to read again.

I hurried over my lunch, and was proof against the landlady's desire that I should visit our Lady of Pradelles, 'who performed many miracles, although she was of wood'; and before three-quarters of an hour I was goading Modestine down the steep descent that leads to Langogne on the Allier. On both sides of the road, in big dusty fields, farmers were preparing for next spring. Every fifty yards a yoke of great-necked stolid oxen were patiently haling at the plough. I saw one of these mild formidable servants of the glebe, who took a sudden interest in Modestine and me. The furrow down which he was journeying lay at an angle to the road, and his head was solidly fixed to the yoke like those of caryatides below a ponderous cornice; but he screwed round his big honest eyes and followed us with a ruminating look, until his master bade him turn the plough and proceed to reascend the field. From all these furrowing plough-shares, from the feet of oxen, from a labourer here and there who was breaking the dry clods with a hoe, the wind carried away a thin dust like so much smoke. It was a fine, busy, breathing, rustic landscape; and as I continued to descend, the highlands of Gévaudan kept mounting in front of me against the sky.

I had crossed the Loire the day before; now I was to cross the Allier; so near are these two confluents in their youth. Just at the bridge of Langogne, as the long-promised rain was beginning to fall, a lassie of some seven or eight addressed me in the sacramental phrase, '*D'où'st-ce-que vous venez?*' She did it with so high an air that she set me laughing; and this cut her to the quick. She was evidently one who reckoned on respect, and stood looking after me in silent dudgeon, as I crossed the bridge and entered the county of Gévaudan.

Upper Gévaudan

The way also here was very wearisome through dirt and slabbiness; nor was there on all this ground so much as one inn or victualling-house wherein to refresh the feebler sort. – *Pilgrim's Progress*

A Camp in the Dark

The next day (Tuesday, September 24th), it was two o'clock in the afternoon before I got my journal written up and my knapsack repaired, for I was determined to carry my knapsack in the future and have no more ado with baskets; and half an hour afterwards I set out for Le Cheylard l'Évêque, a place on the borders of the forest of Mercoire. A man, I was told, should walk there in an hour and a half; and I thought it scarce too ambitious to suppose that a man encumbered with a donkey might cover the same distance in four hours.

All the way up the long hill from Langogne it rained and hailed alternately; the wind kept freshening steadily, although slowly; plentiful hurrying clouds – some dragging veils of straight rain-shower, others massed and luminous as though promising snow – careered out of the north and followed me along my way. I was soon out of the cultivated basin of the Allier, and away from the ploughing oxen, and such-like sights of the country. Moor, heathery marsh, tracts of rock and pines, woods of birch all jewelled with the autumn yellow, here and there a few naked cottages and bleak fields, – these were the characters of the country. Hill and valley followed valley and hill; the little green and stony cattle-tracks wandered in and out of one another, split into three or four, died away in marshy hollows, and began again sporadically on hillsides or at the borders of a wood.

There was no direct road to Cheylard, and it was no easy affair to make a passage in this uneven country and through this intermittent labyrinth of tracks. It must have been about four when I struck Sagnerousse, and went on my way rejoicing in a sure point of departure. Two hours afterwards, the dusk rapidly falling, in a lull of the wind, I issued from a fir-wood where I had long been wandering, and found, not the looked-for village, but another marish bottom among rough-and-tumble hills. For some time past I had heard the ringing of the cattle-bells ahead;

and now, as I came out of the skirts of the wood, I saw near upon a dozen cows and perhaps as many more black figures, which I conjectured to be children, although the mist had almost unrecognisably exaggerated their forms. These were all silently following each other round and round in a circle, now taking hands, now breaking up with chains and reverences. A dance of children appeals to very innocent and lively thoughts; but, at nightfall on the marshes, the thing was eerie and fantastic to behold. Even I, who am well enough read in Herbert Spencer, felt a sort of silence fall for an instant on my mind. The next I was pricking Modestine forward, and guiding her like an unruly ship through the open. In a path, she went doggedly ahead of her own accord, as before a fair wind; but once on the turf or among heather, and the brute became demented. The tendency of lost travellers to go round in a circle was developed in her to the degree of passion, and it took all the steering I had in me to keep even a decently straight course through a single field.

While I was thus desperately tacking through the bog, children and cattle began to disperse, until only a pair of girls remained behind. From these I sought direction on my path. The peasantry in general were but little disposed to counsel a wayfarer. One old devil simply retired into his house, and barricaded the door on my approach; and I might beat and shout myself hoarse, he turned a deaf ear. Another, having given me a direction which, as I found afterwards, I had misunderstood, complacently watched me going wrong without adding a sign. He did not care a stalk of parsley if I wandered all night upon the hills! As for these two girls, they were a pair of impudent sly sluts, with not a thought but mischief. One put out her tongue at me, the other bade me follow the cows, and they both giggled and jogged each other's elbows. The Beast of Gévaudan ate about a hundred children of this district; I began to think of him with sympathy.

Leaving the girls, I pushed on through the bog, and got into another wood and upon a well-marked road. It grew darker and darker. Modestine, suddenly beginning to smell mischief, bettered the pace of her own accord, and from that time forward gave me no trouble. It was the first sign of intelligence I had occasion to remark in her. At the same time, the wind freshened into half a gale, and another heavy discharge of rain came flying up out of the north. At the other side of the wood I sighted some red windows in the dusk. This was the hamlet of Fouzilhic;

three houses on a hillside, near a wood of birches. Here I found a delightful old man, who came a little way with me in the rain to put me safely on the road for Cheylard. He would hear of no reward, but shook his hands above his head almost as if in menace, and refused volubly and shrilly, in unmitigated *patois*.

All seemed right at last. My thoughts began to turn upon dinner and a fireside, and my heart was agreeably softened in my bosom. Alas, and I was on the brink of new and greater miseries! Suddenly, at a single swoop, the night fell. I have been abroad in many a black night, but never in a blacker. A glimmer of rocks, a glimmer of the track where it was well beaten, a certain fleecy density, or night within night, for a tree, – this was all that I could discriminate. The sky was simply darkness overhead; even the flying clouds pursued their way invisibly to human eyesight. I could not distinguish my hand at arm's-length from the track, nor my goad, at the same distance, from the meadows or the sky.

Soon the road that I was following split, after the fashion of the country, into three or four in a piece of rocky meadow. Since Modestine had shown such a fancy for beaten roads, I tried her instinct in this predicament. But the instinct of an ass is what might be expected from the name; in half a minute she was clambering round and round among some boulders, as lost a donkey as you would wish to see. I should have camped long before had I been properly provided; but as this was to be so short a stage, I had brought no wine, no bread for myself, and little over a pound for my lady friend. Add to this, that I and Modestine were both handsomely wetted by the showers. But now, if I could have found some water, I should have camped at once in spite of all. Water, however, being entirely absent, except in the form of rain, I determined to return to Fouzilhic, and ask a guide a little farther on my way – 'a little farther lend thy guiding hand.'

The thing was easy to decide, hard to accomplish. In this sensible roaring blackness I was sure of nothing but the direction of the wind. To this I set my face. The road had disappeared, and I went across country, now in marshy opens, now baffled by walls unscalable to Modestine, until I came once more in sight of some red windows. This time they were differently disposed. It was not Fouzilhic, but Fouzilhac, a hamlet little distant from the other in space, but worlds away in the spirit of its inhabitants. I tied Modestine to a gate, and groped forward, stumbling among rocks, plunging mid-leg in bog, until I gained the entrance of the village. In the first lighted house there was a woman who would not open to me. She could do nothing, she cried to me through the door, being alone and lame; but if I would apply at the next house, there was a man who could help me if he had a mind.

They came to the next door in force, a man, two women, and a girl, and brought a pair of lanterns to examine the wayfarer. The man was not ill-looking, but had a shifty smile. He leaned against the doorpost, and heard me state my case. All I asked was a guide as far as Cheylard.

'*C'est que, voyez-vous, il fait noir,*' said he.

I told him that was just my reason for requiring help.

'I understand that,' said he, looking uncomfortable; '*mais – c'est – de la peine.*'

I was willing to pay, I said. He shook his head. I rose as high as ten francs; but he continued to shake his head.

'Name your own price, then,' said I.

'*Ce n'est pas ça,*' he said at length, and with evident difficulty; 'but I am not going to cross the door – *mais je ne sortirai pas de la porte.*'

I grew a little warm, and asked him what he proposed that I should do.

'Where are you going beyond Cheylard?' he asked by way of answer.

'That is no affair of yours,' I returned, for I was not going to indulge his bestial curiosity; 'it changes nothing in my present predicament.'

'*C'est vrai, ça,*' he acknowledged, with a laugh; '*oui, c'est vrai. Et d'où venez-vous?*'

A better man than I might have felt nettled.

'Oh,' said I, 'I am not going to answer any of your questions, so you may spare yourself the trouble of putting them. I am late enough already; I want help. If you will not guide me yourself, at least help me to find someone else who will.'

'Hold on,' he cried suddenly. 'Was it not you who passed in the meadow while it was still day?'

'Yes, yes,' said the girl, whom I had not hitherto recognised; 'it was monsieur; I told him to follow the cows.'

'As for you, mademoiselle,' said I, 'you are a *farceuse.*'

'And,' added the man, 'what the devil have you done to be still here?'

What the devil, indeed! But there I was.

'The great thing,' said I, 'is to make an end of it'; and once more proposed that he should help me to find a guide.

'*C'est que*,' he said again, '*c'est que – il fait noir.*'

'Very well,' said I; 'take one of your lanterns.'

'No,' he cried, drawing a thought backward, and again intrenching himself behind one of his former phrases; 'I will not cross the door.'

I looked at him. I saw unaffected terror struggling on his face with unaffected shame; he was smiling pitifully and wetting his lip with his tongue, like a detected schoolboy. I drew a brief picture of my state, and asked him what I was to do.

'I don't know,' he said; 'I will not cross the door.'

Here was the Beast of Gévaudan, and no mistake.

'Sir,' said I, with my most commanding manners, 'you are a coward.'

And with that I turned my back upon the family party, who hastened to retire within their fortifications; and the famous door was closed again, but not till I had overheard the sound of laughter. *Filia barbara pater barbarior.* Let me say it in the plural: the Beasts of Gévaudan.

The lanterns had somewhat dazzled me, and I ploughed distressfully among stones and rubbish-heaps. All the other houses in the village were both dark and silent; and though I knocked at here and there a door, my knocking was unanswered. It was a bad business; I gave up Fouzilhac with my curses. The rain had stopped, and the wind, which still kept rising, began to dry my coat and trousers. 'Very well,' thought I, 'water or no water, I must camp.' But the first thing was to return to Modestine. I am pretty sure I was twenty minutes groping for my lady in the dark; and if it had not been for the unkindly services of the bog, into which I once more stumbled, I might have still been groping for her at the dawn. My next business was to gain the shelter of a wood, for the wind was cold as well as boisterous. How, in this well-wooded district, I should have been so long in finding one, is another of the insoluble mysteries of this day's adventures; but I will take my oath that I put near an hour to the discovery.

At last black trees began to show upon my left, and, suddenly crossing the road, made a cave of unmitigated blackness right in front. I call it a cave without exaggeration; to pass below that arch of leaves was like entering a dungeon. I felt about until my hand encountered a stout branch, and to this I tied Modestine, a haggard, drenched, desponding donkey. Then I lowered my pack, laid it along the wall on the margin of the road, and unbuckled the straps. I knew well enough where the lantern was; but where were the candles? I groped and groped among the tumbled articles, and, while I was thus groping, suddenly I touched the spirit-lamp. Salvation! This would serve my turn as well. The wind roared unwearyingly among the trees; I could hear the boughs tossing and the leaves churning through half a mile of forest; yet the scene of my encampment was not only as black as the pit, but admirably sheltered. At the second match the wick caught flame. The light was both livid and shifting; but it cut me off from the universe, and doubled the darkness of the surrounding night.

I tied Modestine more conveniently for herself, and broke up half the black bread for her supper, reserving the other half against the morning. Then I gathered what I should want within reach, took off my wet boots and gaiters, which I wrapped in my waterproof, arranged my knapsack for a pillow under the flap of my sleeping-bag, insinuated my limbs into the interior, and buckled myself in like a *bambino*. I opened a tin of Bologna sausage and broke a cake of chocolate, and that was all I had to eat. It may sound offensive, but I ate them together, bite by bite, by way of bread and meat. All I had to wash down this revolting mixture was neat brandy; a revolting beverage in itself. But I was rare and hungry; ate well, and smoked one of the best cigarettes in my experience. Then I put a stone in my straw hat, pulled the flap of my fur cap over my neck and eyes, put my revolver ready to my hand, and snuggled well down among the sheepskins.

I questioned at first if I were sleepy, for I felt my heart beating faster than usual, as if with an agreeable excitement to which my mind remained a stranger. But as soon as my eyelids touched, that subtle glue leaped between them, and they would no more come separate. The wind among the trees was my lullaby. Sometimes it sounded for minutes together with a steady, even rush, not rising nor abating; and again it would swell and burst like a great crashing breaker, and the trees would patter me all over with big drops from the rain of the afternoon. Night after night, in my own bedroom in the country, I have given ear to this perturbing concert of the wind among the woods; but whether it was a difference in the trees, or the lie of the ground, or because I was myself outside and in the midst of it, the fact remains that the wind sang to a different tune among these woods of Gévaudan. I hearkened and hearkened: and meanwhile sleep took gradual possession of my body and subdued my thoughts and senses; but still my last waking effort was to listen and distinguish, and my last conscious state was one of wonder at the foreign clamour in my ears.

Twice in the course of the dark hours – once when a stone galled me underneath the sack, and again when the poor patient Modestine, growing angry, pawed and stamped upon the road – I was recalled for a brief while to consciousness, and saw a star or two overhead, and the lace-like edge of the foliage against the sky. When I awoke for the third time (Wednesday, September 25th), the world was flooded with a blue light, the mother of the dawn. I saw the leaves labouring in the wind and the ribbon of the road; and, on turning my head, there was Modestine tied to a beech, and standing half across the path in an attitude of inimitable patience. I closed my eyes again, and set to thinking over the experience of the night. I was surprised to find how easy and pleasant it had been, even in this tempestuous weather. The stone which annoyed me would not have been there, had I not been forced to camp blindfold in the opaque night; and I had felt no other inconvenience, except when my feet encountered the lantern or the second volume of Peyrat's *Pastors of the Desert* among the mixed contents of my sleeping-bag; nay, more, I had felt not a touch of cold, and awakened with unusually lightsome and clear sensations.

With that, I shook myself, got once more into my boots and gaiters, and, breaking up the rest of the bread for Modestine, strolled about to see in what part of the world I had awakened. Ulysses, left on Ithaca, and with a mind unsettled by the goddess, was not more pleasantly astray. I have been after an adventure all my life, a pure dispassionate adventure, such as befell early and heroic voyagers; and thus to be found by morning in a random woodside nook in Gévaudan – not knowing north from south, as strange to my surroundings as the first man upon the earth, an inland castaway – was to find a fraction of my daydreams realised. I was on the skirts of a little wood of birch, sprinkled with a few beeches; behind, it adjoined another wood of fir; and in front, it broke up and went down in open order into a shallow and meadowy dale. All around there were bare hilltops, some near, some far away, as the perspective closed or opened, but none apparently much higher than the rest. The wind huddled the trees. The golden specks of autumn in the birches tossed shiveringly. Overhead the sky was full of strings and shreds of vapour, flying, vanishing, reappearing, and turning about an axis like tumblers, as the wind hounded them through heaven. It was wild weather and famishing cold. I ate some chocolate, swallowed a mouthful of brandy, and smoked a cigarette before the cold should have time to disable my fingers. And by the time I had got all this done, and had made my pack and bound it on the pack-saddle, the day was tiptoe on the threshold of the east. We had not gone many steps along the lane before the sun, still invisible to me, sent a glow of gold over some cloud mountains that lay ranged along the eastern sky.

The wind had us on the stern, and hurried us bitingly forward. I buttoned myself into my coat, and walked on in a pleasant frame of mind with all men, when suddenly, at a corner, there was Fouzilhic once more in front of me. Nor only that, but there was the old gentleman who had escorted me so far the night before, running out of his house at sight of me, with hands upraised in horror.

'My poor boy!' he cried, 'what does this mean?'

I told him what had happened. He beat his old hands like clappers in a mill, to think how lightly he had let me go; but when he heard of the man in Fouzilhac, anger and depression seized upon his mind.

'This time, at least,' said he, 'there shall be no mistake.'

And he limped along, for he was very rheumatic, for about half a mile, and until I was almost within sight of Cheylard, the destination I had hunted for so long.

Cheylard and Luc

Candidly, it seemed little worthy of all this searching. A few broken ends of village, with no particular street, but a succession of open places heaped with logs and faggots; a couple of tilted crosses, a shrine to Our Lady of all Graces on the summit of a little hill; and all this, upon a rattling highland river, in the corner of a naked valley. What went ye out for to see? thought I to myself. But the place had a life of its own. I found a board, commemorating the liberalities of Cheylard for the past year, hung up, like a banner, in the diminutive and tottering church. In 1877, it appeared, the inhabitants subscribed forty-eight francs ten centimes for the 'Work of the Propagation of the Faith'. Some of this, I could not help hoping, would be applied to my native land. Cheylard scrapes together halfpence for the darkened souls in Edinburgh; while Balquhidder and Dunrossness bemoan the ignorance of Rome. Thus, to the high entertainment of the angels, do we pelt each other with evangelists, like schoolboys bickering in the snow.

The inn was again singularly unpretentious. The whole furniture of a not ill-to-do family was in the kitchen: the beds, the cradle, the clothes, the plate-rack, the meal-chest, and the photograph of the parish priest. There were five children, one of whom was set to its morning prayers at the stair-foot soon after my arrival, and a sixth would ere long be forthcoming. I was kindly received by these good folk. They were much interested in my misadventure. The wood in which I had slept belonged to them; the man of Fouzilhac they thought a monster of iniquity, and counselled me warmly to summon him at law – 'because I might have died'. The good wife was horror-stricken to see me drink over a pint of uncreamed milk.

'You will do yourself an evil,' she said. 'Permit me to boil it for you.'

After I had begun the morning on this delightful liquor, she having an infinity of things to arrange, I was permitted, nay

requested, to make a bowl of chocolate for myself. My boots
and gaiters were hung up to dry, and, seeing me trying to write
my journal on my knee, the eldest daughter let down a hinged
table in the chimney-corner for my convenience. Here I wrote,
drank my chocolate, and finally ate an omelette before I left.
The table was thick with dust; for, as they explained, it was not
used except in winter weather. I had a clear look up the vent,
through brown agglomerations of soot and blue vapour, to the
sky; and whenever a handful of twigs was thrown on to the fire,
my legs were scorched by the blaze.

The husband had begun life as a muleteer, and when I came
to charge Modestine showed himself full of the prudence of his
art. 'You will have to change this package,' said he; 'it ought to
be in two parts, and then you might have double the weight.'

I explained that I wanted no more weight; and for no donkey
hitherto created would I cut my sleeping-bag in two.

'It fatigues her, however,' said the innkeeper; 'it fatigues her
greatly on the march. Look.'

Alas, there were her two forelegs no better than raw beef on
the inside, and blood was running from under her tail. They
told me when I started, and I was ready to believe it, that before
a few days I should come to love Modestine like a dog. Three
days had passed, we had shared some misadventures, and my
heart was still as cold as a potato towards my beast of burden.
She was pretty enough to look at; but then she had given proof
of dead stupidity, redeemed indeed by patience, but aggravated
by flashes of sorry and ill-judged light-heartedness. And I own
this new discovery seemed another point against her. What the
devil was the good of a she-ass if she could not carry a sleeping-
bag and a few necessaries? I saw the end of the fable rapidly
approaching, when I should have to carry Modestine. Æsop was
the man to know the world! I assure you I set out with heavy
thoughts upon my short day's march.

It was not only heavy thoughts about Modestine that
weighted me upon the way; it was a leaden business altogether.
For first, the wind blew so rudely that I had to hold on the pack
with one hand from Cheylard to Luc; and second, my road lay
through one of the most beggarly countries in the world. It was
like the worst of the Scottish Highlands, only worse; cold,
naked, and ignoble, scant of wood, scant of heather, scant of
life. A road and some fences broke the unvarying waste, and the

line of the road was marked by upright pillars, to serve in time of snow.

Why anyone should desire to visit either Luc or Cheylard is more than my much-inventing spirit can suppose. For my part, I travel not to go anywhere, but to go. I travel for travel's sake. The great affair is to move; to feel the needs and hitches of our life more nearly; to come down off this feather-bed of civilisation, and find the globe granite underfoot and strewn with cutting flints. Alas, as we get up in life, and are more preoccupied with our affairs, even a holiday is a thing that must be worked for. To hold a pack upon a pack-saddle against a gale out of the freezing north is no high industry, but it is one that serves to occupy and compose the mind. And when the present is so exacting, who can annoy himself about the future?

I came out at length above the Allier. A more unsightly prospect at this season of the year it would be hard to fancy. Shelving hills rose round it on all sides, here dabbled with wood and fields, there rising to peaks alternately naked and hairy with pines. The colour throughout was black or ashen, and came to a point in the ruins of the castle of Luc, which pricked up impudently from below my feet, carrying on a pinnacle a tall white statue of Our Lady, which, I heard with interest, weighed fifty quintals, and was to be dedicated on the 6th of October. Through this sorry landscape trickled the Allier and a tributary of nearly equal size, which came down to join it through a broad nude valley in Vivarais. The weather had somewhat lightened, and the clouds massed in squadron; but the fierce wind still hunted them through heaven, and cast great ungainly splashes of shadow and sunlight over the scene.

Luc itself was a straggling double file of houses wedged between hill and river. It had no beauty, nor was there any notable feature, save the old castle overhead with its fifty quintals of brand-new Madonna. But the inn was clean and large. The kitchen, with its two box-beds hung with clean check curtains, with its wide stone chimney, its chimney-shelf four yards long and garnished with lanterns and religious statuettes, its array of chests and pair of ticking clocks, was the very model of what a kitchen ought to be – a melodrama kitchen, suitable for bandits or noblemen in disguise. Nor was the scene disgraced by the landlady, a handsome, silent, dark old woman, clothed and hooded in black like a nun. Even the public bedroom had a character of its own, with the long deal tables and benches, where fifty might have dined, set out as for a harvest-home, and the three box-beds along the wall. In one of these, lying on straw and covered with a pair of table-napkins, did I do penance all night long in goose-flesh and chattering teeth, and sigh, from time to time as I awakened, for my sheepskin sack and the lee of some great wood.

Our Lady
of the Snows

I behold
The House, the Brotherhood austere –
And what am I, that I am here ? – *Matthew Arnold*

Father Apollinaris

Next morning (Thursday, 26th September) I took the road in a new order. The sack was no longer doubled, but hung at full length across the saddle, a green sausage six feet long with a tuft of blue wool hanging out of either end. It was more picturesque, it spared the donkey, and, as I began to see, it would ensure stability, blow high, blow low. But it was not without a pang that I had so decided. For although I had purchased a new cord, and made all as fast as I was able, I was yet jealously uneasy lest the flaps should tumble out and scatter my effects along the line of march.

My way lay up the bald valley of the river, along the march of Vivarais and Gévaudan. The hills of Gévaudan on the right were a little more naked, if anything, than those of Vivarais upon the left, and the former had a monopoly of a low dotty underwood that grew thickly in the gorges and died out in solitary burrs upon the shoulders and the summits. Black bricks of fir-wood were plastered here and there upon both sides, and here and there were cultivated fields. A railway ran beside the river; the only bit of railway in Gévaudan, although there are many proposals afoot and surveys being made, and even, as they tell me, a station standing ready built in Mende. A year or two hence and this may be another world. The desert is beleaguered. Now may some Languedocian Wordsworth turn the sonnet into *patois*: 'Mountains and vales and floods, heard YE that whistle?'

At a place called La Bastide I was directed to leave the river, and follow a road that mounted on the left among the hills of Vivarais, the modern Ardèche; for I was now come within a little way of my strange destination, the Trappist monastery of Our Lady of the Snows. The sun came out as I left the shelter of a pine-wood, and I beheld suddenly a fine wild landscape to the south. High rocky hills, as blue as sapphire, closed the view, and between these lay ridge upon ridge, heathery, craggy, the sun glittering on veins of rock, the underwood clambering in the hollows, as rude as God made them at the first. There was not a sign of man's hand in all the prospect; and, indeed, not a trace of his passage, save where generation after generation had walked in twisted footpaths, in and out among the beeches, and up and down upon the channelled slopes. The mists, which had hitherto beset me, were now broken into clouds, and fled swiftly and shone brightly in the sun. I drew a long breath. It was grateful to come, after so long, upon a scene of some attraction for the human heart. I own I like definite form in what my eyes are to rest upon; and if landscapes were sold, like the sheets of characters of my boyhood, one penny plain and twopence coloured, I should go the length of twopence every day of my life.

But if things had grown better to the south, it was still desolate and inclement near at hand. A spidery cross on every hilltop marked the neighbourhood of a religious house; and a quarter of a mile beyond, the outlook southward opening out and growing bolder with every step, a white statue of the Virgin at the corner of a young plantation directed the traveller to Our Lady of the Snows. Here, then, I struck leftward, and pursued my way, driving my secular donkey before me, and creaking in my secular boots and gaiters, towards the asylum of silence.

I had not gone very far ere the wind brought to me the clanging of a bell, and somehow, I can scarce tell why, my heart sank within me at the sound. I have rarely approached anything with more unaffected terror than the monastery of Our Lady of the Snows. This it is to have had a Protestant education. And suddenly, on turning a corner, fear took hold on me from head to foot – slavish, superstitious fear; and though I did not stop in my advance, yet I went on slowly, like a man who should have passed a bourne unnoticed, and strayed into the country of the dead. For there, upon the narrow new-made road, between the stripling pines, was a mediæval friar, fighting with a barrowful of turfs. Every Sunday of my childhood I used to study the Hermits of Marco Sadeler – enchanting prints, full of wood and field and mediæval landscapes, as large as a county, for the imagination to go a-travelling in; and here, sure enough, was one of Marco Sadeler's heroes. He was robed in white like any spectre, and the hood falling back, in the instancy of his contention with the barrow, disclosed a pate as bald and yellow as a skull. He might have been buried any time these thousand years, and all the lively parts of him resolved into earth and broken up with the farmer's harrow.

I was troubled besides in my mind as to etiquette. Durst I address a person who was under a vow of silence? Clearly not. But drawing near, I doffed my cap to him with a far-away superstitious reverence. He nodded back, and cheerfully addressed me. Was I going to the monastery? Who was I? An Englishman? Ah, an Irishman, then?

'No,' I said, 'a Scotsman.'

A Scotsman? Ah, he had never seen a Scotsman before. And he looked me all over, his good, honest, brawny countenance shining with interest, as a boy might look upon a lion or an alligator. From him I learned with disgust that I could not be received at Our Lady of the Snows; I might get a meal, perhaps, but that was all. And then, as our talk ran on, and it turned out that I was not a pedlar, but a literary man, who drew landscapes and was going to write a book, he changed his manner of thinking as to my reception (for I fear they respect persons even in a Trappist monastery), and told me I must be sure to ask for the Father Prior, and state my case to him in full. On second thoughts he determined to go down with me himself; he thought he could manage for me better. Might he say that I was a geographer?

No; I thought, in the interests of truth, he positively might not.

'Very well, then,' (with disappointment) 'an author.'

It appeared he had been in a seminary with six young Irishmen, all priests long since, who had received newspapers and kept him informed of the state of ecclesiastical affairs in England. And he asked me eagerly after Dr Pusey, for whose conversion the good man had continued ever since to pray night and morning.

'I thought he was very near the truth,' he said; 'and he will reach it yet; there is so much virtue in prayer.'

He must be a stiff, ungodly Protestant who can take anything but pleasure in this kind and hopeful story. While he was thus near the subject, the good father asked me if I were a Christian; and when he found I was not, or not after his way, he glossed it over with great good-will.

The road which we were following, and which this stalwart father had made with his own two hands within the space of a year, came to a corner, and showed us some white buildings a little farther on beyond the wood. At the same time the bell once more sounded abroad. We were hard upon the monastery. Father Apollinaris (for that was my companion's name) stopped me.

'I must not speak to you down there,' he said. 'Ask for the Brother Porter, and all will be well. But try to see me as you go out again through the wood, where I may speak to you. I am charmed to have made your acquaintance.'

And then suddenly raising his arms, flapping his fingers, and crying out twice, 'I must not speak, I must not speak!' he ran away in front of me, and disappeared into the monastery door.

I own this somewhat ghastly eccentricity went a good way to revive my terrors. But where one was so good and simple, why should not all be alike? I took heart of grace, and went forward to the gate as fast as Modestine, who seemed to have a disaffection for monasteries, would permit. It was the first door, in my acquaintance of her, which she had not shown an indecent haste to enter. I summoned the place in form, though with a quaking heart. Father Michael, the Father-Hospitaller, and a pair of brown-robed brothers came to the gate and spoke with me a while. I think my sack was the great attraction; it had already beguiled the heart of poor Apollinaris, who had charged me on my life to show it to the Father Prior. But whether it was my address, or the sack, or the idea speedily published among that part of the brotherhood who attend on strangers that I was not a pedlar after all, I found no difficulty as to my reception. Modestine was led away by a layman to the stables, and I and my pack were received into Our Lady of the Snows.

The Monks

Father Michael, a pleasant, fresh-faced, smiling man, perhaps of thirty-five, took me to the pantry, and gave me a glass of liqueur to stay me until dinner. We had some talk, or rather I should say he listened to my prattle indulgently enough, but with an abstracted air, like a spirit with a thing of clay. And truly, when I remember that I descanted principally on my appetite, and that it must have been by that time more than eighteen hours since Father Michael had so much as broken bread, I can well understand that he would find an earthly savour in my conversation. But his manner, though superior, was exquisitely gracious; and I find I have a lurking curiosity as to Father Michael's past.

The whet administered, I was left alone for a little in the monastery garden. This is no more than the main court, laid out in sandy paths and beds of parti-coloured dahlias, and with a fountain and a black statue of the Virgin in the centre. The buildings stand around it four-square, bleak, as yet unseasoned by the years and weather, and with no other features than a belfry and a pair of slated gables. Brothers in white, brothers in brown, passed silently along the sanded alleys; and when I first came out, three hooded monks were kneeling on the terrace at their prayers. A naked hill commands the monastery upon one side, and the wood commands it on the other. It lies exposed to wind; the snow falls off and on from October to May, and sometimes lies six weeks on end; but if they stood in Eden, with a climate like heaven's, the buildings themselves would offer the same wintry and cheerless aspect; and for my part, on this wild September day, before I was called to dinner, I felt chilly in and out.

When I had eaten well and heartily, Brother Ambrose, a hearty conversable Frenchman (for all those who wait on strangers have the liberty to speak), led me to a little room in that part of the building which is set apart for *MM les retraitants*. It was clean and whitewashed, and furnished with strict necessaries, a crucifix, a bust of the late Pope, the *Imitation* in French, a book of religious meditations, and the *Life of Elizabeth Seton*, evangelist, it would appear, of North America and of New England in particular. As far as my experience goes, there is a fair field for some more evangelisation in these quarters; but think of Cotton Mather! I should like to give him a reading of this little work in heaven, where I hope he dwells; but perhaps he knows all that already, and much more; and perhaps he and Mrs Seton are the dearest friends, and gladly unite their voices in the everlasting psalm. Over the table, to conclude the inventory of the room, hung a set of regulations for *MM les retraitants*: what services they should attend, when they were to tell their beads or meditate, and when they were to rise and go to rest. At the foot was a notable NB: '*Le temps libre est employé à l'examen de conscience, à la confession, à faire de bonnes résolutions,*' etc. To make good resolutions, indeed! You might talk as fruitfully of making the hair grow on your head.

I had scarce explored my niche when Brother Ambrose returned. An English boarder, it appeared, would like to speak with me. I professed my willingness, and the friar ushered in a fresh, young, little Irishman of fifty, a deacon of the Church, arrayed in strict canonicals, and wearing on his head what, in default of knowledge, I can only call the ecclesiastical shako. He had lived seven years in retreat at a convent of nuns in Belgium, and now five at Our Lady of the Snows; he never saw an English newspaper; he spoke French imperfectly, and had he spoken it like a native there was not much chance of conversation where he dwelt. With this, he was a man eminently sociable, greedy of news, and simple-minded like a child. If I was pleased to have a guide about the monastery, he was no less delighted to see an English face and hear an English tongue.

He showed me his room, where he passed his time among breviaries, Hebrew Bibles, and the Waverley Novels. Thence he led me to the cloisters, into the chapter-house, through the vestry, where the brothers' gowns and broad straw hats were hanging up, each with his religious name upon a board – names full of legendary suavity and interest, such as Basil, Hilarion, Raphael, or Pacifique; into the library, where were all the works of Veuillot and Chateaubriand, and the *Odes et Ballades*, if you please, and even Molière, to say nothing of innumerable fathers and a great variety of local and general historians. Thence my good Irishman took me round the workshops, where brothers bake bread, and make cartwheels, and take photographs; where one superintends a collection of curiosities, and another a gallery of rabbits. For in a Trappist monastery each monk has an occupation of his own choice, apart from his religious duties and the general labours of the house. Each must sing in the choir, if he has a voice and ear, and join in the hay-making if he has a hand to stir; but in his private hours, although he must be occupied, he may be occupied on what he likes. Thus I was told that one brother was engaged with literature; while Father Apollinaris busies himself in making roads, and the Abbot employs himself in binding books. It is not so long since this Abbot was consecrated, by the way; and on that occasion, by a special grace, his mother was permitted to enter the chapel and witness the ceremony of consecration. A proud day for her to have a son a mitred abbot; it makes you glad to think they let her in.

In all these journeyings to and fro, many silent fathers and brethren fell in our way. Usually they paid no more regard to our passage than if we had been a cloud; but sometimes the good deacon had a permission to ask of them, and it was granted by a peculiar movement of the hands, almost like that of a dog's paws in swimming, or refused by the usual negative signs, and in either case with lowered eyelids and a certain air of contrition, as of a man who was steering very close to evil.

The monks, by special grace of their Abbot, were still taking two meals a day; but it was already time for their grand fast, which begins somewhere in September and lasts till Easter, and during which they eat but once in the twenty-four hours, and that at two in the afternoon, twelve hours after they have begun the toil and vigil of the day. Their meals are scanty, but even of these they eat sparingly; and though each is allowed a small carafe of wine, many refrain from this indulgence. Without doubt, the most of mankind grossly overeat themselves; our meals serve not only for support, but as a hearty and natural diversion from the labour of life. Yet, though excess may be hurtful, I should have thought this Trappist regimen defective. And I am astonished, as I look back, at the freshness of face and cheerfulness of manner of all whom I beheld. A happier nor a healthier company I should scarce suppose that I have ever seen. As a matter of fact, on this bleak upland, and with the incessant occupation of the monks, life is of an uncertain tenure, and death no infrequent visitor, at Our Lady of the Snows. This, at least, was what was told me. But if they die easily, they must live healthily in the meantime, for they seemed all firm of flesh and high in colour; and the only morbid sign that I could observe, an unusual brilliancy of eye, was one that served rather to increase the general impression of vivacity and strength.

Those with whom I spoke were singularly sweet-tempered, with what I can only call a holy cheerfulness in air and conversation. There is a note, in the direction to visitors, telling them not to be offended at the curt speech of those who wait upon them, since it is proper to monks to speak little. The note might have been spared; to a man the hospitallers were all brimming with innocent talk, and, in my experience of the monastery, it was easier to begin than to break off a conversation. With the exception of Father Michael, who was a man of the world, they showed themselves full of kind and healthy interest in all sorts of subjects – in politics, in voyages, in my sleeping-sack – and not without a certain pleasure in the sound of their own voices.

As for those who are restricted to silence, I can only wonder how they bear their solemn and cheerless isolation. And yet, apart from any view of mortification, I can see a certain policy, not only in the exclusion of women, but in this vow of silence. I have had some experience of lay phalansteries, of an artistic, not to say a bacchanalian, character; and seen more than one association easily formed and yet more easily dispersed. With a Cistercian rule, perhaps they might have lasted longer. In the neighbourhood of women it is but a touch-and-go association that can be formed among defenceless men; the stronger electricity is sure to triumph; the dreams of boyhood, the schemes of youth, are abandoned after an interview of ten minutes, and the arts and sciences, and professional male jollity, deserted at once for two sweet eyes and a caressing accent. And next after this, the tongue is the great divider.

I am almost ashamed to pursue this worldly criticism of a religious rule; but there is yet another point in which the Trappist order appeals to me as a model of wisdom. By two in the morning the clapper goes upon the bell, and so on, hour by hour, and sometimes quarter by quarter, till eight, the hour of rest; so infinitesimally is the day divided among different occupations. The man who keeps rabbits, for example, hurries from his hutches to the chapel, the chapter-room, or the refectory, all day long: every hour he has an office to sing, a duty to perform; from two, when he rises in the dark, till eight, when he returns to receive the comfortable gift of sleep, he is upon his feet and occupied with manifold and changing business. I know many persons, worth several thousands in the year, who are not so fortunate in the disposal of their lives. Into how many houses would not the note of the monastery bell, dividing the day into manageable portions, bring peace of mind and healthful activity of body! We speak of hardships, but the true hardship is to be a dull fool, and permitted to mismanage life in our own dull and foolish manner.

From this point of view, we may perhaps better understand the monk's existence. A long novitiate and every proof of constancy of mind and strength of body is required before admission to the order; but I could not find that many were discouraged. In the photographer's studio, which figures so strangely among the outbuildings, my eye was attracted by the portrait of a young fellow in the uniform of a private of foot. This was one of the novices, who came of age for service, and marched and drilled and mounted guard for the proper time among the garrison of Algiers. Here was a man who had surely seen both sides of life before deciding; yet as soon as he was set free from service he returned to finish his novitiate.

This austere rule entitles a man to heaven as by right. When the Trappist sickens, he quits not his habit; he lies in the bed of death as he has prayed and laboured in his frugal and silent existence; and when the Liberator comes, at the very moment, even before they have carried him in his robe to lie his little last in the chapel among continual chantings, joy-bells break forth, as if for a marriage, from the slated belfry, and proclaim throughout the neighbourhood that another soul has gone to God.

At night, under the conduct of my kind Irishman, I took my place in the gallery to hear compline and *Salve Regina*, with which the Cistercians bring every day to a conclusion. There were none of those circumstances which strike the Protestant as childish or as tawdry in the public offices of Rome. A stern simplicity, heightened by the romance of the surroundings, spoke directly to the heart. I recall the whitewashed chapel, the hooded figures in the choir, the lights alternately occluded and revealed, the strong manly singing, the silence that ensued, the sight of cowled heads bowed in prayer, and then the clear trenchant beating of the bell, breaking in to show that the last office was over and the hour of sleep had come; and when I remember, I am not surprised that I made my escape into the court with somewhat whirling fancies, and stood like a man bewildered in the windy starry night.

But I was weary; and when I had quieted my spirits with Elizabeth Seton's memoirs – a dull work – the cold and the raving of the wind among the pines (for my room was on that side of the monastery which adjoins the woods) disposed me readily to slumber. I was wakened at black midnight, as it seemed, though it was really two in the morning, by the first stroke upon the bell. All the brothers were then hurrying to the chapel; the dead in life, at this untimely hour, were already beginning the uncomforted labours of their day. The dead in life – there was a chill reflection. And the words of a French song came back into my memory, telling of the best of our mixed existence :

> Que t'as de belles filles,
> Giroflé !
> Girofla !
> Que t'as de belles filles,
> *L'Amour les comptera* !

And I blessed God that I was free to wander, free to hope, and free to love.

The Boarders

But there was another side to my residence at Our Lady of the Snows. At this late season there were not many boarders; and yet I was not alone in the public part of the monastery. This itself is hard by the gate, with a small dining-room on the ground-floor and a whole corridor of cells similar to mine upstairs. I have stupidly forgotten the board for a regular *retraitant*; but it was somewhere between three and five francs a day, and I think most probably the first. Chance visitors like myself might give what they chose as a free-will offering, but nothing was demanded. I may mention that when I was going away, Father Michael refused twenty francs as excessive. I explained the reasoning which led me to offer him so much; but even then, from a curious point of honour, he would not accept it with his own hand. 'I have no right to refuse for the monastery,' he explained, 'but I should prefer if you would give it to one of the brothers.'

I had dined alone, because I arrived late; but at supper I found two other guests. One was a country parish priest, who had walked over that morning from the seat of his cure near Mende to enjoy four days of solitude and prayer. He was a grenadier in person, with the hale colour and circular wrinkles of a peasant; and as he complained much of how he had been impeded by his skirts upon the march, I have a vivid fancy portrait of him, striding along, upright, big-boned, with kilted cassock, through the bleak hills of Gévaudan. The other was a short, grizzling, thick-set man, from forty-five to fifty, dressed in tweed with a knitted spencer, and the red ribbon of a decoration in his button-hole. This last was a hard person to classify. He was an old soldier, who had seen service and risen to the rank of commandant; and he retained some of the brisk decisive manners of the camp. On the other hand, as soon as his resignation was accepted, he had come to Our Lady of the Snows as a boarder, and, after a brief experience of its ways,

had decided to remain as a novice. Already the new life was
beginning to modify his appearance; already he had acquired
somewhat of the quiet and smiling air of the brethren; and he
was yet neither an officer nor a Trappist, but partook of the
character of each. And certainly here was a man in an interesting
nick of life. Out of the noise of cannon and trumpets, he was in
the act of passing into this still country bordering on the grave,
where men sleep nightly in their grave-clothes, and, like phan-
toms, communicate by signs.

At supper we talked politics. I make it my business, when I
am in France, to preach political good-will and moderation, and
to dwell on the example of Poland, much as some alarmists in
England dwell on the example of Carthage. The priest and the
commandant assured me of their sympathy with all I said, and
made a heavy sighing over the bitterness of contemporary
feeling.

'Why, you cannot say anything to a man with which he does
not absolutely agree,' said I, 'but he flies up at you in a temper.'

They both declared that such a state of things was anti-
christian.

While we were thus agreeing, what should my tongue stumble
upon but a word in praise of Gambetta's moderation. The old
soldier's countenance was instantly suffused with blood; with
the palms of his hands he beat the table like a naughty child.

'*Comment, monsieur*?' he shouted. '*Comment*? Gambetta
moderate? Will you dare to justify these words?'

But the priest had not forgotten the tenor of our talk. And
suddenly, in the height of his fury, the old soldier found a
warning look directed on his face; the absurdity of his behaviour
was brought home to him in a flash; and the storm came to an
abrupt end, without another word.

It was only in the morning, over our coffee (Friday, 27th
September), that this couple found out I was a heretic. I suppose
I had misled them by some admiring expressions as to the
monastic life around us; and it was only by a point-blank
question that the truth came out. I had been tolerantly used
both by simple Father Apollinaris and astute Father Michael;
and the good Irish deacon, when he heard of my religious
weakness, had only patted me upon the shoulder and said, 'You
must be a Catholic and come to heaven.' But I was now among
a different sect of orthodox. These two men were bitter and

upright and narrow, like the worst of Scotsmen, and indeed upon my heart, I fancy they were worse. The priest snorted, aloud like a battle-horse.

'*Et vous prétendez mourir dans cette espèce de croyance?*' he demanded; and there is no type used by mortal printers large enough to qualify his accent.

I humbly indicated that I had no design of changing.

But he could not away with such a monstrous attitude. 'No, no,' he cried; 'you must change. You have come here, God has led you here, and you must embrace the opportunity.'

I made a slip in policy; I appealed to the family affections, though I was speaking to a priest and a soldier, two classes of men circumstantially divorced from the kind and homely ties of life.

'Your father and mother?' cried the priest. 'Very well; you will convert them in their turn when you go home.'

I think I see my father's face! I would rather tackle the Gætulian lion in his den than embark on such an enterprise against the family theologian.

But now the hunt was up; priest and soldier were in full cry for my conversion; and the Work of the Propagation of the Faith, for which the people of Cheylard subscribed forty-eight francs ten centimes during 1877, was being gallantly pursued against myself. It was an odd but most effective proselytising. They never sought to convince me in argument, where I might have attempted some defence; but took it for granted that I was both ashamed and terrified at my position, and urged me solely on the point of time. Now, they said, when God had led me to Our Lady of the Snows, now was the appointed hour.

'Do not be withheld by false shame,' observed the priest, for my encouragement.

For one who feels very similarly to all sects of religion, and who has never been able, even for a moment, to weigh seriously the merit of this or that creed on the eternal side of things, however much he may see to praise or blame upon the secular and temporal side, the situation thus created was both unfair and painful. I committed my second fault in tact, and tried to plead that it was all the same thing in the end, and we were all drawing near by different sides to the same kind and undiscriminating Friend and Father. That, as it seems to lay spirits, would be the only gospel worthy of the name. But different men think differently; and this revolutionary aspiration brought down the priest with all the terrors of the law. He launched into harrowing details of hell. The damned, he said – on the authority of a little book which he had read not a week before, and which, to add conviction to conviction, he had fully intended to bring along with him in his pocket – were to occupy the same attitude through all eternity in the midst of dismal tortures. And as he thus expatiated, he grew in nobility of aspect with his enthusiasm.

As a result the pair concluded that I should seek out the Prior, since the Abbot was from home, and lay my case immediately before him.

'*C'est mon conseil comme ancien militaire,*' observed the commandant; '*et celui de monsieur comme prêtre.*'

'*Oui,*' added the *curé*, sententiously nodding; '*comme ancien militaire – et comme prêtre.*'

At this moment, whilst I was somewhat embarrassed how to answer, in came one of the monks, a little brown fellow, as lively as a grig, and with an Italian accent, who threw himself at once into the contention, but in a milder and more persuasive vein, as befitted one of these pleasant brethren. Look at *him*, he said. The rule was very hard; he would have dearly liked to stay in his own country, Italy – it was well known how beautiful it was, the beautiful Italy; but then there were no Trappists in Italy; and he had a soul to save; and here he was.

I am afraid I must be at bottom, what a cheerful Indian critic has dubbed me, 'a faddling hedonist', for this description of the brother's motives gave me somewhat of a shock. I should have preferred to think he had chosen the life for its own sake, and not for ulterior purposes; and this shows how profoundly I was out of sympathy with these good Trappists, even when I was doing my best to sympathise. But to the *curé* the argument seemed decisive.

'Hear that!' he cried. 'And I have seen a marquis here, a marquis, a marquis' – he repeated the holy word three times over – 'and other persons high in society; and generals. And here, at your side, is this gentleman, who has been so many years in armies – decorated, an old warrior. And here he is, ready to dedicate himself to God.'

I was by this time so thoroughly embarrassed that I pleaded cold feet, and made my escape from the apartment. It was a furious windy morning, with a sky much cleared, and long and potent intervals of sunshine; and I wandered until dinner in the wild country towards the east, sorely staggered and beaten upon by the gale, but rewarded with some striking views.

At dinner the Work of the Propagation of the Faith was recommenced, and on this occasion still more distastefully to me. The priest asked me many questions as to the contemptible faith of my fathers, and received my replies with a kind of ecclesiastical titter.

'Your sect,' he said once; 'for I think you will admit it would be doing it too much honour to call it a religion.'

'As you please, monsieur,' said I. '*La parole est à vous.*'

At length I grew annoyed beyond endurance; and although he was on his own ground and, what is more to the purpose, an old man, and so holding a claim upon my toleration, I could not avoid a protest against this uncivil usage. He was sadly discountenanced.

'I assure you,' he said, 'I have no inclination to laugh in my heart. I have no other feeling but interest in your soul.'

And there ended my conversion. Honest man! he was no dangerous deceiver; but a country parson, full of zeal and faith. Long may he tread Gévaudan with his kilted skirts – a man strong to walk and strong to comfort his parishioners in death! I daresay he would beat bravely through a snowstorm where his duty called him; and it is not always the most faithful believer who makes the cunningest apostle.

Upper Gévaudan
(continued)

The bed was made, the room was fit,
By punctual eve the stars were lit;
The air was still, the water ran;
No need there was for maid or man,
When we put up, my ass and I,
At God's green caravanserai. – Old Pray.

Across the Goulet

The wind fell during dinner, and the sky remained clear; so it was under better auspices that I loaded Modestine before the monastery gate. My Irish friend accompanied me so far on the way. As we came through the wood, there was Père Apollinaris hauling his barrow; and he too quitted his labours to go with me for perhaps a hundred yards, holding my hand between both of his in front of him. I parted first from one and then from the other with unfeigned regret, but yet with the glee of the traveller who shakes off the dust of one stage before hurrying forth upon another. Then Modestine and I mounted the course of the Allier, which here led us back into Gévaudan towards its sources in the forest of Mercoire. It was but an inconsiderable burn before we left its guidance. Thence, over a hill, our way lay through a naked plateau, until we reached Chasseradès at sundown.

The company in the inn kitchen that night were all men employed in survey for one of the projected railways. They were intelligent and conversable, and we decided the future of France over hot wine, until the state of the clock frightened us to rest. There were four beds in the little upstairs room; and we slept six. But I had a bed to myself, and persuaded them to leave the window open.

'*Hé, bourgeois; il est cinq heures*!' was the cry that wakened me in the morning (Saturday, 28th September). The room was full of a transparent darkness, which dimly showed me the other three beds and the five different nightcaps on the pillows. But out of the window the dawn was growing ruddy in a long belt over the hill-tops, and day was about to flood the plateau. The hour was inspiriting; and there seemed a promise of calm weather, which was perfectly fulfilled. I was soon under way with Modestine. The road lay for a while over the plateau, and then descended through a precipitous village into the valley of the Chassezac. This stream ran among green meadows, well hidden from the world by its steep banks; the broom was in flower, and here and there was a hamlet sending up its smoke.

At last the path crossed the Chassezac upon a bridge, and, forsaking this deep hollow, set itself to cross the mountain of La Goulet. It wound up through Lestampes by upland fields and woods of beech and birch, and with every corner brought me into an acquaintance with some new interest. Even in the gully of the Chassezac my ear had been struck by a noise like that of a great bass bell ringing at the distance of many miles; but this, as I continued to mount and draw nearer to it, seemed to change in character, and I found at length that it came from someone leading flocks afield to the note of a rural horn. The narrow street of Lestampes stood full of sheep, from wall to wall – black sheep and white, bleating with one accord like the birds in spring, and each one accompanying himself upon the sheep-bell round his neck. It made a pathetic concert, all in treble. A little higher, and I passed a pair of men in a tree with pruning-hooks, and one of them was singing the music of a *bourrée*. Still further, and when I was already threading the birches, the crowing of cocks came cheerfully up to my ears, and along with that the voice of a flute discoursing a deliberate and plaintive air from one of the upland villages. I pictured to myself some grizzled, apple-cheeked, country schoolmaster fluting in his bit of a garden in the clear autumn sunshine. All these beautiful and interesting sounds filled my heart with an unwonted expectation; and it appeared to me that, once past this range which I was mounting, I should descend into the garden of the world. Nor was I deceived, for I was now done with rains and winds and a bleak country. The first part of my journey ended here; and this was like an induction of sweet sounds into the other and more beautiful.

There are other degrees of *feyness*, as of punishment, besides the capital; and I was now led by my good spirits into an adventure which I relate in the interest of future donkey-drivers. The road zigzagged so widely on the hillside, that I chose a short cut by map and compass, and struck through the dwarf woods to catch the road again upon a higher level. It was my one serious conflict with Modestine. She would none of my short cut; she turned in my face; she backed, she reared; she, whom I had hitherto imagined to be dumb, actually brayed with a loud hoarse flourish, like a cock crowing for the dawn. I plied the goad with one hand; with the other, so steep was the ascent, I had to hold on the pack-saddle. Half-a-dozen times she was nearly over backwards on the top of me; half-a-dozen times, from sheer weariness of spirit, I was nearly giving it up, and leading her down again to follow the road. But I took the thing as a wager, and fought it through. I was surprised, as I went on my way again, by what appeared to be chill rain-drops falling on my hand, and more than once looked up in wonder at the cloudless sky. But it was only sweat which came dropping from my brow.

Over the summit of the Goulet there was no marked road – only upright stones posted from space to space to guide the drovers. The turf underfoot was springy and well scented. I had no company but a lark or two, and met but one bullock-cart between Lestampes and Bleymard. In front of me I saw a shallow valley, and beyond that the range of the Lozère, sparsely wooded and well enough modelled in the flanks, but straight and dull in outline. There was scarce a sign of culture; only about Bleymard, the white high-road from Villefort to Mende traversed a range of meadows, set with spiry poplars, and sounding from side to side with the bells of flocks and herds.

A Night among The Pines

From Bleymard after dinner, although it was already late, I set out to scale a portion of the Lozère. An ill-marked stony drove-road guided me forward; and I met nearly half-a-dozen bullock-carts descending from the woods, each laden with a whole pine-tree for the winter's firing. At the top of the woods, which do not climb very high upon this cold ridge, I struck leftward by a path among the pines, until I hit on a dell of green turf, where a streamlet made a little spout over some stones to serve me for a water-tap. 'In a more sacred or sequestered bower ... nor nymph nor faunus haunted.' The trees were not old, but they grew thickly round the glade: there was no outlook, except north-eastward upon distant hill-tops, or straight upward to the sky; and the encampment felt secure and private like a room. By the time I had made my arrangements and fed Modestine, the day was already beginning to decline. I buckled myself to the knees into my sack and made a hearty meal; and as soon as the sun went down, I pulled my cap over my eyes and fell asleep.

Night is a dead monotonous period under a roof; but in the open world it passes lightly, with its stars and dews and perfumes, and the hours are marked by changes in the face of Nature. What seems a kind of temporal death to people choked between walls and curtains, is only a light and living slumber to the man who sleeps afield. All night long he can hear Nature breathing deeply and freely; even as she takes her rest, she turns and smiles; and there is one stirring hour unknown to those who dwell in houses, when a wakeful influence goes abroad over the sleeping hemisphere, and all the outdoor world are on their feet. It is then that the cock first crows, not this time to announce the dawn, but like a cheerful watchman speeding the course of night. Cattle awake on the meadows; sheep break their fast on dewy hillsides, and change to a new lair among the ferns; and houseless men, who have lain down with the fowls, open their dim eyes and behold the beauty of the night.

At what inaudible summons, at what gentle touch of Nature, are all these sleepers thus recalled in the same hour to life? Do the stars rain down an influence, or do we share some thrill of mother earth below our resting bodies? Even shepherds and old country-folk, who are the deepest read in these arcana, have not a guess as to the means or purpose of this nightly resurrection. Towards two in the morning they declare the thing takes place; and neither know nor inquire further. And at least it is a pleasant incident. We are disturbed in our slumber only, like the luxurious Montaigne, 'that we may the better and more sensibly relish it.' We have a moment to look upon the stars. And there is a special pleasure for some minds in the reflection that we share the impulse with all outdoor creatures in our neighbourhood, that we have escaped out of the Bastille of civilisation, and are become, for the time being, a mere kindly animal and a sheep of Nature's flock.

When that hour came to me among the pines, I wakened thirsty. My tin was standing by me half full of water. I emptied it at a draught; and feeling broad awake after this internal cold aspersion, sat upright to make a cigarette. The stars were clear, coloured, and jewel-like, but not frosty. A faint silvery vapour stood for the Milky Way. All around me the black fir-points stood upright and stock-still. By the whiteness of the pack-saddle, I could see Modestine walking round and round at the length of her tether; I could hear her steadily munching at the sward; but there was not another sound, save the indescribable quiet talk of the runnel over the stones. I lay lazily smoking and studying the colour of the sky, as we call the void of space, from where it showed a reddish grey behind the pines to where it showed a glossy blue-black between the stars. As if to be more like a pedlar, I wear a silver ring. This I could see faintly shining as I raised or lowered the cigarette; and at each whiff the inside of my hand was illuminated, and became for a second the highest light in the landscape.

A faint wind, more like a moving coolness than a stream of air, passed down the glade from time to time; so that even in my great chamber the air was being renewed all night long. I thought with horror of the inn at Chasseradès and the congregated nightcaps; with horror of the nocturnal prowesses of clerks and students, of hot theatres and pass-keys and close rooms. I have not often enjoyed a more serene possession of myself, nor felt more independent of material aids. The outer world, from which we cower into our houses, seemed after all a gentle habitable place; and night after night a man's bed, it seemed, was laid and waiting for him in the fields, where God keeps an open house. I though I had rediscovered one of those truths which are revealed to savages and hid from political economists; at the least, I had discovered a new pleasure for myself. And yet even while I was exulting in my solitude I became aware of a strange lack. I wished a companion to lie near me in the starlight, silent and not moving, but ever within touch. For there is a fellowship more quiet even than solitude, and which, rightly understood, is solitude made perfect. And to live out of doors with the woman a man loves is of all lives the most complete and free.

As I thus lay, between content and longing, a faint noise stole towards me through the pines. I thought, at first, it was the crowing of cocks or the barking of dogs at some very distant farm; but steadily and gradually it took articulate shape in my ears, until I became aware that a passenger was going by upon the high-road in the valley, and singing loudly as he went. There was more of good-will than grace in his performance; but he trolled with ample lungs; and the sound of his voice took hold upon the hillside and set the air shaking in the leafy glens. I have heard people passing by night in sleeping cities; some of them sang; one, I remember, played loudly on the bagpipes. I have heard the rattle of a cart or carriage spring up suddenly after hours of stillness, and pass, for some minutes, within the range of my hearing as I lay abed. There is a romance about all who are abroad in the black hours, and with something of a thrill we try to guess their business. But here the romance was double: first, this glad passenger, lit internally with wine, who sent up his voice in music through the night; and then I, on the other hand, buckled into my sack, and smoking alone in the pine-woods between four and five thousand feet towards the stars.

When I awoke again (Sunday, 29th September), many of the stars had disappeared; only the stronger companions of the night still burned visibly overhead; and away towards the east I saw a faint haze of light upon the horizon, such as had been the Milky Way when I was last awake. Day was at hand. I lit my lantern, and by its glow-worm light put on my boots and gaiters; then I broke up some bread for Modestine, filled my can at the water-tap, and lit my spirit-lamp to boil myself some chocolate. The blue darkness lay long in the glade where I had so sweetly slumbered; but soon there was a broad streak of orange melting into gold along the mountain-tops of Vivarais. A solemn glee possessed my mind at this gradual and lovely coming in of day. I heard the runnel with delight; I looked round me for something beautiful and unexpected; but the still black pine-trees, the hollow glade, the munching ass, remained unchanged in figure. Nothing had altered but the light, and that, indeed, shed over all a spirit of life and of breathing peace, and moved me to a strange exhilaration.

I drank my water-chocolate, which was hot if it was not rich, and strolled here and there, and up and down about the glade. While I was thus delaying, a gush of steady wind, as long as a heavy sigh, poured direct out of the quarter of the morning. It was cold, and set me sneezing. The trees near at hand tossed their black plumes in its passage; and I could see the thin distant spires of pine along the edge of the hill rock slightly to and fro against the golden east. Ten minutes after, the sunlight spread at a gallop along the hillside, scattering shadows and sparkles, and the day had come completely.

I hastened to prepare my pack, and tackle the steep ascent that lay before me, but I had something on my mind. It was only a fancy; yet a fancy will sometimes be importunate. I had been most hospitably received and punctually served in my green caravanserai. The room was airy, the water excellent, and the dawn had called me to a moment. I say nothing of the tapestries or the inimitable ceiling, nor yet of the view which I commanded from the windows; but I felt I was in someone's debt for all this liberal entertainment. And so it pleased me, in a half-laughing way, to leave pieces of money on the turf as I went along, until I had left enough for my night's lodging. I trust they did not fall to some rich and churlish drover.

The Country
of the Camisards

We travelled in the print of olden wars;
　　　　Yet all the land was green;
　　　　And love we found, and peace,
　　　　Where fire and war had been.
They pass and smile, the children of the sword –
　　　　No more the sword they wield;
　　　　And O, how deep the corn
　　　　Along the battlefield!

– George Bannatyne

Across the Lozère

The track that I had followed in the evening soon died out, and I continued to follow over a bald turf ascent a row of stone pillars, such as had conducted me across the Goulet. It was already warm. I tied my jacket on the pack, and walked in my knitted waistcoat. Modestine herself was in high spirits, and broke of her own accord, for the first time in my experience, into a jolting trot that sent the oats swashing in the pocket of my coat. The view, back upon the northern Gévaudan, extended with every step; scarce a tree, scarce a house, appeared upon the fields of wild hill that ran north, east, and west, all blue and gold in the haze and sunlight of the morning. A multitude of little birds kept sweeping and twittering about my path; they perched on the stone pillars, they pecked and strutted on the turf, and I saw them circle in volleys in the blue air, and show, from time to time, translucent flickering wings between the sun and me.

Almost from the first moment of my march, a faint large noise, like a distant surf, had filled my ears. Sometimes I was tempted to think it the voice of a neighbouring waterfall, and sometimes a subjective result of the utter stillness of the hill. But as I continued to advance, the noise increased, and became like the hissing of an enormous tea-urn, and at the same time breaths of cool air began to reach me from the direction of the summit. At length I understood. It was blowing stiffly from the south upon the other slope of the Lozère, and every step that I took I was drawing nearer to the wind.

Although it had been long desired, it was quite unexpectedly at last that my eyes rose above the summit. A step that seemed no way more decisive than many other steps that had preceded it – and, 'like stout Cortez when, with eagle eyes, he stared on the Pacific,' I took possession, in my own name, of a new quarter of the world. For behold, instead of the gross turf rampart I had been mounting for so long, a view into the hazy air of heaven, and a land of intricate blue hills below my feet.

The Lozère lies nearly east and west, cutting Gévaudan into two unequal parts; its highest point, this Pic de Finiels, on which I was then standing, rises upwards of five thousand six hundred feet above the sea, and in clear weather commands a view over all lower Languedoc to the Mediterranean Sea. I have spoken with people who either pretended or believed that they had seen, from the Pic de Finiels, white ships sailing by Montpellier and Cette. Behind was the upland northern country through which my way had lain, peopled by a dull race, without wood, without much grandeur of hill-form, and famous in the past for little beside wolves. But in front of me, half veiled in sunny haze, lay a new Gévaudan, rich, picturesque, illustrious for stirring events. Speaking largely, I was in the Cévennes at Monastier, and during all my journey; but there is a strict and local sense in which only this confused and shaggy country at my feet has any title to the name, and in this sense the peasantry employ the word. These are the Cévennes with an emphasis: the Cévennes of the Cévennes. In that undecipherable labyrinth of hills, a war of bandits, a war of wild beasts, raged for two years between the Grand Monarch with all his troops and marshals on the one hand, and a few thousand Protestant mountaineers upon the other. A hundred and eighty years ago, the Camisards held a station even on the Lozère, where I stood; they had an organisation, arsenals, a military and religious hierarchy; their affairs were 'the discourse of every coffee-house' in London; England sent fleets in their support; their leaders prophesied and murdered; with colours and drums, and the singing of old French psalms, their bands sometimes affronted daylight, marched before walled cities, and dispersed the generals of the king; and sometimes at night, or in masquerade, possessed themselves of strong castles, and avenged treachery upon their allies and cruelty upon their foes. There, a hundred and eighty years ago, was the chivalrous Roland, 'Count and Lord Roland, generalissimo of the Protestants in France,' grave, silent, imperious, pock-marked ex-dragoon, whom a lady followed in his wanderings out of love. There was Cavalier, a baker's apprentice with a genius for war, elected brigadier of Camisards at seventeen, to die at fifty-five the English governor of Jersey. There again was Castanet, a partisan leader in a voluminous peruke and with a taste for controversial divinity. Strange generals, who moved apart to take counsel with the God of Hosts, and fled or offered battle, set sentinels or slept in an unguarded camp, as the Spirit whispered to their hearts! And there, to follow these and other leaders, was the rank and file of prophets and disciples, bold, patient, indefatigable, hardy to run upon the mountains, cheering their rough life with psalms, eager to fight, eager to pray, listening devoutly to the oracles of brain-sick children, and mystically putting a grain of wheat among the pewter balls with which they charged their muskets.

I had travelled hitherto through a dull district, and in the track of nothing more notable than the child-eating Beast of Gévaudan, the Napoleon Bonaparte of wolves. But now I was to go down into the scene of a romantic chapter – or, better, a romantic footnote – in the history of the world. What was left of all this bygone dust and heroism? I was told that Protestantism still survived in this head seat of Protestant resistance; so much the priest himself had told me in the monastery parlour. But I had yet to learn if it were a bare survival, or a lively and generous tradition. Again, if in the northern Cévennes the people are narrow in religious judgments, and more filled with zeal than charity, what was I to look for in this land of persecution and reprisal – in a land where the tyranny of the Church produced the Camisard rebellion, and the terror of the Camisards threw the Catholic peasantry into legalised revolt upon the other side, so that Camisard and Florentin skulked for each other's lives among the mountains?

Just on the brow of the hill, where I paused to look before me, the series of stone pillars came abruptly to an end; and only a little below, a sort of track appeared and began to go down a breakneck slope, turning like a corkscrew as it went. It led into a valley between falling hills, stubbly with rocks like a reaped field of corn, and floored farther down with green meadows. I followed the track with precipitation; the steepness of the slope, the continual agile turning of the line of the descent, and the old unwearied hope of finding something new in a new country, all conspired to lend me wings. Yet a little lower and a stream began, collecting itself together out of many fountains, and soon making a glad noise among the hills. Sometimes it would cross the track in a bit of waterfall, with a pool, in which Modestine refreshed her feet.

The whole descent is like a dream to me, so rapidly was it

accomplished. I had scarcely left the summit ere the valley had closed round my path, and the sun beat upon me, walking in a stagnant lowland atmosphere. The track became a road, and went up and down in easy undulations. I passed cabin after cabin, but all seemed deserted; and I saw not a human creature, nor heard any sound except that of the stream. I was, however, in a different country from the day before. The stony skeleton of the world was here vigorously displayed to sun and air. The slopes were steep and changeful. Oak-trees clung along the hills, well grown, wealthy in leaf, and touched by the autumn with strong and luminous colours. Here and there another stream would fall in from the right or the left, down a gorge of snow-white and tumultuary boulders. The river in the bottom (for it was rapidly growing a river, collecting on all hands as it trotted on its way) here foamed a while in desperate rapids, and there lay in pools of the most enchanting sea-green shot with watery browns. As far as I have gone, I have never seen a river of so changeful and delicate a hue; crystal was not more clear, the meadows were not by half so green; and at every pool I saw I felt a thrill of longing to be out of these hot, dusty, and material garments, and bathe my naked body in the mountain air and water. All the time as I went on I never forgot it was the Sabbath; the stillness was a perpetual reminder, and I heard in spirit the church-bells clamouring all over Europe, and the psalms of a thousand churches.

At length a human sound struck upon my ear – a cry strangely modulated between pathos and derision; and looking across the valley, I saw a little urchin sitting in a meadow, with his hands about his knees, and dwarfed to almost comical smallness by the distance. But the rogue had picked me out as I went down the road, from oak wood on to oak wood, driving Modestine; and he made me the compliments of the new country in this tremulous high-pitched salutation. And as all noises are lovely and natural at a sufficient distance, this also, coming through so much clean hill air and crossing all the green valley, sounded pleasant to my ear, and seemed a thing rustic, like the oaks or the river.

A little after, the stream that I was following fell into the Tarn at Pont de Montvert of bloody memory.

Pont de Montvert

One of the first things I encountered in Pont de Montvert was,
if I remember rightly, the Protestant temple; but this was but
the type of other novelties. A subtle atmosphere distinguishes a
town in England from a town in France, or even in Scotland. At
Carlisle you can see you are in one country; at Dumfries, thirty
miles away, you are as sure that you in the other. I should find
it difficult to tell in what particulars Pont de Montvert differed
from Monastier or Langogne, or even Bleymard; but the difference existed, and spoke eloquently to the eyes. The place, with
its houses, its lanes, its glaring river-bed, wore an indescribable
air of the South.

All was Sunday bustle in the streets and in the public-house,
as all had been Sabbath peace among the mountains. There must
have been near a score of us at dinner by eleven before noon;
and after I had eaten and drunken, and sat writing up my
journal, I suppose as many more came dropping in one after
another, or by twos and threes. In crossing the Lozère I had not
only come among new natural features, but moved into the
territory of a different race. These people, as they hurriedly
despatched their viands in an intricate sword-play of knives,
questioned and answered me with a degree of intelligence which
excelled all that I had met, except among the railway folk at
Chasseradès. They had open telling faces, and were lively both
in speech and manner. They not only entered thoroughly into
the spirit of my little trip, but more than one declared, if he were
rich enough, he would like to set forth on such another.

Even physically there was a pleasant change. I had not seen a
pretty woman since I left Monastier, and there but one. Now of
the three who sat down with me to dinner, one was certainly
not beautiful – a poor timid thing of forty, quite troubled at this
roaring *table d'hôte*, whom I squired and helped to wine, and
pledged and tried generally to encourage, with quite a contrary
effect; but the other two, both married, were both more

handsome than the average of women. And Clarisse? What shall I say of Clarisse? She waited the table with a heavy placable nonchalance, like a performing cow; her great grey eyes were steeped in amorous languor; her features, although fleshy, were of an original and accurate design; her mouth had a curl; her nostrils spoke of dainty pride; her cheek fell into strange and interesting lines. It was a face capable of strong emotion, and, with training, it offered the promise of delicate sentiment. It seemed pitiful to see so good a model left to country admirers and a country way of thought. Beauty should at least have touched society; then, in a moment, it throws off a weight that lay upon it, it becomes conscious of itself, it puts on an elegance, learns a gait and a carriage of the head, and, in a moment, *patet dea*. Before I left I assured Clarisse of my hearty admiration. She took it like milk, without embarrassment or wonder, merely looking at me steadily with her great eyes; and I own the result upon myself was some confusion. If Clarisse could read English, I should not dare to add that her figure was unworthy of her face. Hers was a case for stays; but that may perhaps grow better as she gets up in years.

Pont de Montvert, or Greenhill Bridge, as we might say at home, is a place memorable in the story of the Camisards. It was here that the war broke out; here that those southern Covenanters slew their Archbishop Sharpe. The persecution on the one hand, the febrile enthusiasm on the other, are almost equally difficult to understand in these quiet modern days, and with our easy modern beliefs and disbeliefs. The Protestants were one and all beside their right minds with zeal and sorrow. They were all prophets and prophetesses. Children at the breast would exhort their parents to good works. 'A child of fifteen months at Quissac spoke from its mother's arms, agitated and sobbing, distinctly and with a loud voice.' Marshal Villars has seen a town where all the women 'seemed possessed by the devil,' and had trembling fits, and uttered prophecies publicly upon the streets. A prophetess of Vivarais was hanged at Montpellier because blood flowed from her eyes and nose, and she declared that she was weeping tears of blood for the misfortunes of the Protestants. And it was not only women and children. Stalwart dangerous fellows, used to swing the sickle or to wield the forest axe, were likewise shaken with strange paroxysms, and spoke oracles with sobs and streaming tears. A persecution unsurpassed in violence had lasted near a score of years, and this was the result upon the persecuted; hanging, burning, breaking on the wheel, had been in vain; the dragoons had left their hoof-marks over all the countryside; there were men rowing in the galleys, and women pining in the prisons of the Church; and not a thought was changed in the heart of any upright Protestant.

Now the head and forefront of the persecution – after Lamoignon de Bâvile – François de Langlade du Chayla (pronounce Chéïla), Archpriest of the Cévennes and Inspector of Missions in the same country, had a house in which he sometimes dwelt in the town of Pont de Montvert. He was a conscientious person, who seems to have been intended by nature for a pirate, and now fifty-five, an age by which a man has learned all the moderation of which he is capable. A missionary in his youth in China, he there suffered martyrdom, was left for dead, and only succoured and brought back to life by the charity of a pariah. We must suppose the pariah devoid of second-sight, and not purposely malicious in this act. Such an experience, it might be thought, would have cured a man of the desire to persecute; but the human spirit is a thing strangely put together; and, having been a Christian martyr, Du Chayla became a Christian persecutor. The Work of the Propagation of the Faith went roundly forward in his hands. His house in Pont de Montvert served him as a prison. There he closed the hands of his prisoners upon live coal, and plucked out the hairs of their beard, to convince them that they were deceived in their opinions. And yet had not he himself tried and proved the inefficacy of these carnal arguments among the Buddhists in China?

Not only was life made intolerable in Languedoc, but flight was rigidly forbidden. One Massip, a muleteer, and well acquainted with the mountain-paths, had already guided several troops of fugitives in safety to Geneva; and on him, with another convoy, consisting mostly of women dressed as men, Du Chayla, in an evil hour for himself, laid his hands. The Sunday following there was a conventicle of Protestants in the woods of Altefage upon Mount Bougès; where there stood up one Séguier – Spirit Séguier, as his companions called him – a wool-carder, tall, black-faced, and toothless, but a man full of prophecy. He declared, in the name of God, that the time for submission had gone by, and they must betake themselves to arms for the deliverance of their brethren and the destruction of the priests.

The next night, 24th July, 1702, a sound disturbed the Inspector of Missions as he sat in his prison-house at Pont de Montvert: the voices of many men upraised in psalmody drew nearer and nearer through the town. It was ten at night; he had his court about him, priests, soldiers, and servants, to the number of twelve or fifteen; and now dreading the insolence of a conventicle below his very windows, he ordered forth his soldiers to report. But the psalm-singers were already at his door, fifty strong, led by the inspired Séguier, and breathing death. To their summons, the archpriest made answer like a stout old persecutor, and bade his garrison fire upon the mob. One Camisard (for, according to some, it was in this night's work that they came by the name) fell at this discharge: his comrades burst in the door with hatchets and a beam of wood, overran the lower storey of the house, set free the prisoners, and finding one of them in the *vine*, a sort of Scavenger's Daughter of the place and period, redoubled in fury against Du Chayla, and sought by repeated assaults to carry the upper floors. But he, on his side, had given absolution to his men, and they bravely held the staircase.

'Children of God,' cried the prophet, 'hold your hands. Let us burn the house, with the priest and the satellites of Baal.'

The fire caught readily. Out of an upper window Du Chayla and his men lowered themselves into the garden by means of knotted sheets; some escaped across the river under the bullets of the insurgents; but the archpriest himself fell, broke his thigh, and could only crawl into the hedge. What were his reflections as this second martyrdom drew near? A poor, brave, besotted, hateful man, who had done his duty resolutely according to his light both in the Cévennes and China. He found at least one telling word to say in his defence; for when the roof fell in and the upbursting flames discovered his retreat, and they came and dragged him to the public place of the town, raging and calling him damned – 'If I be damned,' said he, 'why should you also damn yourselves?'

Here was a good reason for the last; but in the course of his inspectorship he had given many stronger which all told in a contrary direction; and these he was now to hear. One by one,

Séguier first, the Camisards drew near and stabbed him. 'This,' they said, 'is for my father broken on the wheel. This for my brother in the galleys. That for my mother or my sister imprisoned in your cursed convents.' Each gave his blow and his reason; and then all kneeled and sang psalms around the body till the dawn. With the dawn, still singing, they defiled away towards Frugères, farther up the Tarn, to pursue the work of vengeance, leaving Du Chayla's prison-house in ruins, and his body pierced with two-and-fifty wounds upon the public place.

'Tis a wild night's work, with its accompaniment of psalms; and it seems as if a psalm must always have a sound of threatening in that town upon the Tarn. But the story does not end, even so far as concerns Pont de Montvert, with the departure of the Camisards. The career of Séguier was brief and bloody. Two more priests and a whole family at Ladevèze, from the father to the servants, fell by his hand or by his orders; and yet he was but a day or two at large, and restrained all the time by the presence of the soldiery. Taken at length by a famous soldier of fortune, Captain Poul, he appeared unmoved before his judges.

'Your name?' they asked.

'Pierre Séguier.'

'Why are you called Spirit?'

'Because the Spirit of the Lord is with me.'

'Your domicile?'

'Lately in the desert, and soon in heaven.'

'Have you no remorse for your crimes?'

'I have committed none. *My soul is like a garden full of shelter and of fountains.*'

At Pont de Montvert, on the 12th of August, he had his right hand stricken from his body, and was burned alive. And his soul was like a garden? So perhaps was the soul of Du Chayla, the Christian martyr. And perhaps if you could read in my soul, or I could read in yours, our own composure might seem little less surprising.

Du Chayla's house still stands, with a new roof, beside one of the bridges of the town; and if you are curious you may see the terrace-garden into which he dropped.

In the Valley of the Tarn

A new road leads from Pont de Montvert to Florac by the valley of the Tarn; a smooth sandy ledge, it runs about half-way between the summit of the cliffs and the river in the bottom of the valley; and I went in and out, as I followed it, from bays of shadow into promontories of afternoon sun. This was a pass like that of Killiecrankie; a deep turning gully in the hills, with the Tarn making a wonderful hoarse uproar far below, and craggy summits standing in the sunshine high above. A thin fringe of ash-trees ran about the hill-tops, like ivy on a ruin; but on the lower slopes, and far up every glen, the Spanish chestnut-trees stood each four-square to heaven under its tented foliage. Some were planted, each on its own terrace no larger than a bed; some, trusting in their roots, found strength to grow and prosper and be straight and large upon the rapid slopes of the valley; others, where there was a margin to the river, stood marshalled in a line and mighty like cedars of Lebanon. Yet even where they grew most thickly they were not to be thought of as a wood, but as a herd of stalwart individuals; and the dome of each tree stood forth separate and large, and as it were a little hill, from among the domes of its companions. They gave forth a faint sweet perfume which pervaded the air of the afternoon; autumn had put tints of gold and tarnish in the green; and the sun so shone through and kindled the broad foliage that each chestnut was relieved against another, not in shadow, but in light. A humble sketcher here laid down his pencil in despair.

I wish I could convey a notion of the growth of these noble trees; of how they strike out boughs like the oak, and trail sprays of drooping foliage like the willow; of how they stand on upright fluted columns like the pillars of a church; or like the olive, from the most shattered bole can put out smooth and youthful shoots, and begin a new life upon the ruins of the old. Thus they partake of the nature of many different trees; and even their prickly top-knots, seen near at hand against the sky, have a certain palm-like air that impresses the imagination. But their individuality, although compounded of so many elements, is but the richer and the more original. And to look down upon a level filled with these knolls of foliage, or to see a clan of old unconquerable chestnuts cluster 'like herded elephants' upon the spur of a mountain, is to rise to higher thoughts of the powers that are in Nature.

Between Modestine's laggard humour and the beauty of the scene, we made little progress all that afternoon; and at last finding the sun, although still far from setting, was already beginning to desert the narrow valley of the Tarn, I began to cast about for a place to camp in. This was not easy to find; the terraces were too narrow, and the ground, where it was unter-raced, was usually too steep for a man to lie upon. I should have slipped all night, and awakened towards morning with my feet or my head in the river.

After perhaps a mile, I saw, some sixty feet above the road, a little plateau large enough to hold my sack, and securely parapeted by the trunk of an aged and enormous chestnut. Thither, with infinite trouble, I goaded and kicked the reluctant Modestine, and there I hastened to unload her. There was only room for myself upon the plateau, and I had to go nearly as high again before I found so much as standing room for the ass. It was on a heap of rolling stones, on an artificial terrace, certainly not five feet square in all. Here I tied her to a chestnut, and having given her corn and bread and made a pile of chestnut-leaves, of which I found her greedy, I descended once more to my own encampment.

The position was unpleasantly exposed. One or two carts went by upon the road; and as long as daylight lasted I concealed myself, for all the world like a hunted Camisard, behind my fortification of vast chestnut trunk; for I was passionately afraid of discovery and the visit of jocular persons in the night. Moreover, I saw that I must be early awake; for these chestnut gardens had been the scene of industry no further gone than on the day before. The slope was strewn with lopped branches, and here and there a great package of leaves was propped against a trunk; for even the leaves are serviceable, and the peasants use them in winter by way of fodder for their animals. I picked a meal in fear and trembling, half lying down to hide myself from the road; and I daresay I was as much concerned as if I had been a scout from Joani's band above upon the Lozère, or from Salomon's across the Tarn, in the old times of psalm-singing and blood. Or, indeed, perhaps more; for the Camisards had a remarkable confidence in God; and a tale comes back into my memory of how the Count of Gévaudan, riding with a party of dragoons and a notary at his saddlebow to enforce the oath of fidelity in all the country hamlets, entered a valley in the woods, and found Cavalier and his men at dinner, gaily seated on the grass, and their hats crowned with box-tree garlands, while fifteen women washed their linen in the stream. Such was a field festival in 1703; at that date Antony Watteau would be painting similar subjects.

This was a very different camp from that of the night before in the cool and silent pine-woods. It was warm and even stifling in the valley. The shrill song of frogs, like the tremolo note of a whistle with a pea in it, rang up from the riverside before the sun was down. In the growing dusk, faint rustlings began to run to and fro among the fallen leaves; from time to time a faint chirping or cheeping noise would fall upon my ear; and from time to time I thought I could see the movement of something swift and indistinct between the chestnuts. A profusion of large ants swarmed upon the ground; bats whisked by, and mosquitoes droned overhead. The long boughs with their bunches of leaves hung against the sky like garlands; and those immediately above and around me had somewhat the air of a trellis which should have been wrecked and half overthrown in a gale of wind.

Sleep for a long time fled my eyelids; and just as I was beginning to feel quiet stealing over my limbs, and settling densely on my mind, a noise at my head startled me broad awake again, and, I will frankly confess it, brought my heart into my mouth. It was such a noise as a person would make scratching loudly with a finger-nail; it came from under the knapsack which served me for a pillow, and it was thrice repeated before I had time to sit up and turn about. Nothing was to be seen, nothing more was to be heard, but a few of these mysterious rustlings far and near, and the ceaseless accompaniment of the river and the frogs. I learned next day that the chestnut gardens are infested by rats; rustling, chirping, and scraping were probably all due to these; but the puzzle, for the moment, was insoluble, and I had to compose myself for sleep, as best I could, in wondering uncertainty about my neighbours.

I was wakened in the grey of the morning (Monday, 30th September) by the sound of footsteps not far off upon the stones, and opening my eyes, I beheld a peasant going by among the chestnuts by a footpath that I had not hitherto observed. He turned his head neither to the right nor to the left, and disappeared in a few strides among the foliage. Here was an escape! But it was plainly more than time to be moving. The peasantry were abroad; scarce less terrible to me in my nondescript position than the soldiers of Captain Poul to an undaunted Camisard. I fed Modestine with what haste I could; but as I was returning to my sack, I saw a man and a boy come down the hillside in a direction crossing mine. They unintelligibly hailed me, and I replied with inarticulate but cheerful sounds, and hurried forward to get into my gaiters.

The pair, who seemed to be father and son, came slowly up to the plateau, and stood close beside me for some time in silence. The bed was open, and I saw with regret my revolver lying patently disclosed on the blue wool. At last, after they had looked me all over, and the silence had grown laughably embarrassing, the man demanded in what seemed unfriendly tones:

'You have slept here?'

'Yes,' said I. 'As you see.'

'Why?' he asked.

'My faith,' I answered lightly, 'I was tired.'

He next inquired where I was going and what I had had for dinner; and then, without the least transition, '*C'est bien*,' he added, 'come along.' And he and his son, without another word, turned off to the next chestnut-tree but one, which they set to pruning. The thing had passed off more simply than I hoped. He was a grave, respectable man; and his unfriendly voice did not imply that he thought he was speaking to a criminal, but merely to an inferior.

I was soon on the road, nibbling a cake of chocolate and seriously occupied with a case of conscience. Was I to pay for my night's lodging? I had slept ill, the bed was full of fleas in the shape of ants, there was no water in the room, the very dawn had neglected to call me in the morning. I might have missed a train, had there been any in the neighbourhood to catch. Clearly, I was dissatisfied with my entertainment; and I decided I should not pay unless I met a beggar.

The valley looked even lovelier by morning; and soon the road descended to the level of the river. Here, in a place where many straight and prosperous chestnuts stood together, making an isle upon a swarded terrace, I made my morning toilette in the water of the Tarn. It was marvellously clear, thrillingly cool; the soap-suds disappeared as if by magic in the swift current, and the white boulders gave one a model for cleanliness. To wash in one of God's rivers in the open air seems to me a sort of cheerful solemnity or semi-pagan act of worship. To dabble among dishes in a bedroom may perhaps make clean the body; but the imagination takes no share in such a cleansing. I went on with a light and peaceful heart, and sang psalms to the spiritual ear as I advanced.

Suddenly up came an old woman, who point-blank demanded alms.

'Good,' thought I; 'here comes the waiter with the bill.'

And I paid for my night's lodging on the spot. Take it how you please, but this was the first and the last beggar that I met with during all my tour.

A step or two farther I was overtaken by an old man in a brown nightcap, clear-eyed, weather-beaten, with a faint excited smile. A little girl followed him, driving two sheep and a goat; but she kept in our wake, while the old man walked beside me and talked about the morning and the valley. It was not much past six; and for healthy people who have slept enough, that is an hour of expansion and of open and trustful talk.

'*Connaissez-vous le Seigneur?*' he said at length.

I asked him what Seigneur he meant; but he only repeated the question with more emphasis and a look in his eyes denoting hope and interest.

'Ah,' said I, pointing upwards, 'I understand you now. Yes, I know Him; He is the best of acquaintances.'

The old man said he was delighted. 'Hold,' he added, striking his bosom; 'it makes me happy here.' There were a few who knew the Lord in these valleys, he went on to tell me; not many, but a few. 'Many are called,' he quoted, 'and few chosen.'

'My father,' said I, 'it is not easy to say who know the Lord; and it is none of our business. Protestants and Catholics, and even those who worship stones, may know Him and be known by Him; for He has made all.'

I did not know I was so good a preacher.

The old man assured me he thought as I did, and repeated his expressions of pleasure at meeting me. 'We are so few,' he said. 'They call us Moravians here; but down in the Department of Gard, where there are also a good number, they are called Derbists, after an English pastor.'

I began to understand that I was figuring, in questionable taste, as a member of some sect to me unknown; but I was more pleased with the pleasure of my companion than embarrassed by my own equivocal position. Indeed, I can see no dishonesty in not avowing a difference; and especially in these high matters, where we have all a sufficient assurance that, whoever may be in the wrong, we ourselves are not completely in the right. The truth is much talked about; but this old man in a brown nightcap showed himself so simple, sweet, and friendly, that I am not unwilling to profess myself his convert. He was, as a matter of fact, a Plymouth Brother. Of what that involves in the way of doctrine I have no idea nor the time to inform myself; but I know right well that we are all embarked upon a troublesome world, the children of one Father, striving in many essential points to do and to become the same. And although it was somewhat in a mistake that he shook hands with me so often and showed himself so ready to receive my words, that was a mistake of the truth-finding sort. For charity begins blindfold; and only through a series of similar misapprehensions rises at length into a settled principle of love and patience, and a firm belief in all our fellow-men. If I deceived this good old man, in the like manner I would willingly go on to deceive others. And if ever at length, out of our separate and sad ways, we should all come together into one common house, I have a hope, to which I cling dearly, that my mountain Plymouth Brother will hasten to shake hands with me again.

Thus, talking like Christian and Faithful by the way, he and I came down upon a hamlet by the Tarn. It was but a humble place, called La Vernède, with less than a dozen houses, and a Protestant chapel on a knoll. Here he dwelt; and here, at the inn, I ordered my breakfast. The inn was kept by an agreeable young man, a stone-breaker on the road, and his sister, a pretty and engaging girl. The village schoolmaster dropped in to speak with the stranger. And these were all Protestants – a fact which pleased me more than I should have expected; and, what pleased me still more, they seemed all upright and simple people. The Plymouth Brother hung round me with a sort of yearning interest, and returned at least thrice to make sure I was enjoying my meal. His behaviour touched me deeply at the time, and even now moves me in recollection. He feared to intrude, but he would not willingly forgo one moment of my society; and he seemed never weary of shaking me by the hand.

When all the rest had drifted off to their day's work, I sat for near half an hour with the young mistress of the house, who talked pleasantly over her seam of the chestnut harvest, and the beauties of the Tarn, and old family affections, broken up when young folk go from home, yet still subsisting. Hers, I am sure, was a sweet nature, with a country plainness and much delicacy underneath; and he who takes her to his heart will doubtless be a fortunate young man.

The valley below La Vernède pleased me more and more as I went forward. Now the hills approached from either hand, naked and crumbling, and walled in the river between cliffs; and now the valley widened and became green. The road led me past the old castle of Miral on a steep; past a battlemented monastery, long since broken up and turned into a church and parsonage; and past a cluster of black roofs, the village of Cocurès, sitting among vineyards, and meadows, and orchards thick with red apples, and where, along the highway, they were knocking down walnuts from the roadside trees, and gathering them in sacks and baskets. The hills, however much the vale might open, were still tall and bare, with cliffy battlements and here and there a pointed summit; and the Tarn still rattled through the stones with a mountain noise. I had been led, by bagmen of a picturesque turn of mind, to expect a horrific country after the heart of Byron; but to my Scottish eyes it seemed smiling and plentiful, as the weather still gave an impression of high summer to my Scottish body; although the chestnuts were already picked out by the autumn, and the poplars, that here began to mingle with them, had turned into pale gold against the approach of winter.

There was something in this landscape, smiling although wild, that explained to me the spirit of the Southern Covenanters. Those who took to the hills for conscience' sake in Scotland had all gloomy and bedevilled thoughts; for once that they received God's comfort they would be twice engaged with Satan; but the Camisards had only bright and supporting visions. They dealt much more in blood, both given and taken; yet I find no obsession of the Evil One in their records. With a light conscience, they pursued their life in these rough times and circumstances. The soul of Séguier, let us not forget, was like a garden. They knew they were on God's side, with a knowledge that has no parallel among the Scots; for the Scots, although they might be certain of the cause, could never rest confident of the person.

'We flew,' says one old Camisard, 'when we heard the sound of psalm-singing, we flew as if with wings. We felt within us an animating ardour, a transporting desire. The feeling cannot be expressed in words. It is a thing that must have been experienced to be understood. However weary we might be, we thought no more of our weariness, and grew light so soon as the psalms fell upon our ears.'

The valley of the Tarn and the people whom I met at La Vernède not only explain to me this passage, but the twenty years of suffering which those, who were so stiff and so bloody when once they betook themselves to war, endured with the meekness of children and the constancy of saints and peasants.

Florac

On a branch of the Tarn stands Florac, the seat of a sub-prefecture, with an old castle, an alley of planes, many quaint street-corners, and a live fountain welling from the hill. It is notable, besides, for handsome women, and as one of the two capitals, Alais being the other, of the country of the Camisards.

The landlord of the inn took me, after I had eaten, to an adjoining *café*, where I, or rather my journey, became the topic of the afternoon. Everyone had some suggestion for my guidance; and the sub-prefectorial map was fetched from the sub-prefecture itself, and much thumbed among coffee-cups and glasses of liqueur. Most of these kind advisers were Protestant, though I observed that Protestant and Catholic intermingled in a very easy manner; and it surprised me to see what a lively memory still subsisted of the religious war. Among the hills of the south-west, by Mauchline, Cumnock, or Carsphairn, in isolated farms or in the manse, serious Presbyterian people still recall the days of the great persecution, and the graves of local martyrs are still piously regarded. But in towns and among the so-called better classes, I fear that these old doings have become an idle tale. If you met a mixed company in the King's Arms at Wigtown, it is not likely that the talk would run on Covenanters. Nay, at Muirkirk of Glenluce, I found the beadle's wife had not so much as heard of Prophet Peden. But these Cévenols were proud of their ancestors in quite another sense; the war was their chosen topic; its exploits were their own patent of nobility; and where a man or a race has had but one adventure, and that heroic, we must expect and pardon some prolixity of reference. They told me the country was still full of legends hitherto uncollected; I heard from them about Cavalier's descendants – not direct descendants, be it understood, but only cousins or nephews – who were still prosperous people in the scene of the boy-general's exploits; and one farmer had seen the bones of old combatants dug up into the air of an afternoon in the nineteenth century, in a field where the ancestors had fought, and the great-grandchildren were peaceably ditching.

Later in the day one of the Protestant pastors was so good as to visit me: a young man, intelligent and polite, with whom I passed an hour or two in talk. Florac, he told me, is part Protestant, part Catholic; and the difference in religion is usually doubled by a difference in politics. You may judge of my surprise, coming as I did from such a babbling purgatorial Poland of a place as Monastier, when I learned that the population lived together on very quiet terms; and there was even an exchange of hospitalities between households thus doubly separated. Black Camisard and White Camisard, militiaman and Miquelet and dragoon, Protestant prophet and Catholic cadet of the White Cross, they had all been sabring and shooting, burning, pillaging, and murdering, their hearts hot with indignant passion; and here, after a hundred and seventy years, Protestant is still Protestant, Catholic still Catholic, in mutual toleration and mild amity of life. But the race of man, like that indomitable nature whence it sprang, has medicating virtues of its own; the years and seasons bring various harvests; the sun returns after the rain; and mankind outlives secular animosities, as a single man awakens from the passions of a day. We judge our ancestors from a more divine position; and the dust being a little laid with several centuries, we can see both sides adorned with human virtues and fighting with a show of right.

I have never thought it easy to be just, and find it daily even harder than I thought. I own I met these Protestants with delight and a sense of coming home. I was accustomed to speak their language, in another and deeper sense of the word than that which distinguishes between French and English; for the true Babel is a divergence upon morals. And hence I could hold more free communication with the Protestants, and judge them more justly, than the Catholics. Father Apollinaris may pair off with my mountain Plymouth Brother as two guileless and devout old men; yet I ask myself if I had as ready a feeling for the virtues of the Trappist; or, had I been a Catholic, if I should have felt so warmly to the dissenter of La Vernède. With the first I was on terms of mere forbearance; but, with the other, although only on a misunderstanding and by keeping on selected points, it was still possible to hold converse and exchange some honest thoughts. In this world of imperfection we gladly welcome even partial intimacies. And if we find but one to whom we can speak out of our heart freely, with whom we can walk in love and simplicity without dissimulation, we have no ground of quarrel with the world or God.

In the Valley of the Mimente

On Tuesday, 1st October, we left Florac late in the afternoon, a tired donkey and tired donkey-driver. A little way up the Tarnon, a covered bridge of wood introduced us into the valley of the Mimente. Steep rocky red mountains overhung the stream; great oaks and chestnuts grew upon the slopes or in stony terraces; here and there was a red field of millet or a few apple-trees studded with red apples; and the road passed hard by two black hamlets, one with an old castle atop to please the heart of the tourist.

It was difficult here again to find a spot fit for my encampment. Even under the oaks and chestnuts the ground had not only a very rapid slope, but was heaped with loose stones; and where there was no timber the hills descended to the stream in a red precipice tufted with heather. The sun had left the highest peak in front of me, and the valley was full of the lowing sound of herdsmen's horns as they recalled the flocks into the stable, when I spied a bight of meadow some way below the roadway in an angle of the river. Thither I descended, and, tying Modestine provisionally to a tree, proceeded to investigate the neighbourhood. A grey pearly evening shadow filled the glen; objects at a little distance grew indistinct and melted bafflingly into each other; and the darkness was rising steadily like an exhalation. I approached a great oak which grew in the meadow, hard by the river's brink; when to my disgust the voices of children fell upon my ear, and I beheld a house round the angle on the other bank. I had half a mind to pack and be gone again, but the growing darkness moved me to remain. I had only to make no noise until the night was fairly come, and trust to the dawn to call me early in the morning. But it was hard to be annoyed by neighbours in such a great hotel.

A hollow underneath the oak was my bed. Before I had fed Modestine and arranged my sack, three stars were already brightly shining, and the others were beginning dimly to appear.

I slipped down to the river, which looked very black among its rocks, to fill my can; and dined with a good appetite in the dark, for I scrupled to light a lantern while so near a house. The moon, which I had seen a pallid crescent all afternoon, faintly illuminated the summit of the hills, but not a ray fell into the bottom of the glen where I was lying. The oak rose before me like a pillar of darkness; and overhead the heartsome stars were set in the face of the night. No one knows the stars who has not slept, as the French happily put it, *à la belle étoile.* He may know all their names and distances and magnitudes, and yet be ignorant of what alone concerns mankind, – their serene and gladsome influence on the mind. The greater part of poetry is about the stars; and very justly, for they are themselves the most classical of poets. These same far-away worlds, sprinkled like tapers or shaken together like a diamond dust upon the sky, had looked not otherwise to Roland or Cavalier, when, in the words of the latter, they had 'no other tent but the sky, and no other bed than my mother earth.'

All night a strong wind blew up the valley, and the acorns fell pattering over me from the oak. Yet, on this first night of October, the air was as mild as May, and I slept with the fur thrown back.

I was much disturbed by the barking of a dog, an animal that I fear more than any wolf. A dog is vastly braver, and is besides supported by the sense of duty. If you kill a wolf, you meet with encouragement and praise; but if you kill a dog, the sacred rights of property and the domestic affections come clamouring round you for redress. At the end of a fagging day, the sharp cruel note of a dog's bark is in itself a keen annoyance; and to a tramp like myself, he represents the sedentary and respectable world in its most hostile form. There is something of the clergyman or the lawyer about this engaging animal; and if he were not amenable to stones, the boldest man would shrink from travelling afoot. I respect dogs much in the domestic circle; but on the highway, or sleeping afield, I both detest and fear them.

I was wakened next morning (Wednesday, 2nd October) by the same dog – for I knew his bark – making a charge down the bank, and then, seeing me sit up, retreating again with great alacrity. The stars were not yet quite extinguished. The heaven was of that enchanting mild grey-blue of the early morn. A still clear light began to fall, and the trees on the hillside were outlined sharply against the sky. The wind had veered more to the north, and no longer reached me in the glen; but as I was going on with my preparations, it drove a white cloud very swiftly over the hill-top; and looking up, I was surprised to see the cloud dyed with gold. In these high regions of the air, the sun was already shining as at noon. If only the clouds travelled high enough, we should see the same thing all night long. For it is always daylight in the fields of space.

As I began to go up the valley, a draught of wind came down it out of the seat of the sunrise, although the clouds continued to run overhead in an almost contrary direction. A few steps farther, and I saw a whole hillside gilded with the sun; and still a little beyond, between two peaks, a centre of dazzling brilliancy appeared floating in the sky, and I was once more face to face with the big bonfire that occupies the kernel of our system.

I met but one human being that forenoon, a dark military-looking wayfarer, who carried a game-bag on a baldric; but he made a remark that seems worthy of record. For when I asked him if he were Protestant or Catholic –

'Oh,' said he, 'I make no shame of my religion. I am a Catholic.'

He made no shame of it! The phrase is a piece of natural statistics; for it is the language of one in a minority. I thought with a smile of Bavile and his dragoons, and how you may ride rough-shod over a religion for a century, and leave it only the more lively for the friction. Ireland is still Catholic; the Cévennes still Protestant. It is not a basketful of law-papers, nor the hoofs and pistol-butts of a regiment of horse, that can change one tittle of a ploughman's thoughts. Outdoor rustic people have not many ideas, but such as they have are hardy plants, and thrive flourishingly in persecution. One who has grown a long while in the sweat of laborious noons, and under the stars at night, a frequenter of hills and forests, an old honest country-man, has, in the end, a sense of communion with the powers of the universe, and amicable relations towards his God. Like my mountain Plymouth Brother, he knows the Lord. His religion does not repose upon a choice of logic; it is the poetry of the man's experience, the philosophy of the history of his life. God, like a great power, like a great shining sun, has appeared to this simple fellow in the course of years, and become the ground and essence of his least reflections; and you may change creeds and dogmas by authority, or proclaim a new religion with the sound of trumpets, if you will; but here is a man who has his own thoughts, and will stubbornly adhere to them in good and evil. He is a Catholic, a Protestant, or a Plymouth Brother, in the same indefeasible sense that a man is not a woman, or a woman not a man. For he could not vary from his faith, unless he could eradicate all memory of the past, and, in a strict and not a conventional meaning, change his mind.

The Heart of the Country

I was now drawing near to Cassagnas, a cluster of black roofs upon the hillside, in this wild valley, among chestnut gardens, and looked upon in the clear air by many rocky peaks. The road along the Mimente is yet new, nor have the mountaineers recovered their surprise when the first cart arrived at Cassagnas. But although it lay thus apart from the current of men's business, this hamlet had already made a figure in the history of France. Hard by, in caverns of the mountain, was one of the five arsenals of the Camisards; where they laid up clothes and corn and arms against necessity, forged bayonets and sabres, and made themselves gunpowder with willow charcoal and saltpetre boiled in kettles. To the same caves, amid this multifarious industry, the sick and wounded were brought up to heal; and there they were visited by the two surgeons, Chabrier and Tavan, and secretly nursed by women of the neighbourhood.

Of the five legions into which the Camisards were divided, it was the oldest and the most obscure that had its magazines by Cassagnas. This was the band of Spirit Séguier; men who had joined their voices with his in the 68th Psalm as they marched down by night on the Archpriest of the Cévennes. Séguier, promoted to heaven, was succeeded by Salomon Couderc, whom Cavalier treats in his memoirs as chaplain-general to the whole army of the Camisards. He was a prophet; a great reader of the heart, who admitted people to the sacrament or refused them, by 'intentively viewing every man' between the eyes; and had the most of the Scriptures off by rote. And this was surely happy; since in a surprise in August, 1703, he lost his mule, his portfolios, and his Bible. It is only strange that they were not surprised more often and more effectually; for this legion of Cassagnas was truly patriarchal in its theory of war, and camped without sentries, leaving that duty to the angels of the God for whom they fought. This is a token, not only of their faith, but of the trackless country where they harboured. M. de Caladon, taking a stroll one fine day, walked without warning into their midst, as he might have walked into 'a flock of sheep in a plain,' and found some asleep and some awake and psalm-singing. A traitor had need of no recommendation to insinuate himself among their ranks, beyond 'his faculty of singing psalms'; and even the prophet Salomon 'took him into a particular friendship.' Thus, among their intricate hills, the rustic troop subsisted; and history can attribute few exploits to them but sacraments and ecstasies.

People of this tough and simple stock will not, as I have just been saying, prove variable in religion; nor will they get nearer to apostasy than a mere external conformity like that of Naaman in the house of Rimmon. When Louis XVI, in the words of the edict, 'convinced by the uselessness of a century of persecutions, and rather from necessity than sympathy,' granted at last a royal grace of toleration, Cassagnas was still Protestant; and to a man, it is so to this day. There is, indeed, one family that is not Protestant, but neither is it Catholic. It is that of a Catholic *curé* in revolt, who has taken to his bosom a school-mistress. And his conduct, it is worth noting, is disapproved by the Protestant villagers.

'It is a bad idea for a man,' said one, 'to go back from his engagements.'

The villagers whom I saw seemed intelligent after a countrified fashion, and were all plain and dignified in manner. As a Protestant myself, I was well looked upon, and my acquaintance with history gained me further respect. For we had something not unlike a religious controversy at table, a gendarme and a merchant with whom I dined being both strangers to the place, and Catholics. The young men of the house stood round and supported me; and the whole discussion was tolerantly conducted, and surprised a man brought up among the infinitesimal and contentious differences of Scotland. The merchant, indeed, grew a little warm, and was far less pleased than some others with my historical acquirements. But the gendarme was mighty easy over it all.

'It's a bad idea for a man to change,' said he; and the remark was generally applauded.

That was not the opinion of the priest and soldier at Our Lady of the Snows. But this is a different race; and perhaps the same great-heartedness that upheld them to resist, now enables them to differ in a kind spirit. For courage respects courage; but where a faith has been trodden out, we may look for a mean and narrow population. The true work of Bruce and Wallace was the union of the nations; not that they should stand apart a while longer, skirmishing upon their borders; but that, when the time came, they might unite with self-respect.

The merchant was much interested in my journey, and thought it dangerous to sleep afield.

'There are the wolves,' said he; 'and then it is known you are an Englishman. The English have always long purses, and it might very well enter into someone's head to deal you an ill blow some night.'

I told him I was not much afraid of such accidents; and at any rate judged it unwise to dwell upon alarms or consider small perils in the arrangement of life. Life itself, I submitted, was a far too risky business as a whole to make each additional particular of danger worth regard. 'Something,' said I, 'might burst in your inside any day of the week, and there would be an end of you, if you were locked into your room with three turns of the key.'

'*Cependant*,' said he, '*coucher dehors*!'

'God,' said I, 'is everywhere.'

'*Cependant, coucher dehors*!' he repeated, and his voice was eloquent of terror.

He was the only person, in all my voyage, who saw anything hardy in so simple a proceeding; although many considered it superfluous. Only one, on the other hand, professed much delight in the idea; and that was my Plymouth Brother, who cried out, when I told him I sometimes preferred sleeping under the stars to a close and noisy alehouse, 'Now I see that you know the Lord!'

The merchant asked me for one of my cards as I was leaving, for he said I should be something to talk of in the future, and desired me to make a note of his request and reason; a desire with which I have thus complied.

A little after two I struck across the Mimente, and took a rugged path southward up a hillside covered with loose stones and tufts of heather. At the top, as is the habit of the country, the path disappeared; and I left my she-ass munching heather, and went forward alone to seek a road.

I was now on the separation of two vast watersheds; behind

me all the streams were bound for the Garonne and the Western Ocean; before me was the basin of the Rhône. Hence, as from the Lozère, you can see in the clear weather the shining of the Gulf of Lyons; and perhaps from here the soldiers of Salomon may have watched for the topsails of Sir Cloudesley Shovel, and the long-promised aid from England. You may take this ridge as lying in the heart of the country of the Camisards; four of the five legions camped all round it and almost within view — Salomon and Joani to the north, Castanet and Roland to the south; and when Julien had finished his famous work, the devastation of the High Cévennes, which lasted all through October and November 1703, and during which four hundred and sixty villages and hamlets were, with fire and pickaxe, utterly subverted, a man standing on this eminence would have looked forth upon a silent, smokeless, and dispeopled land. Time and man's activity have now repaired these ruins; Cassagnas is once more roofed and sending up domestic smoke; and in the chestnut gardens, in low and leafy corners, many a prosperous farmer returns, when the day's work is done, to his children and bright hearth. And still it was perhaps the wildest view of all my journey. Peak upon peak, chain upon chain of hills ran surging southward, channelled and sculptured by the winter streams, feathered from head to foot with chestnuts, and here and there breaking out into a coronal of cliffs. The sun, which was still far from setting, sent a drift of misty gold across the hill-tops, but the valleys were already plunged in a profound and quiet shadow.

A very old shepherd, hobbling on a pair of sticks, and wearing a black cap of liberty, as if in honour of his nearness to the grave, directed me to the road for St Germain de Calberte. There was something solemn in the isolation of this infirm and ancient creature. Where he dwelt, how he got upon this high ridge, or how he proposed to get down again, were more than I could fancy. Not far off upon my right was the famous Plan de Font Morte, where Poul with his Armenian sabre slashed down the Camisards of Séguier. This, methought, might be some Rip Van Winkle of the war, who had lost his comrades, fleeing before Poul, and wandered ever since upon the mountains. It might be news to him that Cavalier had surrendered, or Roland had fallen fighting with his back against an olive. And while I was thus working on my fancy, I heard him hailing in broken tones, and saw him waving me to come back with one of his two sticks. I had already got some way past him; but, leaving Modestine once more, retraced my steps.

Alas, it was a very commonplace affair. The old gentleman had forgot to ask the pedlar what he sold, and wished to remedy this neglect.

I told him sternly, 'Nothing.'

'Nothing?' cried he.

I repeated 'Nothing,' and made off.

It's odd to think of, but perhaps I thus became as inexplicable to the old man as he had been to me.

The road lay under chestnuts, and though I saw a hamlet or two below me in the vale, and many lone houses of the chestnut farmers, it was a very solitary march all afternoon; and the evening began early underneath the trees. But I heard the voice of a woman singing some sad, old, endless ballad not far off. It seemed to be about love and a *bel amoureux*, her handsome sweetheart; and I wished I could have taken up the strain and answered her, as I went on upon my invisible woodland way, weaving, like Pippa in the poem, my own thoughts with hers. What could I have told her? Little enough; and yet all the heart requires. How the world gives and takes away, and brings sweethearts near only to separate them again into distant and strange lands; but to love is the great amulet which makes the world a garden; and 'hope, which comes to all', outwears the accidents of life, and reaches with tremulous hand beyond the grave and death. Easy to say: yea, but also, by God's mercy, both easy and grateful to believe!

We struck at last into a wide white high-road carpeted with noiseless dust. The night had come; the moon had been shining for a long while upon the opposite mountain; when on turning a corner my donkey and I issued ourselves into her light. I had emptied out my brandy at Florac, for I could bear the stuff no longer, and replaced it with some generous and scented Volnay; and now I drank to the moon's sacred majesty upon the road. It was but a couple of mouthfuls; yet I became thenceforth unconscious of my limbs, and my blood flowed with luxury. Even Modestine was inspired by this purified nocturnal sun-shine, and bestirred her little hoofs as to a livelier measure. The road wound and descended swiftly among masses of chestnuts. Hot dust rose from our feet and flowed away. Our two shadows

– mine deformed with the knapsack, hers comically bestridden by the pack – now lay before us clearly outlined on the road, and now, as we turned a corner, went off into the ghostly distance, and sailed along the mountain like clouds. From time to time a warm wind rustled down the valley, and set all the chestnuts dangling their bunches of foliage and fruit; the ear was filled with whispering music, and the shadows danced in tune. And next moment the breeze had gone by, and in all the valley nothing moved except our travelling feet. On the opposite slope, the monstrous ribs and gullies of the mountain were faintly designed in the moonshine; and high overhead, in some lone house, there burned one lighted window, one square spark of red in the huge field of sad nocturnal colouring.

At a certain point, as I went downward, turning many acute angles, the moon disappeared behind the hill; and I pursued my way in great darkness, until another turning shot me without preparation into St Germain de Calberte. The place was asleep and silent, and buried in opaque night. Only from a single open door, some lamplight escaped upon the road to show me that I was come among men's habitations. The two last gossips of the evening, still talking by a garden wall, directed me to the inn. The landlady was getting her chicks to bed; the fire was already out, and had, not without grumbling, to be rekindled; half an hour later, and I must have gone supperless to roost.

The Last Day

When I awoke (Thursday, 3rd October), and, hearing a great flourishing of cocks and chuckling of contented hens, betook me to the window of the clean and comfortable room where I had slept the night, I looked forth on a sunshiny morning in a deep vale of chestnut gardens. It was still early, and the cock-crows, and the slanting lights, and the long shadows, encouraged me to be out and look around me.

St Germain de Calberte is a great parish nine leagues round about. At the period of the wars, and immediately before the devastation, it was inhabited by two hundred and seventy-five families, of which only nine were Catholic; and it took the *curé* seventeen September days to go from house to house on horseback for a census. But the place itself, although capital of a canton, is scarce larger than a hamlet. It lies terraced across a steep slope in the midst of mighty chestnuts. The Protestant chapel stands below upon a shoulder; in the midst of the town is the quaint old Catholic church.

It was here that poor Du Chayla, the Christian martyr, kept his library and held a court of missionaries; here he had built his tomb, thinking to lie among a grateful population whom he had redeemed from error; and hither on the morrow of his death they brought the body, pierced with two-and-fifty wounds, to be interred. Clad in his priestly robes, he was laid out in state in the church. The *curé*, taking his text from Second Samuel, twentieth chapter and twelfth verse, 'And Amasa wallowed in his blood in the highway,' preached a rousing sermon, and exhorted his brethren to die each at his post, like their unhappy and illustrious superior. In the midst of this eloquence there came a breeze that Spirit Séguier was near at hand; and behold! all the assembly took to their horses' heels, some east, some west, and the *curé* himself as far as Alais.

Strange was the position of this little Catholic metropolis, a thimbleful of Rome, in such a wild and contrary neighbourhood.

On the one hand, the legion of Salomon overlooked it from Cassagnas; on the other it was cut off from assistance by the legion of Roland at Mialet. The *curé* Louvrelenil, although he took a panic at the archpriest's funeral, and so hurriedly decamped to Alais, stood well by his isolated pulpit, and thence uttered fulminations against the crimes of the Protestants. Salomon besieged the village for an hour and a half, but was beaten back. The militiamen, on guard before the *curé*'s door, could be heard, in the black hours, singing Protestant psalms and holding friendly talk with the insurgents. And in the morning, although not a shot had been fired, there would not be a round of powder in their flasks. Where was it gone? All handed over to the Camisards for a consideration. Untrusty guardians for an isolated priest!

That these continual stirs were once busy in St Germain de Calberte, the imagination with difficulty receives; all is now so quiet, the pulse of human life now beats so low and still in this hamlet of the mountains. Boys followed me a great way off, like a timid sort of lion-hunters; and people turned round to have a second look, or came out of their houses, as I went by. My passage was the first event, you would have fancied, since the Camisards. There was nothing rude or forward in this observation; it was but a pleased and wondering scrutiny, like that of oxen or the human infant; yet it wearied my spirits, and soon drove me from the street.

I took refuge on the terraces, which are here greenly carpeted with sward, and tried to imitate with a pencil the inimitable attitudes of the chestnuts as they bear up their canopy of leaves. Ever and again a little wind went by, and the nuts dropped all around me, with a light and dull sound, upon the sward. The noise was as of a thin fall of great hailstones; but there went with it a cheerful human sentiment of an approaching harvest and farmers rejoicing in their gains. Looking up, I could see the brown nut peering through the husk, which was already gaping; and between the stems the eye embraced an amphitheatre of hill, sunlit and green with leaves.

I have not often enjoyed a place more deeply. I moved in an atmosphere of pleasure, and felt light and quiet and content. But perhaps it was not the place alone that so disposed my spirit. Perhaps someone was thinking of me in another country; or perhaps some thought of my own had come and gone unnoticed, and yet done me good. For some thoughts, which sure would be the most beautiful, vanish before we can rightly scan their features; as though a god, travelling by our green highways, should but ope the door, give one smiling look into the house, and go again for ever. Was it Apollo, or Mercury, or Love with folded wings? Who shall say? But we go the lighter about our business, and feel peace and pleasure in our hearts.

I dined with a pair of Catholics. They agreed in the condemnation of a young man, a Catholic, who had married a Protestant girl and gone over to the religion of his wife. A Protestant born they could understand and respect; indeed, they seemed to be of the mind of an old Catholic woman, who told me that same day there was no difference between the two sects, save that 'wrong was more wrong for the Catholic', who had more light and guidance; but this of a man's desertion filled them with contempt.

'It is a bad idea for a man to change,' said one.

It may have been accidental, but you see how this phrase pursued me; and for myself, I believe it is the current philosophy in these parts. I have some difficulty in imagining a better. It's not only a great flight of confidence for a man to change his creed and go out of his family for heaven's sake; but the odds are – nay, and the hope is – that, with all this great transition in the eyes of man, he has not changed himself a hairbreadth to the eyes of God. Honour to those who do so, for the wrench is sore. But it argues something narrow, whether of strength or weakness, whether of the prophet or the fool, in those who can take a sufficient interest in such infinitesimal and human operations, or who can quit a friendship for a doubtful process of the mind. And I think I should not leave my old creed for another, changing only words for other words; but by some brave reading, embrace it in spirit and truth, and find wrong as wrong for me as for the best of other communions.

The phylloxera was in the neighbourhood; and instead of wine we drank at dinner a more economical juice of the grape – La Parisienne, they call it. It is made by putting the fruit whole into a cask with water; one by one the berries ferment and burst; what is drunk during the day is supplied at night in water: so, with ever another pitcher from the well, and ever another grape exploding and giving out its strength, one cask of

Parisienne may last a family till spring. It is, as the reader will anticipate, a feeble beverage, but very pleasant to the taste.

What with dinner and coffee, it was long past three before I left St Germain de Calberte. I went down beside the Gardon of Mialet, a great glaring watercourse devoid of water, and through St Étienne-Vallée Française, or Val Francesque, as they used to call it; and towards evening began to ascend the hill of St Pierre. It was a long and steep ascent. Behind me an empty carriage returning to St Jean du Gard kept hard upon my tracks, and near the summit overtook me. The driver, like the rest of the world, was sure I was a pedlar; but, unlike others, he was sure of what I had to sell. He had noticed the blue wool which hung out of my pack at either end; and from this he had decided, beyond my power to alter his decision, that I dealt in blue-wool collars, such as decorate the neck of the French draught-horse.

I had hurried to the topmost powers of Modestine, for I dearly desired to see the view upon the other side before the day had faded. But it was night when I reached the summit; the moon was riding high and clear; and only a few grey streaks of twilight lingered in the west. A yawning valley, gulfed in blackness, lay like a hole in created nature at my feet; but the outline of the hills was sharp against the sky. There was Mount Aigoal, the stronghold of Castanet. And Castanet, not only as an active undertaking leader, deserves some mention among Camisards; for there is a spray of rose among his laurel; and he showed how, even in a public tragedy, love will have its way. In the high tide of war he married, in his mountain citadel, a young and pretty lass called Mariette. There were great rejoicings; and the bridegroom released five-and-twenty prisoners in honour of the glad event. Seven months afterwards, Mariette, the Princess of the Cévennes, as they called her in derision, fell into the hands of the authorities, where it was like to have gone hard with her. But Castanet was a man of execution, and loved his wife. He fell on Valleraugue, and got a lady there for a hostage; and for the first and last time in that war there was an exchange of prisoners. Their daughter, pledge of some starry night upon Mount Aigoal, has left descendants to this day.

Modestine and I – it was our last meal together – had a snack upon the top of St Pierre, I on a heap of stones, she standing by me in the moonlight and decorously eating bread out of my hand. The poor brute would eat more heartily in this manner; for she had a sort of affection for me, which I was soon to betray.

It was a long descent upon St Jean du Gard, and we met no one but a carter, visible afar off by the glint of the moon on his extinguished lantern.

Before ten o'clock we had got in and were at supper; fifteen miles and a stiff hill in little beyond six hours!

Farewell, Modestine!

On examination, on the morning of 4th October, Modestine was pronounced unfit for travel. She would need at least two days' repose, according to the ostler; but I was now eager to reach Alais for my letters; and, being in a civilised country of stage-coaches, I determined to sell my lady friend and be off by the diligence that afternoon. Our yesterday's march, with the testimony of the driver who had pursued us up the long hill of St Pierre, spread a favourable notion of my donkey's capabilities. Intending purchasers were aware of an unrivalled opportunity. Before ten I had an offer of twenty-five francs; and before noon, after a desperate engagement, I sold her, saddle and all, for five-and-thirty. The pecuniary gain is not obvious, but I had bought freedom into the bargain.

St Jean du Gard is a large place, and largely Protestant. The *maire*, a Protestant, asked me to help him in a small matter which is itself characteristic of the country. The young women of the Cévennes profit by the common religion and the difference of the language to go largely as governesses into England; and here was one, a native of Mialet, struggling with English circulars from two different agencies in London. I gave what help I could; and volunteered some advice, which struck me as being excellent.

One thing more I note. The phylloxera has ravaged the vineyards in this neighbourhood; and in the early morning, under some chestnuts by the river, I found a party of men working with a cider-press. I could not at first make out what they were after, and asked one fellow to explain.

'Making cider,' he said. '*Oui, c'est comme ça. Comme dans le nord!*'

There was a ring of sarcasm in his voice: the country was going to the devil.

It was not until I was fairly seated by the driver, and rattling through a rocky valley with dwarf olives, that I became aware of my bereavement. I had lost Modestine. Up to that moment I had thought I hated her; but now she was gone,

> And oh!
> The difference to me!

For twelve days we had been fast companions; we had travelled upwards of a hundred and twenty miles, crossed several respectable ridges, and jogged along with our six legs by many a rocky and many a boggy by-road. After the first day, although sometimes I was hurt and distant in manner, I still kept my patience; and as for her, poor soul! she had come to regard me as a god. She loved to eat out of my hand. She was patient, elegant in form, the colour of an ideal mouse, and inimitably small. Her faults were those of her race and sex; her virtues were her own. Farewell, and if for ever –

Father Adam wept when he sold her to me; after I had sold her in my turn, I was tempted to follow his example; and being alone with a stage-driver and four or five agreeable young men, I did not hesitate to yield to my emotion.

The End

THE SILVERADO
SQUATTERS

Vixerunt nonnulli in agris, delectati re sua familiari. His idem propositum fuit quod regibus, ut ne qua re egerent, ne cui parerent, libertate uterentur: cujus proprium est sic vivere ut velis. – Cɪc., *De Off.*, I. xx.

CONTENTS

The Silverado Squatters

The scene of this little book is on a high mountain. There are, indeed, many higher; there are many of a nobler outline. It is no place of pilgrimage for the summary globe-trotter; but to one who lives upon its sides, Mount Saint Helena soon becomes a centre of interest. It is the Mont Blanc of one section of the Californian Coast Range, none of its near neighbours rising to one-half its altitude. It looks down on much green, intricate country. It feeds in the spring-time many splashing brooks. From its summit you must have an excellent lesson of geography: seeing, to the south, San Francisco Bay, with Tamalpais on the one hand and Monte Diablo on the other; to the west and thirty miles away, the open ocean; eastward, across the cornlands and thick tule swamps of Sacramento Valley, to where the Central Pacific railroad begins to climb the sides of the Sierras; and northward, for what I know, the white head of Shasta looking down on Oregon. Three counties, Napa County, Lake County, and Sonoma County, march across its cliffy shoulders. Its naked peak stands nearly four thousand five hundred feet above the sea; its sides are fringed with forest; and the soil, where it is bare, glows warm with cinnabar.

Life in its shadow goes rustically forward. Bucks, and bears, and rattlesnakes, and former mining operations, are the staple of men's talk. Agriculture has only begun to mount above the valley. And though in a few years from now the whole district may be smiling with farms, passing trains shaking the mountain to the heart, many-windowed hotels lighting up the night like factories, and a prosperous city occupying the site of sleepy Calistoga; yet in the meantime, around the foot of that mountain the silence of nature reigns in a great measure unbroken, and the people of hill and valley go sauntering about their business as in the days before the flood.

To reach Mount Saint Helena from San Francisco the traveller has twice to cross the bay: once by the busy Oakland Ferry, and again, after an hour or so of the railway, from Vallejo junction to Vallejo. Thence he takes rail once more to mount the long green strath of Napa Valley.

In all the contractions and expansions of that inland sea, the Bay of San Francisco, there can be few drearier scenes than the Vallejo Ferry. Bald shores and a low, bald islet enclose the sea; through the narrows the tide bubbles, muddy like a river. When we made the passage (bound, although yet we knew it not, for Silverado) the steamer jumped, and the black buoys were dancing in the jabble; the ocean breeze blew killing chill; and, although the upper sky was still unflecked with vapour, the sea fogs were pouring in from seaward, over the hilltops of Marin County, in one great, shapeless, silver cloud.

South Vallejo is typical of many Californian towns. It was a blunder; the site had proved untenable; and, although it is still such a young place by the scale of Europe, it has already begun to be deserted for its neighbour and namesake, North Vallejo. A long pier, a number of drinking saloons, a hotel of a great size, marshy pools where the frogs keep up their croaking, and even at high noon the entire absence of any human face or voice – these are the marks of South Vallejo. Yet there was a tall building beside the pier, labelled the *Star Flour Mills*; and sea-going, full-rigged ships lay close along shore, waiting for their cargo. Soon these would be plunging round the Horn, soon the flour from the *Star Flour Mills* would be landed on the wharves of Liverpool. For that, too, is one of England's outposts; thither, to this gaunt mill, across the Atlantic and Pacific deeps and round about the icy Horn, this crowd of great, three-masted, deep-sea ships come, bringing nothing, and return with bread.

The Frisby House, for that was the name of the hotel, was a place of fallen fortunes, like the town. It was now given up to labourers, and partly ruinous. At dinner there was the ordinary display of what is called in the west a *two-bit house*: the tablecloth checked red and white, the plague of flies, the wire hencoops over the dishes, the great variety and invariable vileness of the food and the rough coatless men devouring it in silence. In our bedroom, the stove would not burn, though it would smoke; and while one window would not open, the other would not shut. There was a view on a bit of empty road, a few dark houses, a donkey wandering with its shadow on a slope, and a blink of sea, with a tall ship lying anchored in the moonlight. All about that dreary inn frogs sang their ungainly chorus.

Early the next morning we mounted the hill along a wooden footway, bridging one marish spot after another. Here and there, as we ascended, we passed a house embowered in white roses. More of the bay became apparent, and soon the blue peak of Tamalpais rose above the green level of the island opposite. It told us we were still but a little way from the city of the Golden Gates, already, at that hour, beginning to awake among the sand-hills. It called to us over the waters as with the voice of a bird. Its stately head, blue as a sapphire on the paler azure of the sky, spoke to us of wider outlooks and the bright Pacific. For Tamalpais stands sentry, like a lighthouse, over the Golden Gates, between the bay and the open ocean, and looks down indifferently on both. Even as we saw and hailed it from Vallejo, seamen, far out at sea, were scanning it with shaded eyes; and, as if to answer to the thought, one of the great ships below began silently to clothe herself with white sails, homeward bound for England.

For some way beyond Vallejo the railway led us through bald green pastures. On the west the rough highlands of Marin shut off the ocean; in the midst, in long, straggling, gleaming arms, the bay died out among the grass; there were few trees and few enclosures; the sun shone wide over open uplands, the dis-plumed hills stood clear against the sky. But by-and-by these hills began to draw nearer on either hand, and first thicket and then wood began to clothe their sides; and soon we were away from all signs of the sea's neighbourhood, mounting an inland, irrigated valley. A great variety of oaks stood, now severally, now in a becoming grove, among the fields and vineyards. The towns were compact, in about equal proportions, of bright, new wooden houses and great and growing forest trees; and the chapel bell on the engine sounded most festally that sunny Sunday, as we drew up at one green town after another, with the townsfolk trooping in their Sunday's best to see the strangers, with the sun sparkling on the clean houses, and great domes of foliage humming overhead in the breeze.

This pleasant Napa valley is, at its north end, blockaded by our mountain. There, at Calistoga, the railroad ceases, and the traveller who intends faring farther, to the Geysers or to the springs in Lake County, must cross the spurs of the mountain by stage. Thus, Mount Saint Helena is not only a summit, but frontier; and, up to the time of writing, it has stayed the progress of the iron horse.

In the Valley

I

Calistoga

It is difficult for a European to imagine Calistoga, the whole place is so new, and of such an occidental pattern; the very name, I hear, was invented at a supper-party by the man who found the springs.

The railroad and the highway come up the valley about parallel to one another. The street of Calistoga joins them, perpendicular to both – a wide street, with bright, clean, lowhouses, here and there a verandah over the sidewalk, here and there a horse-post, here and there lounging townsfolk. Other streets are marked out, and most likely named; for these towns in the New World begin with a firm resolve to grow larger, Washington and Broadway, and then First and Second, and so forth, being boldly plotted out as soon as the community indulges in a plan. But, in the meanwhile, all the life and most of the houses of Calistoga are concentrated upon that street between the railway station and the road. I never heard it called by any name, but I will hazard a guess that it is either Washington or Broadway. Here are the blacksmith's, the chemist's, the general merchant's, and Kong Sam Kee, the Chinese laundryman's; here, probably, is the office of the local paper (for the place has a paper – they all have papers); and here certainly is one of the hotels, Cheeseborough's, whence the daring Foss, a man dear to legend, starts his horses for the Geysers.

It must be remembered that we are in a land of stage-drivers and highwaymen: a land, in that sense, like England a hundred years ago. The highway robber – road-agent, he is quaintly called – is still busy in these parts. The fame of Vasquez is still young. Only a few years ago, the Lakeport stage was robbed a mile or two from Calistoga. In 1879, the dentist of Mendocino City, fifty miles away upon the coast, suddenly threw off the garments of his trade, like Grindoff in *The Miller and his Men*, and flamed forth in his second dress as a captain of banditti. A great robbery was followed by a long chase, a chase of days if not of weeks, among the intricate hill-country; and the chase was followed by much desultory fighting, in which several – and the dentist, I believe, amongst the number – bit the dust. The grass was springing for the first time, nourished upon their blood, when I arrived in Calistoga. I am reminded of another highwayman of that same year. 'He had been unwell,' so ran his humorous defence, 'and the doctor told him to take something, so he took the express-box.'

The cultus of the stage-coachman always flourishes highest where there are thieves on the road, and where the guard travels armed, and the stage is not only a link between country and city, and the vehicle of news, but has a faint warfaring aroma, like a man who should be brother to a soldier. California boasts her famous stage-drivers, and among the famous Foss is not forgotten. Along the unfenced, abominable mountain roads, he launches his team with small regard to human life or the doctrine of probabilities. Flinching travellers, who behold themselves coasting eternity at every corner, look with natural admiration at their driver's huge, impassive, fleshy countenance. He has the very face for the driver in Sam Weller's anecdote, who upset the election party at the required point. Wonderful tales are current of his readiness and skill. One in particular, of how one of his horses fell at a ticklish passage of the road, and how Foss let slip the reins, and, driving over the fallen animal arrived at the next stage with only three. This I relate as I heard it, without guarantee.

I only saw Foss once, though, strange as it may sound, I have twice talked with him. He lives out of Calistoga, at a ranche called Fossville. One evening, after he was long gone home, I dropped into Cheeseborough's, and was asked if I should like to speak with Mr Foss. Supposing that the interview was impossible, and that I was merely called upon to subscribe the general sentiment, I boldly answered 'Yes.' Next moment, I had one instrument at my ear, another at my mouth, and found myself, with nothing in the world to say, conversing with a man several miles off among desolate hills. Foss rapidly and somewhat plaintively brought the conversation to an end; and he returned to his night's grog at Fossville, while I strolled forth again on Calistoga high street. But it was an odd thing that here, on what we are accustomed to consider the very skirts of civilisation, I should have used the telephone for the first time in my civilised career. So it goes in these young countries; telephones, and telegraphs, and newspapers, and advertisements running far ahead among the Indians and the grizzly bears.

Alone, on the other side of the railway, stands the Springs Hotel, with its attendant cottages. The floor of the valley is extremely level to the very roots of the hills; only here and there a hillock, crowned with pines, rises like the barrow of some chieftain framed in war; and right against one of these hillocks is the Spring Hotel – is or was; for since I was there the place has been destroyed by fire, and has risen again from its ashes. A lawn runs about the house, and the lawn is in its turn surrounded by a system of little five-roomed cottages, each with a verandah and a weedy palm before the door. Some of the cottages are let to residents, and these are wreathed in flowers. The rest are occupied by ordinary visitors to the hotel; and a very pleasant way this is, by which you have a little country cottage of your own, without domestic burthens, and by the day or week.

The whole neighbourhood of Mount Saint Helena is full of sulphur and of boiling springs. The Geysers are famous; they were the great health resort of the Indians before the coming of the whites. Lake County is dotted with spas; Hot Springs and White Sulphur Springs are the names of two stations on the Napa Valley railroad; and Calistoga itself seems to repose on a mere film above a boiling, subterranean lake. At one end of the hotel enclosure are the springs from which it takes its name, hot enough to scald a child seriously while I was there. At the other end, the tenant of a cottage sank a well, and there also the water came up boiling. It keeps this end of the valley as warm as a toast. I have gone across to the hotel a little after five in the morning, when a sea fog from the Pacific was hanging thick and grey, and dark and dirty overhead, and found the thermometer had been up before me, and had already climbed among the nineties; and in the stress of the day it was sometimes too hot to move about.

But in spite of this heat from above and below, doing one on both sides, Calistoga was a pleasant place to dwell in; beautifully green, for it was then that favoured moment in the Californian year, when the rains are over and the dusty summer has not yet set in; often visited by fresh airs, now from the mountain, now across Sonoma from the sea; very quiet, very idle, very silent but for the breezes and the cattle bells afield. And there was something satisfactory in the sight of that great mountain that enclosed us to the north: whether it stood, robed in sunshine, quaking to its topmost pinnacle with the heat and brightness of the day; or whether it set itself to weaving vapours, wisp after wisp growing, trembling, fleeting, and fading blue.

The tangled, woody, and almost trackless foot-hills that enclose the valley, shutting it off from Sonoma on the West, and from Yolo on the east – rough as they were in outline, dug out by winter streams, crowned by cliffy bluffs and nodding pine trees – were dwarfed into satellites by the bulk and bearing of Mount Saint Helena. She over-towered them by two-thirds of her own stature. She excelled them by the boldness of her profile. Her great bald summit, clear of trees and pasture, a cairn of quartz and cinnabar, rejected kinship with the dark and shaggy wilderness of lesser hill-tops.

II
The Petrified Forest

We drove off from the Springs Hotel about three in the afternoon. The sun warmed me to the heart. A broad, cool wind streamed pauselessly down the valley, laden with perfume. Up at the top stood Mount Saint Helena, a bulk of mountain, bare atop, with tree-fringed spurs, and radiating warmth. Once we saw it framed in a grove of tall and exquisitely graceful white oaks, in line and colour a finished composition. We passed a cow stretched by the roadside, her bell slowly beating time to the movement of her ruminating jaw, her big red face crawled over by half-a-dozen flies, a monument of content.

A little farther, and we struck to the left up a mountain road, and for two hours threaded one valley after another, green, tangled, full of noble timber, giving us every now and again a sight of Mount Saint Helena and the blue hilly distance, and crossed by many streams, through which we splashed to the carriage-step. To the right or the left, there was scarce any trace of man but the road we followed; I think we passed but one ranchero's house in the whole distance, and that was closed and smokeless. But we had the society of these bright streams – dazzlingly clear, as is their wont, splashing from the wheels in diamonds, and striking a lively coolness through the sunshine. And what with the innumerable variety of greens, the masses of foliage tossing in the breeze, the glimpses of distance, the descents into seemingly impenetrable thickets, the continual dodging of the road, which made haste to plunge again into the covert, we had a fine sense of woods, and spring-time, and the open air.

Our driver gave me a lecture by the way on Californian trees – a thing I was much in need of, having fallen among painters who know the name of nothing, and Mexicans who know the name of nothing in English. He taught me the madrona, the manzanita, the buck-eye, the maple; he showed me the crested mountain quail; he showed me where some young redwoods were already spiring heavenwards from the ruins of the old; for in this district all had already perished: redwoods and redskins, the two noblest indigenous living things, alike condemned.

At length, in a lonely dell, we came on a huge wooden gate with a sign upon it like an inn. 'The Petrified Forest. Proprietor: C. Evans', ran the legend. Within, on a knoll of sward, was the house of the proprietor, and another smaller house hard by to serve as a museum, where photographs and petrifactions were retailed. It was a pure little isle of touristry among these solitary hills.

The proprietor was a brave old white-faced Swede. He had wandered this way, Heaven knows how, and taken up his acres – I forget how many years ago – all alone, bent double with sciatica, and with six bits in his pocket and an axe upon his shoulder. Long, useless years of seafaring had thus discharged him at the end, penniless and sick. Without doubt he had tried his luck at the diggings, and got no good from that; without doubt he had loved the bottle, and lived the life of Jack ashore. But at the end of these adventures, here he came; and, the place hitting his fancy, down he sat to make a new life of it, far from crimps and the salt sea. And the very sight of his ranche had done him good. It was 'the handsomest spot in the Californy mountains.' 'Isn't it handsome, now?' he said. Every penny he makes goes into that ranche to make it handsomer. Then the climate, with the sea-breeze every afternoon in the hottest summer weather, had gradually cured the sciatica; and his sister and niece were now domesticated with him for company – or, rather, the niece came only once in the two days, teaching music the meanwhile in the valley. And then, for a last piece of luck, 'the handsomest spot in the Californy mountains' had produced a petrified forest, which Mr Evans now shows at the modest figure of half a dollar a head, or two-thirds of his capital when he first came there with an axe and a sciatica.

This tardy favourite of fortune – hobbling a little, I think, as if in memory of the sciatica, but with not a trace that I can remember of the sea – thoroughly ruralised from head to foot, proceeded to escort us up the hill behind his house.

'Who first found the forest?' asked my wife.

'The first? I was that man,' said he. 'I was cleaning up the pasture for my beasts, when I found *this*' – kicking a great redwood, seven feet in diameter, that lay there on its side, hollow heart, clinging lumps of bark, all changed into grey stone, with veins of quartz between what had been the layers of the wood.

'Were you surprised?'

'Surprised? No! What would I be surprised about? What did I know about petrifactions – following the sea? Petrifaction! There was no such word in my language! I knew about putrefaction, though! I thought it was a stone; so would you, if you was cleaning up pasture.'

And now he had a theory of his own, which I did not quite grasp, except that the trees had not 'grewed' there. But he mentioned, with evident pride, that he differed from all the scientific people who had visited the spot; and he flung about such words as 'tufa' and 'scilica' with careless freedom.

When I mentioned I was from Scotland, 'My old country,' he said; 'my old country' – with a smiling look and a tone of real affection in his voice. I was mightily surprised, for he was obviously Scandinavian, and begged him to explain. It seemed he had learned his English and done nearly all his sailing in Scotch ships. 'Out of Glasgow,' said he, 'or Greenock; but that's all the same – they all hail from Glasgow.' And he was so pleased with me for being a Scotsman, and his adopted compatriot, that he made me a present of a very beautiful piece of petrifaction – I believe the most beautiful and portable he had.

Here was a man, at least, who was a Swede, a Scot, and an American, acknowledging some kind allegiance to three lands.

Mr Wallace's Scoto-Circassian will not fail to come before the reader. I have myself met and spoken with a Fifeshire German, whose combination of abominable accents struck me dumb. But, indeed, I think we all belong to many countries. And perhaps this habit of much travel, and the engendering of scattered friendships, may prepare the euthanasia of ancient nations.

And the forest itself? Well, on a tangled, briery hillside – for the pasture would bear a little further cleaning up, to my eyes – there he scattered thickly various lengths of petrified trunk, such as the one already mentioned. It is very curious, of course, and ancient enough if that were all. Doubtless, the heart of the geologist beats quicker at the sight; but, for my part, I was mightily unmoved. Sight-seeing is the art of disappointment.

> There's nothing under heaven so blue,
> That's fairly worth the travelling to.

But, fortunately, Heaven rewards us with many agreeable prospects and adventures by the way; and sometimes, when we go out to see a petrified forest, prepares a far more delightful curiosity in the form of Mr Evans, whom may all prosperity attend throughout a long and green old age.

III
Napa Wine

I was interested in Californian wine. Indeed, I am interested in all wines, and have been all my life, from the raisin wine that a schoolfellow kept secreted in his play-box up to my last discovery, those notable Valtellines, that once shone upon the board of Cæsar.

Some of us, kind old Pagans, watch with dread the shadows falling on the age: how the unconquerable worm invades the sunny terraces of France, and Bordeaux is no more, and the Rhône a mere Arabia Petræa. Château Neuf is dead, and I have never tasted it; Hermitage – a hermitage indeed from all life's sorrows – lies expiring by the river. And in the place of these imperial elixirs, beautiful to every sense, gem-hued, flower-scented, dream-compellers: – behold upon the quays at Cette the chemicals arrayed; behold the analyst at Marseilles, raising hands in obsecration, attesting god Lyœus, and the vats staved in, and the dishonest wines poured forth among the sea. It is not Pan only: Bacchus, too, is dead.

If wine is to withdraw its most poetic countenance, the sun of the white dinner-cloth, a deity to be invoked by two or three, all fervent, hushing their talk, degusting tenderly, and storing reminiscences – for a bottle of good wine, like a good act, shines ever in the retrospect – if wine is to desert us, go thy ways, old Jack! Now we begin to have compunctions, and look back at the brave bottles squandered upon dinner-parties, where the guests drank grossly, discussing politics the while, and even the schoolboy 'took his whack', like liquorice water. And at the same time, we look timidly forward, with a spark of hope, to where the new lands, already weary of producing gold, begin to green with vineyards. A nice point in human history falls to be decided by Californian and Australian wines.

Wine in California is still in the experimental stage; and when you taste a vintage, grave economical questions are involved. The beginning of vine-planting is like the beginning of mining for the precious metals: the wine-grower also 'prospects.' One corner of land after another is tried with one kind of grape after another. This is a failure; that is better; a third best. So, bit by bit, they grope about for their Clos Vougeot and Lafite. Those lodes and pockets of earth, more precious than the precious ores, that yield inimitable fragrance and soft fire; those virtuous Bonanzas, where the soil has sublimated under sun and stars to something finer, and the wine is bottled poetry: these still lie undiscovered; chaparral conceals, thicket embowers them; the miner chips the rock and wanders farther, and the grizzly muses undisturbed. But there they bide their hour, awaiting their Columbus; and nature nurses and prepares them. The smack of Californian earth shall linger on the palate of your grandson.

Meanwhile the wine is merely a good wine; the best that I have tasted better than a Beaujolais, and not unlike. But the trade is poor; it lives from hand to mouth, putting its all into experiments, and forced to sell its vintages. To find one properly matured, and bearing its own name, is to be fortune's favourite.

Bearing its own name, I say, and dwell upon the innuendo.

'You want to know why California wine is not drunk in the

States?' a San Francisco wine merchant said to me, after he had shown me through his premises. 'Well, here's the reason.'

And opening a large cupboard, fitted with many little drawers, he proceeded to shower me all over with a great variety of gorgeously tinted labels, blue, red, or yellow, stamped with crown or coronet, and hailing from such a profusion of *clos* and *châteaux*, that a single department could scarce have furnished forth the names. But it was strange that all looked unfamiliar.

'Château X – ?' said I. 'I never heard of that.'

'I dare say not,' said he. 'I have been reading one of X – 's novels.'

They were all castles in Spain! But that sure enough is the reason why California wine is not drunk in the States.

Napa Valley has been long a seat of the wine-growing industry. It did not here begin, as it does too often, in the low valley lands along the river, but took at once to the rough foot-hills, where alone it can expect to prosper. A basking inclination, and stones, to be a reservoir of the day's heat, seem necessary to the soil for wine; the grossness of the earth must be evaporated, its marrow daily melted and refined for ages; until at length these clods that break below our footing, and to the eye appear but common earth, are truly and to the perceiving mind, a masterpiece of nature. The dust of Richebourg, which the wind carries away, what an apotheosis of the dust! Not man himself can seem a stranger child of that brown, friable powder, than the blood and sun in that old flask behind the faggots.

A Californian vineyard, one of man's outposts in the wilder-ness, has features of its own. There is nothing here to remind you of the Rhine or Rhône, of the low *côte d'or*, or the infamous and scabby deserts of Champagne; but all is green, solitary, covert. We visited two of them, Mr Schram's and Mr M'Eck-ron's, sharing the same glen.

Some way down the valley below Calistoga, we turned sharply to the south and plunged into the thick of the wood. A rude trail rapidly mounting; a little stream tinkling by on the one hand, big enough perhaps after the rains, but already yielding up its life; overhead and on all sides, a bower of green and tangled thicket, still fragrant, and still flower-bespangled by the early season, where thimble-berry played the part of our English hawthorn, and the buck-eyes were putting forth their twisted horns of blossom: through all this, we struggled toughly upwards, canted to and fro by the roughness of the trail, and continually switched across the face by sprays of leaf or blossom. The last is no great inconvenience at home; but here in California it is a matter of some moment. For in all woods and by every wayside there prospers an abominable shrub or weed, called poison oak, whose very neighbourhood is venomous to some, and whose actual touch is avoided by the most impervious.

The two houses, with their vineyards, stood each in a green niche of its own in this steep and narrow forest dell. Though they were so near, there was already a good difference in level; and Mr M'Eckron's head must be a long way under the feet of Mr Schram. No more had been cleared than was necessary for cultivation; close around each oasis ran the tangled wood; the glen enfolds them; there they lie basking in sun and silence, concealed from all but the clouds and the mountain birds.

Mr M'Eckron's is a bachelor establishment; a little bit of a wooden house, a small cellar hard by in the hillside, and a patch of vines planted and tended single-handed by himself. He had but recently begun; his vines were young, his business young also; but I thought he had the look of the man who succeeds. He hailed from Greenock: he remembered his father putting him inside Mons Meg, and that touched me home; and we exchanged a word or two of Scotch, which pleased me more than you would fancy.

Mr Schram's, on the other hand, is the oldest vineyard in the valley, eighteen years old, I think; yet he began a penniless barber, and even after he had broken ground up here with his black malvoisies, continued for long to tramp the valley with his razor. Now, his place is the picture of prosperity: stuffed birds in the verandah, cellars far dug into the hillside, and resting on pillars like a bandit's cave; – all trimness, varnish, flowers, and sunshine, among the tangled wildwood. Stout, smiling Mrs Schram, who has been to Europe and apparently all about the States for pleasure, entertained Fanny in the verandah, while I was tasting wines in the cellar. To Mr Schram this was a solemn office; his serious gusto warmed my heart; prosperity had not yet wholly banished a certain neophyte and girlish trepidation, and he followed every sip and read my face with proud anxiety. I tasted all. I tasted every variety and shade of Schramberger, red and white Schramberger, Burgundy Schramberger, Schramberger Hock, Schramberger Golden Chasselas, the latter with a notable bouquet, and I fear to think how many more. Much of it goes to London – most, I think; and Mr Schram has a great notion of the English taste.

In this wild spot, I did not feel the sacredness of ancient cultivation. It was still raw, it was no Marathon, and no Johannisberg; yet the stirring sunlight, and the growing vines, and the vats and bottles in the cavern, made a pleasant music for the mind. Here, also, earth's cream was being skimmed and garnered; and the London customers can taste, such as it is, the tang of the earth in this green valley. So local, so quintessential is a wine, that it seems the very birds in the verandah might communicate a flavour, and that romantic cellar influence the bottle next to be uncorked in Pimlico, and the smile of jolly Mr Schram might mantle in the glass.

But these are but experiments. All things in this new land are moving farther on: the wine-vats and the miner's blasting tools but picket for a night, like Bedouin pavilions; and to-morrow, to fresh woods! This stir of change and these perpetual echoes of the moving football, haunt the land. Men move eternally, still chasing Fortune; and, Fortune found, still wander. As we drove back to Calistoga, the road lay empty of mere passengers, but its green side was dotted with the camps of travelling families: one cumbered with a great waggonful of household stuff, settlers going to occupy a ranche they had taken up in Mendocino, or perhaps Tehama County; another, a party in dust coats, men and women, whom we found camped in a grove on the roadside, all on pleasure bent, with a China-man to cook for them, and who waved their hands to us as we drove by.

IV
The Scot Abroad

A few pages back, I wrote that a man belonged, in these days, to a variety of countries; but the old land is still the true love, the others are but pleasant infidelities. Scotland is indefinable; it has no unity except upon the map. Two languages, many dialects, innumerable forms of piety, and countless local patriotisms and prejudices, part us among ourselves more widely than the extreme east and west of that great continent of America. When I am at home, I feel a man from Glasgow to be something like a rival, a man from Barra to be more than half a foreigner. Yet let us meet in some far country, and, whether we hail from the braes of Manor or the braes of Mar, some ready-made affection joins us on the instant. It is not race. Look at us. One is Norse, one is Celtic, and another Saxon. It is not community of tongue. We have it not among ourselves; and we have it almost to perfection, with English, or Irish, or American. It is no tie of faith, for we detest each other's errors. And yet somewhere, deep down in the heart of each one of us, something yearns for the old land, and the old kindly people.

Of all mysteries of the human heart, this is perhaps the most inscrutable. There is no special loveliness in that grey country, with its rainy, sea-beat archipelago; its fields of dark mountains; its unsightly places, black with coal; its treeless, sour unfriendly-looking cornlands; its quaint, grey, castled city, where the bells clash of a Sunday, and the wind squalls, and the salt showers fly and beat. I do not even know if I desire to live there; but let me hear, in some far land, a kindred voice sing out, 'Oh, why left I my hame?' and it seems at once as if no beauty under the kind heavens, and no society of the wise and good, can repay me for my absence from my country. And though I think I would rather die elsewhere, yet in my heart of hearts I long to be buried among good Scots clods. I will say it fairly, it grows on me with every year: there are no stars so lovely as Edinburgh street-lamps. When I forget thee, Auld Reekie, may my right hand forget its cunning!

The happiest lot on earth is to be born a Scotchman. You must pay for it in many ways, as for all other advantages on earth. You have to learn the paraphrases and the shorter catechism; you generally take to drink; your youth, as far as I can find out, is a time of louder war against society, of more outcry and tears and turmoil, than if you had been born, for instance, in England. But somehow life is warmer and closer; the hearth burns more redly; the lights of home shine softer on the rainy street; the very names, endeared in verse and music, cling nearer round our hearts. An Englishman may meet an Englishman to-morrow, upon Chimborazo, and neither of them care; but when the Scotch wine-grower told me of Mons Meg, it was like magic.

> From the dim shieling on the misty island
>> Mountains divide us, and a world of seas;
> Yet still our hearts are true, our hearts are Highland,
>> And we, in dreams, behold the Hebrides.

And, Highland and Lowland, all our hearts are Scotch.

Only a few days after I had seen M'Eckron, a message reached me in my cottage. It was a Scotchman who had come down a long way from the hills to market. He had heard there was a countryman in Calistoga, and came round to the hotel to see him. We said a few words to each other; we had not much to say – should never have seen each other had we stayed at home, separated alike in space and in society; and then we shook hands, and he went his way again to his ranche among the hills, and that was all.

Another Scotchman there was, a resident, who for the mere love of the common country, douce, serious, religious man, drove me all about the valley, and took as much interest in me as if I had been his son: more, perhaps; for the son has faults too keenly felt, while the abstract countryman is perfect – like a whiff of peats.

And there was yet another. Upon him I came suddenly, as he was calmly entering my cottage, his mind quite evidently bent on plunder: a man of about fifty, filthy, ragged, roguish, with a chimney-pot hat and a tail coat, and a pursing of his mouth that might have been envied by an elder of the kirk. He had just such a face as I have seen a dozen times behind the plate.

'Hullo, sir!' I cried. 'Where are you going?'

He turned round without a quiver.

'You're a Scotchman, sir?' he said gravely. 'So am I; I come from Aberdeen. This is my card,' presenting me with a piece of pasteboard which he had raked out of some gutter in the period of the rains. 'I was just examining this palm,' he continued, indicating the misbegotten plant before our door, 'which is the largest spacimen I have yet observed in Califoarnia.'

There were four or five larger within sight. But where was the use of argument? He produced a tape-line, made me help him to measure the tree at the level of the ground, and entered the figures in a large and filthy pocket-book, all with the gravity of Solomon. He then thanked me profusely, remarking that such little services were due between countrymen; shook hands with me, 'for auld lang syne,' as he said; and took himself solemnly away, radiating dirt and humbug as he went.

A month or two after this encounter of mine, there came a Scot to Sacramento – perhaps from Aberdeen. Anyway, there never was any one more Scotch in this wide world. He could sing and dance, and drink, I presume; and he played the pipes with vigour and success. All the Scotch in Sacramento became infatuted with him, and spent their spare time and money driving him about in an open cab, between drinks, while he blew himself scarlet at the pipes. This is a very sad story. After he had borrowed money from everyone, he and his pipes suddenly disppeared from Sacramento, and when I last heard, the police were looking for him.

I cannot say how this story amused me, when I felt myself so thoroughly ripe on both sides to be duped in the same way.

It is at least a curious thing, to conclude, that the races which wander widest, Jews and Scotch, should be the most clannish in the world. But perhaps these two are cause and effect: 'For ye were strangers in the land of Egypt.'

With the Children of Israel

I

To Introduce Mr Kelmar

One thing in this new country very particularly strikes a stranger, and that is the number of antiquities. Already there have been many cycles of population succeeding each other, and passing away and leaving behind them relics. These, standing on into changed times, strike the imagination as forcibly as any pyramid or feudal tower. The towns, like the vineyards, are experimentally founded: they grow great and prosper by passing occasions; and when the lode comes to an end, and the miners move elsewhere, the town remains behind them, like Palmyra in the desert. I suppose there are, in no country in the world, so many deserted towns as here in California.

The whole neighbourhood of Mount Saint Helena, now so quiet and sylvan, was once alive with mining camps and villages. Here there would be two thousand souls under canvas; there one thousand or fifteen hundred ensconced, as if for ever, in a town of comfortable houses. But the luck had failed, the mines petered out; and the army of miners had departed, and left this quarter of the world to the rattlesnakes and deer and grizzlies, and to the slower but steadier advance of husbandry.

It was with an eye on one of these deserted places, Pine Flat, on the Geysers road, that we had come first to Calistoga. There is something singularly enticing in the idea of going, rent-free, into a ready-made house. And to the British merchant, sitting at home at ease, it may appear that, with such a roof over your head and a spring of clear water hard by, the whole problem of the squatter's existence would be solved. Food, however, has yet to be considered. I will go as far as most people on tinned meats; some of the brightest moments of my life were passed over tinned mulligatawny in the cabin of a sixteen-ton schooner, storm-stayed in Portree Bay; but after suitable experiments, I pronounce authoritatively that man cannot live by tins alone. Fresh meat must be had on an occasion. It is true that the great Foss, driving by along the Geysers road, wooden-faced, but glorified with legend, might have been induced to bring us meat, but the great Foss could hardly bring us milk. To take a cow would have involved taking a field of grass and a milkmaid; after which it would have been hardly worth while to pause, and we might have added to our colony a flock of sheep and an experienced butcher.

It is really very disheartening how we depend on other people in this life. *Mihi est propositum*, as you may see by the motto, *idem quod regibus*; and behold it cannot be carried out, unless I find a neighbour rolling in cattle.

Now, my principal adviser in this matter was one whom I will call Kelmar. That was not what he called himself, but as soon as I set eyes on him, I knew it was or ought to be his name; I am sure it will be his name among the angels. Kelmar was the store-keeper, a Russian Jew, good-natured, in a very thriving way of business, and, on equal terms, one of the most serviceable of men. He also had something of the expression of a Scotch country elder, who, by some peculiarity, should chance to be a Hebrew. He had a projecting under-lip, with which he continually smiled, or rather smirked. Mrs Kelmar was a singularly kind woman; and the oldest son had quite a dark and romantic bearing, and might be heard on summer evenings playing sentimental airs on the violin.

I had no idea, at the time I made his acquaintance, what an important person Kelmar was. But the Jew store-keepers of California, profiting at once by the needs and habits of the people, have made themselves in too many cases the tyrants of the rural population. Credit is offered, is pressed on the new customer, and when once he is beyond his depth, the tune changes, and he is from thenceforth a white slave. I believe, even from the little I saw, that Kelmar, if he chose to put on the screw, could send half the settlers packing in a radius of seven or eight miles round Calistoga. These are continually paying him, but are never suffered to get out of debt. He palms dull goods upon them, for they dare not refuse to buy; he goes and dines with them when he is on an outing, and no man is loudlier welcomed; he is their family friend, the director of their business, and, to a degree elsewhere unknown in modern days, their king.

For some reason, Kelmar always shook his head at the mention of Pine Flat, and for some days I thought he disapproved of the whole scheme and was proportionately sad. One fine morning, however, he met me, wreathed in smiles. He had found the very place for me – Silverado, another old mining town, right up the mountain. Rufe Hanson, the hunter, could take care of us – fine people the Hansons; we should be close to the Toll House, where the Lakeport stage called daily; it was the best place for my health, besides. Rufe had been consumptive, and was now quite a strong men, ain't it? In short, the place and all its accompaniments seemed made for us on purpose.

He took me to his back door, whence, as from every point of Calistoga, Mount Saint Helena could be seen towering in the air. There, in the nick, just where the eastern foothills joined the mountain, and she herself began to rise above the zone of forest – there was Silverado. The name had already pleased me; the high station pleased me still more. I began to inquire with some eagerness. It was but a little while ago that Silverado was a great place. The mine – a silver mine, of course – had promised great things. There was quite a lively population, with several hotels and boarding-houses; and Kelmar himself had opened a branch store, and done extremely well – 'Ain't it?' he said, appealing to his wife. And she said, 'Yes; extremely well.' Now there was no one living in the town but Rufe the hunter; and once more I heard Rufe's praises by the yard, and this time sung in chorus.

I could not help perceiving at the time that there was something underneath; that no unmixed desire to have us comfortably settled had inspired the Kelmars with this flow of words. But I was impatient to be gone, to be about my kingly project; and when we were offered seats in Kelmar's waggon, I accepted on the spot. The plan of their next Sunday's outing took them, by good fortune, over the border into Lake County. They would carry us so far, drop us at the Toll House, present us to the Hansons, and call for us again on Monday morning early.

II
First Impressions of Silverado

We were to leave by six precisely; that was solemnly pledged on
both sides; and a messenger came to us the last thing at night to
remind us of the hour. But it was eight before we got clear of
Calistoga: Kelmar, Mrs Kelmar, a friend of theirs whom we
named Abramina, her little daughter, my wife, myself, and,
stowed away behind us, a cluster of ship's coffee-kettles. These
last were highly ornamental in the sheen of their bright tin, but
I could invent no reason for their presence. Our carriageful
reckoned up, as near as we could get at it, some three hundred
years to the six of us. Four of the six, besides, were Hebrews.
But I never, in all my life, was conscious of so strong an
atmosphere of holiday. No word was spoken but of pleasure;
and even when we drove in silence, nods and smiles went round
the party like refreshments.

The sun shone out of a cloudless sky. Close at the zenith rode
the belated moon, still clearly visible, and, along one margin,
even bright. The wind blew a gale from the north; the trees
roared; the corn and the deep grass in the valley fled in
whitening surges; the dust towered into the air along the road
and dispersed like the smoke of battle. It was clear in our teeth
from the first, and for all the windings of the road it managed
to keep clear in our teeth until the end.

For some two miles we rattled through the valley, skirting the
eastern foothills; then we struck off to the right, through haugh-
land, and presently, crossing a dry water-course, entered the
Toll road, or, to be more local, entered on 'the grade'. The road
mounts the near shoulder of Mount Saint Helena, bound
northward into Lake County. In one place it skirts along the
edge of a narrow and deep canyon, filled with trees, and I was
glad, indeed, not to be driven at this point by the dashing Foss.
Kelmar, with his unvarying smile, jogging to the motion of the
trap, drove for all the world like a good, plain, country
clergyman at home, and I profess I blessed him unawares for his
timidity.

Vineyards and deep meadows, islanded and framed with
thicket, gave place more and more as we ascended to woods of
oak and madrona, dotted with enormous pines. It was these
pines, as they shot above the lower wood, that produced that

pencilling of single trees I had so often remarked from the valley. Thence, looking up and from however far, each fir stands separate against the sky no bigger than an eyelash; and all together lend a quaint, fringed aspect to the hills. The oak is no baby; even the madrona, upon these spurs of Mount Saint Helena, comes to a fine bulk and ranks with forest trees; but the pines look down upon the rest for underwood. As Mount Saint Helena among her foothills, so these dark giants out-top their fellow-vegetables. Alas! if they had left the redwoods, the pines, in turn, would have been dwarfed. But the redwoods, fallen from their high estate, are serving as family bedsteads, or yet more humbly as field fences, along all Napa Valley.

A rough smack of resin was in the air, and a crystal mountain purity. It came pouring over these green slopes by the oceanful. The woods sang loud, and gave largely of their healthful breath. Gladness seemed to inhabit these upper zones, and we had left indifference behind us in the valley. 'I to the hills will lift mine eyes!' There are days in a life when thus to climb out of the lowland seems like scaling heaven.

As we continued to ascend, the wind fell upon us with increasing strength. It was a wonder how the two stout horses managed to pull us up that steep incline and still face the athletic opposition of the wind, or how their great eyes were able to endure the dust. Ten minutes after we went by, a tree fell, blocking the road, and even before us leaves were thickly strewn, and boughs had fallen, large enough to make the passage difficult. But now we were hard by the summit. The road crosses the ridge, just in the nick that Kelmar showed me from below, and then, without pause, plunges down a deep, thickly-wooded glen on the farther side. At the highest point a trail strikes up the main hill to the leftward; and that leads to Silverado. A hundred yards beyond, and in a kind of elbow of the glen, stands the Toll House Hotel. We came up the one side, were caught upon the summit by the whole weight of the wind as it poured over into Napa Valley, and a minute after had drawn up in shelter, but all buffeted and breathless, at the Toll House door.

A water-tank, and stables, and a grey house of two storeys, with gable ends and a verandah, are jammed hard against the hillside, just where a stream has cut for itself a narrow canyon, filled with pines. The pines go right up overhead; a little more and the stream might have played, like a fire-hose, on the Toll House roof. In front the ground drops as sharply as it rises behind. There is just room for the road and a sort of promontory of croquet ground, and then you can lean over the edge and look deep below you through the wood. I said croquet *ground*, not *green*; for the surface was of brown, beaten earth. The toll-bar itself was the only other note of originality: a long beam, turning on a post, and kept slightly horizontal by a counter-weight of stones. Regularly about sundown this rude barrier was swung, like a derrick, across the road and made fast, I think, to a tree upon the farther side.

On our arrival there followed a gay scene in the bar. I was presented to Mr Corwin, the landlord; to Mr Jennings, the engineer, who lives there for his health; to Mr Hoddy, a most pleasant little gentleman, once a member of the Ohio legislature, again the editor of a local paper, and now, with undiminished dignity, keeping the Toll House bar. I had a number of drinks and cigars bestowed on me, and enjoyed a famous opportunity of seeing Kelmar in his glory, friendly, radiant, smiling, steadily edging one of the ship's kettles on the reluctant Corwin. Corwin, plainly aghast, resisted gallantly, and for that bout victory crowned his arms.

At last we set forth for Silverado on foot. Kelmar and his jolly Jew girls were full of the sentiment of Sunday outings, breathed geniality and vagueness, and suffered a little vile boy from the hotel to lead them here and there about the woods. For three people all so old, so bulky in body, and belonging to a race so venerable, they could not but surprise us by their extreme and almost imbecile youthfulness of spirit. They were only going to stay ten minutes at the Toll House; had they not twenty long miles of road before them on the other side? Stay to dinner? Not they! Put up the horses? Never. Let us attach them to the verandah by a wisp of straw rope, such as would not have held a person's hat on that blustering day. And with all these protestations of hurry, they proved irresponsible like children. Kelmar himself, shrewd old Russian Jew, with a smirk that seemed just to have concluded a bargain to its satisfaction, entrusted himself and us devoutly to that boy. Yet the boy was patently fallacious; and for that matter a most unsympathetic urchin, raised apparently on gingerbread. He was bent on his own pleasure, nothing else; and Kelmar followed him to his ruin, with the same shrewd smirk. If the boy said there was 'a hole there in the hill' – a hole, pure and simple, neither more nor less – Kelmar and his Jew girls would follow him a hundred yards to look complacently down that hole. For two hours we looked for houses; and for two hours they followed us, smelling trees, picking flowers, foisting false botany on the unwary. Had we taken five, with that vile lad to head them off on idle divagations, for five they would have smiled and stumbled through the woods.

However, we came forth at length, and as by accident, upon a lawn, sparse planted like an orchard, but with forest instead of fruit trees. That was the site of Silverado mining town. A piece of ground was levelled up, where Kelmar's store had been; and facing that we saw Rufe Hanson's house, still bearing on its front the legend *Silverado Hotel*. Not another sign of habitation. Silverado town had all been carted from the scene; one of the houses was now the schoolhouse far down the road; one was gone here, one there, but all were gone away. It was now a sylvan solitude, and the silence was unbroken but by the great, vague voice of the wind. Some days before our visit, a grizzly bear had been sporting round the Hansons' chicken-house.

Mrs Hanson was at home alone, we found. Rufe had been out after a 'bar', had risen late, and was now gone, it did not clearly appear whither. Perhaps he had had wind of Kelmar's coming, and was now ensconced among the underwood or watching us from the shoulder of the mountain. We, hearing there were no houses to be had, were for immediately giving up all hopes of Silverado. But this, somehow, was not to Kelmar's fancy. He first proposed that we should 'camp some-veres around, ain't it?' waving his hand cheerily as though to weave a spell; and when that was firmly rejected, he decided that we must take up house with the Hansons. Mrs Hanson had been, from the first, flustered, subdued, and a little pale; but from this proposition she recoiled with haggard indignation. So did we, who would have preferred, in a manner of speaking, death. But Kelmar was not to be put by. He edged Mrs Hanson into a corner, where for a long time he threatened her with his forefinger, like a character in Dickens; and the poor woman, driven to her entrenchments, at last remembered with a shriek that there were still some houses at the tunnel.

Thither we went; the Jews, who should already have been miles into Lake County, still cheerily accompanying us. For about a furlong we followed a good road along the hillside through the forest, until suddenly that road widened out and came abruptly to an end. A canyon, woody below, red, rocky, and naked overhead, was here walled across by a dump of rolling stones, dangerously steep, and from twenty to thirty feet in height. A rusty iron chute on wooden legs came flying, like a monstrous gargoyle, across the parapet. It was down this that they poured the precious ore; and below here the carts stood to wait their lading, and carry it mill-ward down the mountain.

The whole canyon was so entirely blocked, as if by some rude guerilla fortification, that we could only mount by lengths of wooden ladder, fixed in the hillside. These led us round the farther corner of the dump; and when they were at an end, we still persevered over loose rubble and wading deep in poison oak, till we struck a triangular platform, filling up the whole glen, and shut in on either hand by bold projections of the mountain. Only in front the place was open like the proscenium of a theatre, and we looked forth into a great realm of air, and down upon treetops and hilltops, and far and near on wild and varied country. The place still stood as on the day it was deserted: a line of iron rails with a bifurcation; a truck in working order; a world of lumber, old wood, old iron; a blacksmith's forge on one side, half buried in the leaves of dwarf madronas; and on the other, an old brown wooden house.

Fanny and I dashed at the house. It consisted of three rooms, and was so plastered against the hill, that one room was right atop of another, that the upper floor was more than twice as large as the lower, and that all three apartments must be entered from a different side and level. Not a window-sash remained. The door of the lower room was smashed, and one panel hung in splinters. We entered that, and found a fair amount of rubbish: sand and gravel that had been sifted in there by the mountain winds; straw, sticks, and stones; a table, a barrel; a plate-rack on the wall; two home-made bootjacks, signs of miners and their boots; and a pair of papers pinned on the boarding, headed respectively 'Funnel No. 1', and 'Funnel No. 2', but with the tails torn away. The window, sashless of course, was choked with the green and sweetly-smelling foliage of a bay; and through a chink in the floor, a spray of poison oak had shot up and was handsomely prospering in the interior. It was my first care to cut away that poison oak, Fanny standing by at a respectful distance. That was our first improvement by which we took possession.

The room immediately above could only be entered by a plank propped against the threshold, along which the intruder must foot it gingerly, clutching for support to sprays of poison oak, the proper product of the country. Herein was, on either hand, a triple tier of beds, where miners had once lain; and the other gable was pierced by a sashless window and a doorless doorway opening on the air of heaven, five feet above the ground. As for the third room, which entered squarely from the ground level, but higher up the hill and farther up the canyon, it contained only rubbish and the uprights for another triple tier of beds.

The whole building was overhung by a bold, lion-like, red rock. Poison oak, sweet bay trees, calycanthus, brush, and chaparral, grew freely but sparsely all about it. In front, in the strong sunshine, the platform lay overstrewn with busy litter, as though the labours of the mine might begin again to-morrow in the morning.

Following back into the canyon, among the mass of rotting plant and through the flowering bushes, we came to a great crazy staging, with a wry windlass on the top; and clambering up, we could look into an open shaft, leading edgeways down into the bowels of the mountain, trickling with water, and lit by some stray sun-gleams, whence I know not. In that quiet place the still, far-away tinkle of the water-drops was loudly audible. Close by, another shaft led edgeways up into the super-incumbent shoulder of the hill. It lay partly open; and sixty or a hundred feet above our head, we could see the strata propped part by solid wooden wedges, and a pine, half undermined, precariously nodding on the verge. Here also a rugged, horizontal tunnel ran straight into the unsunned bowels of the rock. This secure angle in the mountain's flank was, even on this wild day, as still as my lady's chamber. But in the tunnel a cold, wet draught tempestuously blew. Nor have I ever known that place otherwise than cold and windy.

Such was our first prospect of Juan Silverado. I own I had looked for something different: a clique of neighbourly houses on a village green, we shall say, all empty to be sure, but swept and varnished; a trout stream brawling by; great elms or chestnuts, humming with bees and nested in by song-birds; and the mountains standing round about, as at Jerusalem. Here, mountain and house and the old tools of industry were all alike rusty and downfalling. The hill was here wedged up, and there poured forth its bowels in a spout of broken mineral; man with his picks and powder, and nature with her own great blasting. tools of sun and rain, labouring together at the ruin of that proud mountain. The view up the canyon was a glimpse of devastation; dry red minerals sliding together, here and there a crag, here and there dwarf thicket clinging in the general glissade, and over all a broken outline trenching on the blue of heaven. Downward indeed, from our rock eyrie, we beheld the greener side of nature; and the bearing of the pines and the sweet smell of bays and nutmegs commended themselves gratefully to our senses. One way and another, now the die was cast. Silverado be it!

After we had got back to the Toll House, the Jews were not long of striking forward. But I observed that one of the Hanson lads came down, before their departure, and returned with a ship's kettle. Happy Hansons! Nor was it until after Kelmar was gone, if I remember rightly, that Rufe put in an appearance to arrange the details of our installation.

The latter part of the day, Fanny and I sat in the verandah of the Toll House, utterly stunned by the uproar of the wind among the trees on the other side of the valley. Sometimes, we would have it it was like a sea, but it was not various enough for that; and again, we thought it like the roar of a cataract, but it was too changeful for the cataract; and then we would decide, speaking in sleepy voices, that it could be compared with nothing but itself. My mind was entirely preoccupied by the noise. I hearkened to it by the hour, gapingly hearkened, and let my cigarette go out. Sometimes the wind would make a sally nearer hand, and send a shrill, whistling crash among the foliage on our side of the glen; and sometimes a back draught would strike into the elbow where we sat, and cast the gravel and torn leaves into our faces. But for the most part, this great, streaming gale passed unweariedly by us into Napa Valley, not two hundred yards away, visible by the tossing boughs, stunningly audible, and not yet moving a hair upon our heads. So it blew all night long while I was writing up my journal, and after we were in bed, under a cloudless, starset heaven; and so it was blowing still next morning when we rose.

It was a laughable thought to us, what had become of our cheerful, wandering Hebrews. We could not suppose they had reached a destination. The meanest boy could lead them miles out of their way to see a gopher-hole. Boys, we felt to be their special danger; none others were of that exact pitch of cheerful irrelevancy to exercise a kindred sway upon their minds: but before the attractions of a boy their most settled resolutions would be wax. We thought we could follow in fancy these three aged Hebrew truants wandering in and out on hilltop and in thicket, a demon boy trotting far ahead, their will-o'-the-wisp conductor; and at last about midnight, the wind still roaring in the darkness, we had a vision of all three on their knees upon a mountain-top around a glow-worm.

III
The Return

Next morning we were up by half-past five, according to agreement, and it was ten by the clock before our Jew boys returned to pick us up: Kelmar, Mrs Kelmar, and Abramina, all smiling from ear to ear, and full of tales of the hospitality they had found on the other side. It had not gone unrewarded; for I observed with interest that the ship's kettles, all but one, had been 'placed'. Three Lake County families, at least, endowed for life with a ship's kettle. Come, this was no misspent Sunday. The absence of the kettles told its own story: our Jews said nothing about them: but on the other hand, they said many kind and comely things about the people they had met. The two women, in particular, had been charmed out of themselves by the sight of a young girl surrounded by her admirers; all evening, it appeared, they had been triumphing together in the girl's innocent successes, and to this natural and unselfish joy they gave expression in language that was beautiful by its simplicity and truth.

Take them for all in all, few people have done my heart more good; they seemed so thoroughly entitled to happiness, and to enjoy it in so large a measure and so free from afterthought;

almost they persuaded me to be a Jew. There was, indeed, a chink of money in their talk. They particularly commended people who were well-to-do. '*He* don't care – ain't it?' was their highest word of commendation to an individual fate; and here I seem to grasp the root of their philosophy – it was to be free from care, to be free to make these Sunday wanderings, that they so eagerly pursued after wealth; and all this carefulness was to be careless. The fine good humour of all three seemed to declare they had attained their end. Yet there was the other side to it; and the recipients of kettles perhaps cared greatly.

No sooner had they returned, than the scene of yesterday began again. The horses were not even tied with a straw rope this time – it was not worth while; and Kelmar disappeared into the bar, leaving them under a tree on the other side of the road. I had to devote myself. I stood under the shadow of that tree for, I suppose, hard upon an hour, and had not the heart to be angry. Once someone remembered me, and brought me out half a tumblerful of the playful, innocuous American cocktail. I drank it, and lo! veins of living fire ran down my leg; and then a focus of conflagration remained seated in my stomach, not unpleasantly, for a quarter of an hour. I love these sweet, fiery pangs, but I will not court them. The bulk of the time I spent in repeating as much French poetry as I could remember to the horses, who seemed to enjoy it hugely. And now it went –

> O ma vieille Font-georges
> Où volent les rouges-gorges:

and again, to a more trampling measure –

> Et tout tremble, Irun, Coïmbre,
> Santander, Almodovar,
> Sitôt qu'on entend le timbre
> Des cymbales de Bivar.

The redbreasts and the brooks of Europe, in that dry and songless land; brave old names and wars, strong cities, cymbals, and bright armour, in that nook of the mountain, sacred only to the Indian and the bear! This is still the strangest thing in all man's travelling, that he should carry about with him incongruous memories. There is no foreign land; it is the traveller only that is foreign, and now and again, by a flash of recollection, lights up the contrasts of the earth.

But while I was thus wandering in my fancy, great feats had been transacted in the bar. Corwin the bold had fallen, Kelmar was again crowned with laurels, and the last of the ship's kettles had changed hands. If I had ever doubted the purity of Kelmar's motives, if I had ever suspected him of a single eye to business in his eternal dallyings, now at least, when the last kettle was disposed of, my suspicions must have been allayed. I dare not guess how much more time was wasted; nor how often we drove off, merely to drive back again and renew interrupted conversations about nothing, before the Toll House was fairly left behind. Alas! and not a mile down the grade there stands a ranche in a sunny vineyard, and here we must all dismount again and enter.

Only the old lady was at home, Mrs Guele, a brown old Swiss dame, the picture of honesty; and with her we drank a bottle of wine and had an age-long conversation, which would have been highly delightful if Fanny and I had not been faint with hunger. The ladies each narrated the story of her marriage, our two Hebrews with the prettiest combination of sentiment and financial bathos. Abramina, specially, endeared herself with every word. She was as simple, natural, and engaging as a kid that should have been brought up to the business of a money-changer. One touch was so resplendently Hebraic that I cannot pass it over. When her 'old man' wrote home for her from America, her old man's family would not entrust her with the money for the passage, till she had bound herself by an oath – on her knees, I think she said – not to employ it otherwise. This had tickled Abramina hugely, but I think it tickled me fully more.

Mrs Guele told of her home-sickness up here in the long winters; of her honest, country-woman troubles and alarms upon the journey; how in the bank at Frankfurt she had feared lest the banker, after having taken her cheque, should deny all knowledge of it – a fear I have myself every time I go to a bank; and how crossing the Luneburger Heath, an old lady, witnessing her trouble and finding whither she was bound, had given her 'the blessing of a person eighty years old, which would be sure to bring her safely to the States. And the first thing I did,' added Mrs Guele, 'was to fall downstairs.'

At length we got out of the house, and some of us into the trap, when – judgment of Heaven! – here came Mr Guele from his vineyard. So another quarter of an hour went by; till at length, at our earnest pleading, we set forth again in earnest, Fanny and I whitefaced and silent, but the Jews still smiling. The heart fails me. There was yet another stoppage! And we drove at last into Calistoga past two in the afternoon, Fanny and I having breakfasted at six in the morning, eight mortal hours before. We were a pallid couple; but still the Jews were smiling.

So ended our excursion with the village usurers; and, now that it was done, we had no more idea of the nature of the business, nor of the part we had been playing in it, than the child unborn. That all the people we had met were the slaves of Kelmar, though in various degrees of servitude; that we ourselves had been sent up the mountain in the interests of none but Kelmar; that the money we laid out, dollar by dollar, cent by cent, and through the hands of various intermediaries, should all hop ultimately into Kelmar's till; – these were facts that we only grew to recognise in the course of time and by the accumulation of evidence. At length all doubt was quieted, when one of the kettle-holders confessed. Stopping his trap in the moonlight, a little way out of Calistoga, he told me, in so many words, that he dare not show face there with an empty pocket. 'You see, I don't mind if it was only five dollars, Mr Stevens,' he said, 'but I must give Mr Kelmar *something*.'

Even now, when the whole tyranny is plain to me, I cannot find it in my heart to be as angry as perhaps I should be with the Hebrew tyrant. The whole game of business is beggar my neighbour; and though perhaps that game looks uglier when played at such close quarters and on so small a scale, it is none the more intrinsically inhumane for that. The village usurer is not so sad a feature of humanity and human progress as the millionaire manufacturer, fattening on the toil and loss of thousands, and yet declaiming from the platform against the greed and dishonesty of landlords. If it were fair for Cobden to buy up land from owners whom he thought unconscious of its proper value, it was fair enough for my Russian Jew to give credit to his farmers. Kelmar, if he was unconscious of the beam in his own eye, was at least silent in the matter of his brother's mote.

The Act of Squatting

There were four of us squatters – myself and my wife, the King and Queen of Silverado; Sam, the Crown Prince; and Chuchu, the Grand Duke. Chuchu, a setter crossed with spaniel, was the most unsuited for a rough life. He had been nurtured tenderly in the society of ladies; his heart was large and soft; he regarded the sofa-cushion as a bed-rock necessary of existence. Though about the size of a sheep, he loved to sit in ladies' laps; he never said a bad word in all his blameless days; and if he had seen a flute, I am sure he could have played upon it by nature. It may seem hard to say it of a dog, but Chuchu was a tame cat.

The king and queen, the grand duke, and a basket of cold provender for immediate use, set forth from Calistoga in a double buggy; the crown prince, on horseback, led the way like an outrider. Bags and boxes and a second-hand stove were to follow close upon our heels by Hanson's team.

It was a beautiful still day; the sky was one field of azure, Not a leaf moved, not a speck appeared in heaven. Only from the summit of the mountain one little snowy wisp of cloud after another kept detaching itself, like smoke from a volcano, and blowing southward in some high stream of air: Mount Saint Helena still at her interminable task, making the weather, like a Lapland witch.

By noon we had come in sight of the mill: a great brown building, half-way up the hill, big as a factory, two storeys high, and with tanks and ladders along the roof; which, as a pendicle of Silverado mine, we held to be an outlying province of our own. Thither, then, we went, crossing the valley by a grassy trail; and there lunched out of the basket, sitting in a kind of portico, and wondering, while we ate, at this great bulk of useless building. Through a chink we could look far down into the interior, and see sunbeams floating in the dust and striking on tier after tier of silent, rusty machinery. It cost six thousand dollars, twelve hundred English sovereigns; and now, here it stands deserted, like the temple of a forgotten religion, the busy millers toiling somewhere else. All the time we were there, mill and mill town showed no sign of life; that part of the mountain-side, which is very open and green, was tenanted by no living creature but ourselves and the insects; and nothing stirred but the cloud manufactory upon the mountain summit. It was odd to compare this with the former days, when the engine was in full blast, the mill palpitating to its strokes, and the carts came rattling down from Silverado, charged with ore.

By two we had been landed at the mine, the buggy was gone again, and we were left to our own reflections and the basket of cold provender, until Hanson should arrive. Hot as it was by the sun, there was something chill in such a home-coming, in that world of wreck and rust, splinter and rolling gravel, where for so many years no fire had smoked.

Silverado platform filled the whole width of the canyon. Above, as I have said, this was a wild, red, stony gully in the mountains; but below it was a wooded dingle. And through this, I was told, there had gone a path between the mine and the Toll House – our natural north-west passage to civilisation. I found and followed it, clearing my way as I went through fallen branches and dead trees. It went straight down that steep canyon, till it brought you out abruptly over the roofs of the hotel. There was nowhere any break in the descent. It almost seemed as if, were you to drop a stone down the old iron chute at our platform, it would never rest until it hopped upon the Toll House shingles. Signs were not wanting of the ancient greatness of Silverado. The footpath was well marked, and had been well trodden in the old days by thirsty miners. And far down, buried in foliage, deep out of sight of Silverado, I came on a last outpost of the mine – a mound of gravel, some wreck of wooden aqueduct, and the mouth of a tunnel, like a treasure grotto in a fairy story. A stream of water, fed by the invisible leakage from our shaft, and dyed red with cinnabar or iron, ran trippingly forth out of the bowels of the cave; and, looking far under the arch, I could see something like an iron lantern fastened on the rocky wall. It was a promising spot for the imagination. No boy could have left it unexplored.

The stream thenceforward stole along the bottom of the dingle, and made, for that dry land, a pleasant warbling in the leaves. Once, I suppose, it ran splashing down the whole length of the canyon, but now its head waters had been tapped by the shaft at Silverado, and for a great part of its course it wandered sunless among the joints of the mountain. No wonder that it should better its pace when it sees, far before it, daylight whitening in the arch, or that it should come trotting forth into the sunlight with a song.

The two stages had gone by when I got down, and the Toll House stood, dozing in sun and dust and silence, like a place enchanted. My mission was after hay for bedding, and that I was readily promised. But when I mentioned that we were waiting for Rufe, the people shook their heads. Rufe was not a regular man anyway, it seemed; and if he got playing poker – well, poker was too many for Rufe. I had not yet heard them bracketed together; but it seemed a natural conjunction, and commended itself swiftly to my fears; and as soon as I returned to Silverado and had told my story, we practically gave Hanson up, and set ourselves to do what we could find doable in our desert-island state.

The lower room had been the assayer's office. The floor was thick with débris – part human, from the former occupants; part natural, sifted in by mountain winds. In a sea of red dust there swam or floated sticks, boards, hay, straw, stones, and paper; ancient newspapers, above all – for the newspaper, especially when torn, soon becomes an antiquity – and bills of the Silverado boarding-house, some dated Silverado, some Calistoga Mine. Here is one, verbatim; and if anyone can calculate the scale of charges, he has my envious admiration.

Calistoga Mine, May 3rd, 1875.

JOHN STANLEY

To S. CHAPMAN, Cr.

To board from April 1st to April 30	$25 75
To board from May 1st to 3rd	2 00
	27 75

Where is John Stanley mining now? Where is S. Chapman, within whose hospitable walls we were to lodge? The date was but five years old, but in that time the world had changed for Silverado; like Palmyra in the desert, it had outlived its people and its purpose; we camped, like Layard, amid ruins, and these

names spoke to us of prehistoric time. A bootjack, a pair of
boots, a dog-hutch, and these bills of Mr Chapman's were the
only speaking relics that we disinterred from all that vast
Silverado rubbish-heap; but what would I not have given to
unearth a letter, a pocket-diary, only a ledger, or a roll of names,
to take me back, in a more personal manner, to the past? It
pleases me, besides, to fancy that Stanley or Chapman, or one
of their companions, may light upon this chronicle, and be
struck by the name, and read some news of their anterior home,
coming, as it were, out of a subsequent epoch of history in that
quarter of the world.

As we were tumbling the mingled rubbish on the floor, kicking
it with our feet, and groping for these written evidences of the
past, Sam, with a somewhat whitened face, produced a paper
bag. 'What's this?' said he. It contained granulated powder,
something the colour of Gregory's Mixture, but rosier; and as
there were several of the bags, and each more or less broken,
the powder was spread widely on the floor. Had any of us ever
seen giant powder? No, nobody had; and instantly there grew
up in my mind a shadowy belief, verging with every moment
nearer to certitude, that I had somewhere heard somebody
describe it as just such a powder as the one around us. I have
learnt since that it is a substance not unlike tallow, and is made
up in rolls for all the world like tallow candles.

Fanny, to add to our happiness, told us a story of a gentleman
who had camped one night, like ourselves, by a deserted mine.
He was a handy, thrifty fellow, and looked right and left for
plunder, but all he could lay his hands on was a can of oil. After
dark he had to see to the horses with a lantern; and not to miss
an opportunity, filled up his lamp from the oil can. Thus
equipped, he set forth into the forest. A little while after, his
friends heard a loud explosion; the mountain echoes bellowed,
and then all was still. On examination, the can proved to
contain oil, with the trifling addition of nitro-glycerine; but no
research disclosed a trace of either man or lantern.

It was a pretty sight, after this anecdote, to see us sweeping
out the giant powder. It seemed never to be far enough away.
And after all, it was only some rock pounded for assay.

So much for the lower room. We scraped some of the rougher
dirt off the floor, and left it. That was our sitting-room and
kitchen, though there was nothing to sit upon but the table, and

no provision for a fire except a hole in the roof of the room above, which had once contained the chimney of a stove.

To that upper room we now proceeded. There were the eighteen bunks in a double tier, nine on either hand, where from eighteen to thirty-six miners had once snored together all night long, John Stanley, perhaps, snoring loudest. There was the roof, with a hole in it through which the sun now shot an arrow. There was the floor, in much the same state as the one below, though, perhaps, there was more hay, and certainly there was the added ingredient of broken glass, the man who stole the window-frames having apparently made a miscarriage with this one. Without a broom, without hay or bedding, we could but look about us with a beginning of despair. The one bright arrow of day, in that gaunt and shattered barrack, made the rest look dirtier and darker, and the sight drove us at last into the open.

Here, also, the handiwork of man lay ruined: but the plants were all alive and thriving; the view below was fresh with the colours of nature; and we had exchanged a dim, human garret for a corner, even although it were untidy, of the blue hall of heaven. Not a bird, not a beast, not a reptile. There was no noise in that part of the world, save when we passed beside the staging, and heard the water musically falling in the shaft.

We wandered to and fro. We searched among that drift of lumber – wood and iron, nails and rails, and sleepers and the wheels of trucks. We gazed up the cleft into the bosom of the mountain. We sat by the margin of the dump and saw, far below us, the green treetops, standing still in the clear air. Beautiful perfumes, breaths of bay, resin, and nutmeg, came to us more often and grew sweeter and sharper as the afternoon declined. But still there was no word of Hanson.

I set to with pick and shovel, and deepened the pool behind the shaft, till we were sure of sufficient water for the morning; and by the time I had finished, the sun had begun to go down behind the mountain shoulder, the platform was plunged in quiet shadow, and a chill descended from the sky. Night began early in our cleft. Before us, over the margin of the dump, we could see the sun still striking aslant into the wooded nick below, and on the battlemented, pine-bescattered ridges on the farther side.

There was no stove, of course, and no hearth in our lodging, so we betook ourselves to the blacksmith's forge across the platform. If the platform be taken as a stage, and the outcurving margin of the dump to represent the line of the footlights, then our house would be the first wing on the actor's left, and this blacksmith's forge, although no match for it in size, the foremost on the right. It was a low, brown cottage, planted close against the hill, and overhung by the foliage and peeling boughs of a madrona thicket. Within it was full of dead leaves and mountain dust and rubbish from the mine. But we soon had a good fire brightly blazing, and sat close about it on impromptu seats. Chuchu, the slave of sofa-cushions, whimpered for a softer bed; but the rest of us were greatly revived and comforted by that good creature – fire, which gives us warmth and light and companionable sounds, and colours up the emptiest building with better than frescoes. For a while it was even pleasant in the forge, with the blaze in the midst, and a look over our shoulders on the woods and mountains where the day was dying like a dolphin.

It was between seven and eight before Hanson arrived, with a waggonful of our effects and two of his wife's relatives to lend him a hand. The elder showed surprising strength. He would pick up a huge packing-case, full of books of all things, swing it on his shoulder, and away up the two crazy ladders and the breakneck spout of rolling mineral, familiarly termed a path, that led from the cart-track to our house. Even for a man unburthened, the ascent was toilsome and precarious; but Irvine scaled it with a light foot, carrying box after box, as the hero whisks the stage child up the practicable footway beside the waterfall of the fifth act. With so strong a helper, the business was speedily transacted. Soon the assayer's office was thronged with our belongings, piled higgledy-piggledy, and upside down, about the floor. There were our boxes, indeed, but my wife had left her keys in Calistoga. There was the stove, but, alas! our carriers had forgot the chimney, and lost one of the plates along the road. The Silverado problem was scarce solved.

Rufe himself was grave and good-natured over his share of blame; he even, if I remember right, expressed regret. But his crew, to my astonishment and anger, grinned from ear to ear, and laughed aloud at our distress. They thought it 'real funny' about the stove-pipe they had forgotten; 'real funny' that they should have lost a plate. As for hay, the whole party refused to bring us any till they should have supped. See how late they were! Never had there been such a job as coming up that grade! Nor often, I suspect, such a game of poker as that before they started. But about nine, as a particular favour, we should have some hay.

So they took their departure, leaving me still staring, and we resigned ourselves to wait for their return. The fire in the forge had been suffered to go out, and we were one and all too weary to kindle another. We dined, or, not to take that word in vain, we ate after a fashion, in the nightmare disorder of the assayer's office, perched among boxes. A single candle lighted us. It could scarce be called a house-warming; for there was, of course, no fire, and with the two open doors and the open window gaping on the night, like breaches in a fortress, it began to grow rapidly chill. Talk ceased; nobody moved but the unhappy Chuchu, still in quest of sofa-cushions, who tumbled complainingly among the trunks. It required a certain happiness of disposition to look forward hopefully, from so dismal a beginning, across the brief hours of night, to the warm shining of to-morrow's sun.

But the hay arrived at last, and we turned, with our last spark of courage, to the bedroom. We had improved the entrance, but it was still a kind of rope-walking; and it would have been droll to see us mounting, one after another, by candle-light, under the open stars.

The western door – that which looked up the canyon, and through which we entered by our bridge of flying plank – was still entire, a handsome, panelled door, the most finished piece of carpentry in Silverado. And the two lowest bunks next to this we roughly filled with hay for that night's use. Through the opposite, or eastern-looking gable, with its open door and window, a faint, diffused starshine came into the room like mist; and when we were once in bed, we lay, awaiting sleep, in a haunted incomplete obscurity. At first the silence of the night was utter. Then a high wind began in the distance among the treetops, and for hours continued to grow higher. It seemed to me much such a wind as we had found on our visit; yet here in our open chamber we were fanned only by gentle and refreshing draughts, so deep was the canyon, so close our house was planted under the overhanging rock.

The Hunter's Family

There is quite a large race or class of people in America, for whom we scarcely seem to have a parallel in England. Of pure white blood, they are unknown or unrecognisable in towns; inhabit the fringe of settlements and the deep, quiet places of the country; rebellious to all labour, and pettily thievish, like the English gypsies; rustically ignorant, but with a touch of wood-lore and the dexterity of the savage. Whence they came is a moot point. At the time of the war, they poured north in crowds to escape the conscription; lived during summer on fruits, wild animals, and petty theft; and at the approach of winter, when these supplies failed, built great fires in the forest, and there died stoically by starvation. They are widely scattered, however, and easily recognised. Loutish, but not ill-looking, they will sit all day, swinging their legs on a field fence, the mind seemingly as devoid of all reflection as a Suffolk peasant's, careless of politics, for the most part incapable of reading, but with a rebellious vanity and a strong sense of independence. Hunting is their most congenial business, or, if the occasion offers, a little amateur detection. In tracking a criminal, following a particular horse along a beaten highway, and drawing inductions from a hair or a footprint, one of those somnolent, grinning Hodges will suddenly display activity of body and finesse of mind. By their names ye may know them, the women figuring as Loveina, Larsenia, Serena, Leanna, Orreana; the men answering to Alvin, Alva, or Orion, pronounced Orrion, with the accent on the first. Whether they are indeed a race, or whether this is the form of degeneracy common to all back-woodsmen, they are at least known by a generic byword, as Poor Whites or Low-downers.

I will not say that the Hanson family was Poor White, because the name savours of offence; but I may go as far as this – they were, in many points, not unsimilar to the people usually so called. Rufe himself combined two of the qualifications, for he

THE HUNTER'S FAMILY 261

was both a hunter and an amateur detective. It was he who pursued Russel and Dollar, the robbers of the Lakeport stage, and captured them the very morning after the exploit, while they were still sleeping in a hayfield. Russel, a drunken Scotch carpenter, was even an acquaintance of his own, and he expressed much grave commiseration for his fate. In all that he said and did, Rufe was grave. I never saw him hurried. When he spoke, he took out his pipe with ceremonial deliberation, looked east and west, and then, in quiet tones and few words, stated his business or told his story. His gait was to match; it would never have surprised you if, at any step, he had turned round and walked away again, so warily and slowly, and with so much seeming hesitation did he go about. He lay long in bed in the morning – rarely, indeed, rose before noon; he loved all games, from poker to clerical croquet; and in the Toll House croquet ground I have seen him toiling at the latter with the devotion of a curate. He took an interest in education, was an active member of the local school-board, and when I was there, he had recently lost the school-house key. His waggon was broken, but it never seemed to occur to him to mend it. Like all truly idle people, he had an artistic eye. He chose the print stuff for his wife's dresses, and counselled her in the making of a patchwork quilt, always, as she thought, wrongly, but to the more educated eye, always with bizarre and admirable taste – the taste of an Indian. With all this, he was a perfect, unoffending gentleman in word and act. Take his clay pipe from him, and he was fit for any society but that of fools. Quiet as he was, there burned a deep, permanent excitement in his dark blue eyes; and when this grave man smiled, it was like sunshine in a shady place.

Mrs Hanson (née, if you please, Lovelands) was more commonplace than her lord. She was a comely woman, too, plump, fair-coloured, with wonderful white teeth; and in her print dresses (chosen by Rufe) and with a large sun-bonnet shading her valued complexion, made, I assure you, a very agreeable figure. But she was on the surface, what there was of her, outspoken and loud-spoken. Her noisy laughter had none of the charm of one of Hanson's rare, slow-spreading smiles; there was no reticence, no mystery, no manner about the woman: she was a first-class dairymaid, but her husband was an unknown quantity between the savage and the nobleman. She was often in and out with us, merry, and healthy, and fair; he came far seldomer – only, indeed, when there was business, or now and again, to pay a visit of ceremony, brushed up for the occasion, with his wife on his arm, and a clean clay pipe in his teeth. These visits, in our forest state, had quite the air of an event, and turned our red canyon into a salon.

Such was the pair who ruled in the old Silverado Hotel among the windy trees, on the mountain shoulder overlooking the whole length of Napa Valley, as the man aloft looks down on the ship's deck. There they kept house, with sundry horses and fowls, and a family of sons, Daniel Webster, and I think George Washington, among the number. Nor did they want visitors. An old gentleman, of singular stolidity, and called Breedlove – I think he had crossed the plains in the same caravan with Rufe – housed with them for awhile during our stay; and they had besides a permanent lodger, in the form of Mrs Hanson's brother, Irvine Lovelands. I spell Irvine by guess; for I could get no information on the subject, just as I could never find out, in spite of many inquiries, whether or not Rufe was a contraction for Rufus. They were all cheerfully at sea about their names in that generation. And this is surely the more notable where the names are all so strange, and even the family names appear to have been coined. At one time, at least, the ancestors of all these Alvins and Alvas, Loveinas, Lovelands, and Breedloves, must have taken serious council and found a certain poetry in these denominations; that must have been, then, their form of literature. But still times change; and their next descendants, the George Washingtons and Daniel Websters, will at least be clear upon the point. And anyway, and however his name should be spelt, this Irvine Lovelands was the most unmitigated Caliban I ever knew.

Our very first morning at Silverado, when we were full of business, patching up doors and windows, making beds and seats, and getting our rough lodging into shape, Irvine and his sister made their appearance together, she for neighbourliness and general curiosity; he, because he was working for me, to my sorrow, cutting firewood at I forget how much a day. The way that he set about cutting wood was characteristic. We were at that moment patching up and unpacking in the kitchen. Down he sat on one side, and down sat his sister on the other. Both were chewing pine-tree gum, and he, to my annoyance, accompanied that simple pleasure with profuse expectoration.

She rattled away, talking up hill and down dale, laughing, tossing her head, showing her brilliant teeth. He looked on in silence, now spitting heavily on the floor, now putting his head back and uttering a loud, discordant, joyless laugh. He had a tangle of shock hair, the colour of wool; his mouth was a grin; although as strong as a horse, he looked neither heavy nor yet adroit, only leggy, coltish, and in the road. But it was plain he was in high spirits, thoroughly enjoying his visit; and he laughed frankly whenever we failed to accomplish what we were about. This was scarcely helpful: it was even, to amateur carpenters, embarrassing; but it lasted until we knocked off work and began to get dinner. Then Mrs Hanson remembered she should have been gone an hour ago; and the pair retired, and the lady's laughter died away among the nutmegs down the path. That was Irvine's first day's work in my employment – the devil take him!

The next morning he returned and, as he was this time alone, he bestowed his conversation upon us with great liberality. He prided himself on his intelligence; asked us if we knew the school-ma'am. *He* didn't think much of her, anyway. He had tried her, he had. He had put a question to her. If a tree a hundred feet high were to fall a foot a day, how long would it take to fall right down? She had not been able to solve the problem. 'She don't know nothing,' he opined. He told us how a friend of his kept a school with a revolver, and chuckled mightily over that; his friend could teach school, he could. All the time he kept chewing gum and spitting. He would stand a while looking down; and then he would toss back his shock of hair, and laugh hoarsely, and spit, and bring forward a new subject. A man, he told us, who bore a grudge against him, had poisoned his dog. 'That was a low thing for a man to do now, wasn't it? It wasn't like a man, that, nohow. But I got even with him: I pisoned *his* dog.' His clumsy utterance, his rude embarrassed manner, set a fresh value on the stupidity of his remarks. I do not think I ever appreciated the meaning of two words until I knew Irvine – the verb, loaf, and the noun, oaf; between them, they complete his portrait. He could lounge, and wriggle, and rub himself against the wall, and grin, and be more in everybody's way than any other two people that I ever set my eyes on. Nothing that he did became him; and yet you were conscious that he was one of your own race, that his mind was cumbrously at work, revolving the problem of existence like a quid of gum, and in his cloudy manner enjoying life, and passing judgment on his fellows. Above all things, he was delighted with himself. You would not have thought it, from his uneasy manners and troubled, struggling utterance; but he loved himself to the marrow, and was happy and proud like a peacock on a rail.

His self-esteem was, indeed, the one joint in his harness. He could be got to work, and even kept at work, by flattery. As long as my wife stood over him, crying out how strong he was, so long exactly he would stick to the matter in hand; and the moment she turned her back, or ceased to praise him, he would stop. His physical strength was wonderful; and to have a woman stand by and admire his achievements, warmed his heart like sunshine. Yet he was as cowardly as he was powerful, and felt no shame in owning to the weakness. Something was once wanted from the crazy platform over the shaft, and he at once refused to venture there – 'did not like,' as he said, 'foolen' around them kind o' places,' and let my wife go instead of him, looking on with a grin. Vanity, where it rules, is usually more heroic: but Irvine steadily approved himself, and expected others to approve him; rather looked down upon my wife, and decidedly expected her to look up to him, on the strength of his superior prudence.

Yet the strangest part of the whole matter was perhaps this, that Irvine was as beautiful as a statue. His features were, in themselves, perfect; it was only his cloudy, uncouth, and coarse expression that disfigured them. So much strength residing in so spare a frame was proof sufficient of the accuracy of his shape. He must have been built somewhat after the pattern of Jack Sheppard; but the famous housebreaker, we may be certain, was no lout. It was by the extraordinary powers of his mind no less than by the vigour of his body that he broke his strong prison with such imperfect implements, turning the very obstacles to service. Irvine, in the same case, would have sat down and spat, and grumbled curses. He had the soul of a fat sheep, but, regarded as an artist's model, the exterior of a Greek God. It was a cruel thought to persons less favoured in their birth, that this creature, endowed – to use the language of theatres – with extraordinry 'means', should so manage to misemploy them that he looked ugly and almost deformed. It was only by an effort of abstraction, and after many days, that you discovered what he was.

By playing on the oaf's conceit, and standing closely over him, we got a path made round the corner of the dump to our door, so that we could come and go with decent ease; and he even enjoyed the work, for in that there were boulders to be plucked up bodily, bushes to be uprooted, and other occasions for athletic display: but cutting wood was a different matter. Anybody could cut wood; and, besides, my wife was tired of supervising him, and had other things to attend to. And, in short, days went by, and Irvine came daily, and talked and lounged and spat; but the firewood remained intact as sleepers on the platform or growing trees upon the mountain-side. Irvine, as a woodcutter, we could tolerate; but Irvine as a friend of the family, at so much a day, was too bald an imposition, and at length, on the afternoon of the fourth or fifth day of our connection, I explained to him, as clearly as I could, the light in which I had grown to regard his presence. I pointed out to him that I could not continue to give him a salary for spitting on the floor; and this expression, which came after a good many others, at last penetrated his obdurate wits. He rose at once, and said if that was the way he was going to be spoke to, he reckoned he would quit. And, no one interposing, he departed.

So far, so good. But we had no firewood. The next afternoon, I strolled down to Rufe's and consulted him on the subject. It was a very droll interview, in the large, bare north room of the Silverado Hotel, Mrs Hanson's patchwork on a frame, and Rufe, and his wife, and I, and the oaf himself, all more or less embarrassed. Rufe announced there was nobody in the neighbourhood but Irvine who could do a day's work for anybody. Irvine, thereupon, refused to have any more to do with my service; he 'wouldn't work no more for a man as had spoke to him 's I had done.' I found myself on the point of the last humiliation – driven to beseech the creature whom I had just dismissed with insult: but I took the high hand in despair, said there must be no talk of Irvine coming back unless matters were to be differently managed; that I would rather chop firewood for myself than be fooled; and, in short, the Hansons being eager for the lad's hire, I so imposed upon them with merely affected resolution, that they ended by begging me to re-employ him again, on a solemn promise that he should be more industrious. The promise, I am bound to say, was kept. We soon had a fine pile of firewood at our door; and if Caliban gave me the cold shoulder and spared me his conversation, I thought none the worse of him for that, nor did I find my days much longer for the deprivation.

The leading spirit of the family was, I am inclined to fancy, Mrs Hanson. Her social brilliancy somewhat dazzled the others, and she had more of the small change of sense. It was she who faced Kelmar, for instance; and perhaps, if she had been alone, Kelmar would have had no rule within her doors. Rufe, to be sure, had a fine, sober, open-air attitude of mind, seeing the world without exaggeration – perhaps, we may even say, without enough; for he lacked, along with the others, that commercial idealism which puts so high a value on time and money. Sanity itself is a kind of convention. Perhaps Rufe was wrong; but, looking on life plainly, he was unable to perceive that croquet or poker were in any way less important than, for instance, mending his waggon. Even his own profession, hunting, was dear to him mainly as a sort of play; even that he would have neglected, had it not appealed to his imagination. His hunting-suit, for instance, had cost I should be afraid to say how many bucks – the currency in which he paid his way: it was all befringed, after the Indian fashion, and it was dear to his heart. The pictorial side of his daily business was never forgotten. He was even anxious to stand for his picture in those buckskin hunting clothes; and I remember how he once warmed almost into enthusiasm, his dark blue eyes growing perceptibly larger, as he planned the composition in which he should appear, 'with the horns of some real big bucks, and dogs, and a camp on a crick' (creek, stream).

There was no trace in Irvine of this woodland poetry. He did not care for hunting, nor yet for buckskin suits. He had never observed scenery. The world, as it appeared to him, was almost obliterated by his own great grinning figure in the foreground: Caliban Malvolio. And it seems to me as if, in the persons of these brothers-in-law, we had the two sides of rusticity fairly well represented: the hunter living really in nature; the clodhopper living merely out of society: the one bent up in every corporal agent to capacity in one pursuit, doing at least one thing keenly and thoughtfully, and thoroughly alive to all that touches it; the other in the inert and bestial state, walking in a faint dream, and taking so dim an impression of the myriad sides of life that he is truly conscious of nothing but himself. It is only in the fastnesses of nature, forests, mountains, and the back of man's beyond, that a creature endowed with five senses can grow up into the perfection of this crass and earthy vanity. In towns or the busier countrysides, he is roughly reminded of other men's existence; and if he learns no more, he learns at least to fear contempt. But Irvine had come scathless through life, conscious only of himself, of his great strength and intelligence; and in the silence of the universe, to which he did not listen, dwelling with delight on the sound of his own thoughts.

The Sea Fogs

A change in the colour of the light usually called me in the morning. By a certain hour, the long, vertical chinks in our western gable, where the boards had shrunk and separated, flashed suddenly into my eyes as strips of dazzling blue, at once so dark and splendid that I used to marvel how the qualities could be combined. At an earlier hour, the heavens in that quarter were still quietly coloured, but the shoulder of the mountain which shuts in the canyon already glowed with sunlight in a wonderful compound of gold and rose and green; and this too would kindle, although more mildly and with rainbow tints, the fissures of our crazy gable. If I were sleeping heavily, it was the bold blue that struck me awake; if more lightly, then I would come to myself in that earlier and fairer light.

One Sunday morning, about five, the first brightness called me. I rose and turned to the east, not for my devotions, but for air. The night had been very still. The little private gale that blew every evening in our canyon, for ten minutes or perhaps a quarter of an hour, had swiftly blown itself out; in the hours that followed not a sigh of wind had shaken the treetops; and our barrack, for all its breaches, was less fresh that morning than of wont. But I had no sooner reached the window than I forgot all else in the sight that met my eyes, and I made but two bounds into my clothes, and down the crazy plank to the platform.

The sun was still concealed below the opposite hilltops, though it was shining already, not twenty feet above my head, on our own mountain slope. But the scene, beyond a few near features, was entirely changed. Napa Valley was gone; gone were all the lower slopes and woody foothills of the range; and in their place, not a thousand feet below me, rolled a great level ocean. It was as though I had gone to bed the night before, safe in a nook of inland mountain, and had awakened in a bay upon the coast. I had seen these inundations from below; at Calistoga I had risen and gone abroad in the early morning, coughing and sneezing, under fathoms on fathoms of grey sea vapour, like a cloudy sky – a dull sight for the artist, and a painful experience for the invalid. But to sit aloft one's self in the pure air and under the unclouded dome of heaven, and thus look down on the submergence of the valley, was strangely different and even delightful to the eyes. Far away were hilltops like little islands. Nearer, a smoky surf beat about the foot of precipices and poured into all the coves of these rough mountains. The colour of that fog ocean was a thing never to be forgotten. For an instant, among the Hebrides and just about sundown, I have seen something like it on the sea itself. But the white was not so opaline; nor was there, what surprisingly increased the effect, that breathless, crystal stillness over all. Even in its gentlest moods the salt sea travails, moaning among the weeds or lisping on the sand; but that vast fog ocean lay in a trance of silence, nor did the sweet air of the morning tremble with a sound.

As I continued to sit upon the dump, I began to observe that this sea was not so level as at first sight it appeared to be. Away in the extreme south, a little hill of fog arose against the sky above the general surface, and as it had already caught the sun, it shone on the horizon like the topsails of some giant ship. There were huge waves, stationary, as it seemed, like waves in a frozen sea; and yet, as I looked again. I was not sure but they were moving after all, with a slow and august advance. And while I was yet doubting, a promontory of the hills some four or five miles away, conspicuous by the bouquet of tall pines, was in a single instant overtaken and swallowed up. It reappeared in a little, with its pines, but this time as an islet, and only to be swallowed up once more and then for good. This set me looking nearer, and I saw that in every cove along the line of mountains the fog was being piled in higher and higher, as though by some wind that was inaudible to me. I could trace its progress, one pine tree first growing hazy and then disappearing after another; although sometimes there was none of this forerunning haze, but the whole opaque white ocean gave a start and swallowed a piece of mountain at a gulp. It was to flee these poisonous fogs that I had left the seaboard and climbed so high among the mountains. And now, behold, here came the fog to besiege me in my chosen altitudes, and yet came so beautifully that my first thought was of welcome.

The sun had now gotten much higher, and through all the gaps of the hills it cast long bars of gold across that white ocean. An eagle, or some other very great bird of the mountain, came wheeling over the nearer pine-tops, and hung, poised and something sideways, as if to look abroad on that unwonted desolation, spying, perhaps with terror, for the eyries of her comrades. Then with a long cry, she disappeared again towards Lake County and the clearer air. At length it seemed to me as if the flood were beginning to subside. The old landmarks, by whose disappearance I had measured its advance, here a crag, there a brave pine tree, now began, in the inverse order, to make their reappearance into daylight. I judged all danger of the fog was over. This was not Noah's flood; it was but a morning spring, and would now drift out seaward whence it came. So, mightily relieved, and a good deal exhilarated by the sight, I went into the house to light the fire.

I suppose it was nearly seven when I once more mounted the platform to look abroad. The fog ocean had swelled up enormously since last I saw it; and a few hundred feet below me, in the deep gap where the Toll House stands and the road runs through into Lake County, it had already topped the slope, and was pouring over and down the other side like driving smoke. The wind had climbed along with it; and though I was still in calm air, I could see the trees tossing below me, and their long, strident sighing mounted to me where I stood.

Half-an-hour later, the fog had surmounted all the ridge on the opposite side of the gap, though a shoulder of the mountain still warded it out of our canyon. Napa Valley and its bounding hills were now utterly blotted out. The fog, sunny white in the sunshine, was pouring over into Lake County in a huge, ragged cataract, tossing treetops appearing and disppearing in the spray. The air struck with a little chill, and set me coughing. It smelt strong of the fog, like the smell of a washing-house but with a shrewd tang of the sea salt.

Had it not been for two things – the sheltering spur which answered as a dyke, and the great valley on the other side which rapidly engulfed whatever mounted – our own little platform in the canyon must have been already buried a hundred feet in salt and poisonous air. As it was, the interest of the scene entirely occupied our minds. We were set just out of the wind, and but just above the fog; we could listen to the voice of the one as to music on the stage; we could plunge our eyes down into the other, as into some flowing stream from over the parapet of a bridge; thus we looked on upon a strange, impetuous, silent, shifting exhibition of the powers of nature, and saw the familiar landscape changing from moment to moment like figures in a dream.

The imagination loves to trifle with what is not. Had this been indeed the deluge, I should have felt more strongly, but the emotion would have been similar in kind. I played with the idea, as the child flees in delighted terror from the creations of his fancy. The look of the thing helped me. And when at last I began to flee up the mountain, it was indeed partly to escape from the raw air that kept me coughing, but it was also part in play.

As I ascended the mountain-side, I came once more to overlook the upper surface of the fog; but it wore a different appearance from what I had beheld at daybreak. For, first, the sun now fell on it from high overhead, and its surface shone and undulated like a great nor'land moor country, sheeted with untrodden morning snow. And next the new level must have been a thousand or fifteen hundred feet higher than the old, so that only five or six points of all the broken country below me still stood out. Napa Valley was now one with Sonoma on the west. On the hither side, only a thin scattered fringe of bluffs was unsubmerged; and through all the gaps the fog was pouring over, like an ocean, into the blue, clear, sunny country on the east. There it was soon lost; for it fell instantly into the bottom of the valleys, following the watershed; and the hilltops in that quarter were still clear cut upon the eastern sky.

Through the Toll House gap and over the near ridges on the other side, the deluge was immense. A spray of thin vapour was thrown high above it, rising and falling, and blown into fantastic shapes. The speed of its course was like a mountain torrent. Here and there a few treetops were discovered and then whelmed again; and for one second, the bough of a dead pine beckoned out of the spray like the arm of a drowning man. But still the imagination was dissatisfied, still the ear waited for something more. Had this indeed been water (as it seemed so to the eye), with what a plunge of reverberating thunder would it have rolled upon its course, disembowelling mountains and deracinating pines! And yet water it was, and sea-water at that – true Pacific billows, only somewhat rarefied, rolling in mid-air among the hilltops.

I climbed still higher, among the red rattling gravel and dwarf underwood of Mount Saint Helena, until I could look right down upon Silverado, and admire the favoured nook in which it lay. The sunny plain of fog was several hundred feet higher; behind the protecting spur a gigantic accumulation of cottony vapour threatened, with every second, to blow over and submerge our homestead; but the vortex setting past the Toll House was too strong; and there lay our little platform, in the arms of the deluge, but still enjoying its unbroken sunshine. About eleven, however, thin spray came flying over the friendly buttress, and I began to think the fog had hunted out its Jonah after all. But it was the last effort. The wind veered while we were at dinner, and began to blow squally from the mountain summit; and by half-past one, all that world of sea-fog was utterly routed and flying here and there into the south in little rags of cloud. And instead of a lone sea-beach, we found ourselves once more inhabiting a high mountainside, with the clear green country far below us, and the light smoke of Calistoga blowing in the air.

This was the great Russian campaign for that season. Now and then, in the early morning, a little white lakelet of fog would be seen far down in Napa Valley; but the heights were not again assailed, nor was the surrounding world again shut off from Silverado.

The Toll House

The Toll House, standing alone by the wayside under nodding pines, with its streamlet and water-tank; its backwoods, tollbar, and well-trodden croquet ground; the ostler standing by the stable door, chewing a straw; a glimpse of the Chinese cook in the back parts; and Mr Hoddy in the bar, gravely alert and serviceable, and equally anxious to lend or borrow books; – dozed all day in the dusty sunshine, more than half asleep. There were no neighbours, except the Hansons up the hill. The traffic on the road was infinitesimal; only, at rare intervals, a couple in a waggon, or a dusty farmer on a spring-board, toiling over 'the grade' to that metropolitan hamlet, Calistoga; and, at the fixed hours, the passage of the stages.

The nearest building was the schoolhouse, down the road; and the school-ma'am boarded at the Toll House, walking thence in the morning to the little brown shanty, where she taught the young ones of the district, and returning thither pretty weary in the afternoon. She had chosen this outlying situation, I understood, for her health. Mr Corwin was consumptive; so was Rufe; so was Mr Jennings, the engineer. In short, the place was a kind of small Davos: consumptive folk consorting on a hilltop in the most unbroken idleness. Jennings never did anything that I could see, except now and then to fish, and generally to sit about in the bar and the verandah, waiting for something to happen. Corwin and Rufe did as little as possible; and if the school-ma'am, poor lady, had to work pretty hard all morning, she subsided when it was over into much the same dazed beatitude as all the rest.

Her special corner was the parlour – a very genteel room, with Bible prints, a crayon portrait of Mrs Corwin in the height of fashion a few years ago, another of her son (Mr Corwin was not represented), a mirror, and a selection of dried grasses. A large book was laid religiously on the table – *From Palace to Hovel*, I believe, its name – full of the raciest experiences in

England. The author had mingled freely with all classes, the
nobility particularly meeting him with open arms; and I must
say that traveller had ill requited his reception. His book, in
short, was a capital instance of the Penny Messalina school of
literature; and there rose from it, in that cool parlour, in that
silent, wayside, mountain inn, a rank atmosphere of gold and
blood and 'Jenkins', and the 'Mysteries of London', and sicken-
ing, inverted snobbery, fit to knock you down. The mention of
this book reminds me of another and far racier picture of our
island life. The latter parts of *Rocambole* are surely too sparingly
consulted in the country which they celebrate. No man's education can be said to be complete, nor can he pronounce the
world yet emptied of enjoyment, till he has made the acquaintance of 'the Reverend Patterson, director of the Evangelical
Society'. To follow the evolutions of that reverend gentleman,
who goes through scenes in which even Mr Duffield would
hesitate to place a bishop, is to rise to new ideas. But, alas! there
was no Patterson about the Toll House. Only, alongside of
From Palace to Hovel, a sixpenny 'Ouida' figured. So literature,
you see, was not unrepresented.

The school-ma'am had friends to stay with her, other school-
ma'ams enjoying their holidays, quite a bevy of damsels. They
seemed never to go out, or not beyond the verandah, but sat
close in the little parlour, quietly talking or listening to the wind
among the trees. Sleep dwelt in the Toll House, like a fixture:
summer sleep, shallow, soft, and dreamless. A cuckoo-clock, a
great rarity in such a place, hooted at intervals about the echoing
house; and Mr Jennings would open his eyes for a moment in
the bar, and turn the leaf of a newspaper, and the resting school-
ma'ams in the parlour would be recalled to the consciousness of
their inaction. Busy Mrs Corwin and her busy China-man might
be heard indeed, in the penetralia, pounding dough or rattling
dishes; or perhaps Rufe had called up some of the sleepers for a
game of croquet, and the hollow strokes of the mallet sounded
far away among the woods: but with these exceptions, it was
sleep and sunshine and dust, and the wind in the pine trees, all
day long.

A little before stage time, that castle of indolence awoke. The
ostler threw his straw away and set to his preparations. Mr
Jennings rubbed his eyes; happy Mr Jennings, the something he
had been waiting for all day about to happen at last! The

boarders gathered in the verandah, silently giving ear, and gazing down the road with shaded eyes. And as yet there was no sign for the senses, not a sound, not a tremor of the mountain road. The birds, to whom the secret of the hooting cuckoo is unknown, must have set down to instinct this premonitory bustle.

And then the first of the two stages swooped upon the Toll House with a roar and in a cloud of dust; and the shock had not yet time to subside, before the second was abreast of it. Huge concerns they were, well-horsed and loaded, the men in their shirt-sleeves, the women swathed in veils, the long whip cracking like a pistol; and as they charged upon that slumbering hostelry, each shepherding a dust-storm, the dead place blossomed into life and talk and chatter. This the Toll House? – with its city throng, its jostling shoulders, its infinity of instant business in the bar? The mind would not receive it! The heartfelt bustle of that hour is hardly credible; the thrill of the great shower of letters from the postbag, the childish hope and interest with which one gazed in all these strangers' eyes. They paused there but to pass: the blue-clad China-boy, the San Francisco magnate, the mystery in the dust-coat, the secret memoirs in tweed, the ogling, well-shod lady with her troop of girls; they did but flash and go; they were hull-down for us behind life's ocean, and we but hailed their topsails on the line. Yet, out of our great solitude of four-and-twenty mountain hours, we thrilled to their momentary presence; gauged and divined them, loved and hated; and stood lightheaded in that storm of human electricity. Yes, like Piccadilly Circus, this is also one of life's crossing-places. Here I beheld one man, already famous or infamous, a centre of pistol-shots: and another who, if not yet known to rumour, will fill a column of the Sunday paper when he comes to hang – a burly, thick-set, powerful Chinese desperado, six long bristles upon either lip; redolent of whisky, playing-cards, and pistols; swaggering in the bar with the lowest assumption of the lowest European manners; rapping out blackguard English oaths in his canorous Oriental voice; and combining in one person the depravities of two races and two civilisations. For all his lust and vigour, he seemed to look cold upon me from the valley of the shadow of the gallows. He imagined a vain thing; and while he drained his cock-tail, Holbein's death was at his elbow. Once, too, I fell in talk with another of these flitting strangers – like the rest, in his shirt-sleeves and all begrimed with dust – and the next minute we were discussing Paris and London, theatres and wines. To him, journeying from one human place to another, this was a trifle; but to me! No, Mr Lillie, I have not forgotten it.

And presently the city-tide was at its flood and began to ebb. Life runs in Piccadilly Circus, say, from nine to one, and then, there also, ebbs into the small hours of the echoing policeman and the lamps and stars. But the Toll House is far up-stream, and near its rural springs; the bubble of the tide but touches it. Before you had yet grasped your pleasure, the horses were put to, the loud whips volleyed and the tide was gone. North and south had the two stages vanished, the towering dust subsided in the woods; but there was still an interval before the flush had fallen on your cheeks, before the ear became once more contented with the silence, or the seven sleepers of the Toll House dozed back to their accustomed corners. Yet a little, and the ostler would swing round the great barrier across the road; and in the golden evening, that dreamy inn begin to trim its lamps and spread the board for supper.

As I recall the place – the green dell below; the spires of pine; the sun-warmed, scented air; that grey, gabled inn, with its faint stirrings of life amid the slumber of the mountains – I slowly awake to a sense of admiration, gratitude, and almost love. A fine place, after all, for a wasted life to doze away in – the cuckoo-clock hooting of its far home country; the croquet mallets, eloquent of English lawns; the stages daily bringing news of the turbulent world away below there; and perhaps once in the summer, a salt fog pouring overhead with its tale of the Pacific.

A Starry Drive

In our rule at Silverado there was a melancholy interregnum. The queen and the crown prince with one accord fell sick; and, as I was sick to begin with, our lone position on Mount Saint Helena was no longer tenable, and we had to hurry back to Calistoga and a cottage on the green. By that time we had begun to realise the difficulties of our position. We had found what an amount of labour it cost to support life in our red canyon; and it was the dearest desire of our hearts to get a China-boy to go along with us when we returned. We could have given him a whole house to himself, self-contained, as they say in the advertisements; and on the money question we were prepared to go far. Kong Sam Kee, the Calistoga washerman, was entrusted with the affair, and from day to day it languished on, with protestations on our part and mellifluous excuses on the part of Kong Sam Kee.

At length, about half-past eight of our last evening, with the waggon ready harnessed to convey us up the grade, the washerman, with a somewhat sneering air, produced the boy. He was a handsome, gentlemanly lad, attired in rich dark blue, and shod with snowy white; but alas! he had heard rumours of Silverado. He knew it for a lone place on the mountain-side, with no friendly wash-house near by, where he might smoke a pipe of opium o' nights with other China-boys, and lose his little earnings at the game of tan; and he first backed out for more money; and then, when that demand was satisfied, refused to come point-blank. He was wedded to his wash-houses; he had no taste for the rural life; and we must go to our mountain servantless. It must have been near half-an-hour before we reached that conclusion, standing in the midst of Calistoga high street under the stars, and the China-boy and Kong Sam Kee singing their pidgin-English in the sweetest voices and with the most musical inflections.

We were not, however, to return alone; for we brought with

us Joe Strong, the painter, a most good-natured comrade and a capital hand at an omelette. I do not know in which capacity he was most valued – as a cook or a companion; and he did excellently well in both.

The Kong Sam Kee negotiation had delayed us unduly; it must have been half-past nine before we left Calistoga, and night came fully ere we struck the bottom of the grade. I have never seen such a night. It seemed to throw calumny in the teeth of all the painters that ever dabbled in starlight. The sky itself was of a ruddy, powerful, nameless, changing colour, dark and glossy like a serpent's back. The stars, by innumerable millions, stuck boldly forth like lamps. The milky way was bright, like a moonlit cloud; half heaven seemed milky way. The greater luminaries shone each more clearly than a winter's moon. Their light was dyed in every sort of colour – red, like fire; blue, like steel; green, like the tracks of sunset; and so sharply did each stand forth in its own lustre that there was no appearance of that flat, star-spangled arch we know so well in pictures, but all the hollow of heaven was one chaos of contesting luminaries – a hurly-burly of stars. Against this the hills and rugged treetops stood out redly dark.

As we continued to advance, the lesser lights and milky ways first grew pale, and then vanished; the countless hosts of heaven dwindled in number by successive millions; those that still shone had tempered their exceeding brightness and fallen back into their customary wistful distance; and the sky declined from its first bewildering splendour into the appearance of a common night. Slowly this change proceeded, and still there was no sign of any cause. Then a whiteness like mist was thrown over the spurs of the mountain. Yet a while, and, as we turned a corner, a great leap of silver light and net of forest shadows fell across the road and upon our wondering waggonful; and, swimming low among the trees, we beheld a strange, misshapen, waning moon, half-tilted on her back.

'Where are ye when the moon appears?' so the old poet sang, half-taunting, to the stars, bent upon a courtly purpose.

As the sunlight round the dim earth's midnight tower of shadow pours,
　Streaming past the dim, wide portals,
　Viewless to the eyes of mortals,
Till it floods the moon's pale islet or the morning's golden shores.

So sings Mr Trowbridge, with a noble inspiration. And so had the sunlight flooded that pale islet of the moon, and her lit face put out, one after another, that galaxy of stars. The wonder of the drive was over; but, by some nice conjunction of clearness in the air and fit shadow in the valley where we travelled, we had seen for a little while that brave display of the midnight heavens. It was gone, but it had been; nor shall I ever again behold the stars with the same mind. He who has seen the sea commoved with a great hurricane, thinks of it very differently from him who has seen it only in a calm. And the difference between a calm and a hurricane is not greatly more striking than that between the ordinary face of night and the splendour that shone upon us in that drive. Two in our waggon knew night as she shines upon the tropics, but even that bore no comparison. The nameless colour of the sky, the hues of the starfire, and the incredible projection of the stars themselves, starting from their orbits, so that the eye seemed to distinguish their positions in the hollow of space – these were things that we had never seen before and shall never see again.

Meanwhile, in this altered night, we proceeded on our way among the scents and silence of the forest, reached the top of the grade, wound up by Hanson's, and came at last to a stand under the flying gargoyle of the chute. Sam, who had been lying back, fast asleep, with the moon on his face, got down with the remark that it was pleasant 'to be home.' The waggon turned and drove away, the noise gently dying in the woods, and we clambered up the rough path, Caliban's great feat of engineering, and came home to Silverado.

The moon shone in at the eastern doors and windows, and over the lumber on the platform. The one tall pine beside the ledge was steeped in silver. Away up the canyon, a wild cat welcomed us with three discordant squalls. But once we had lit a candle, and began to review our improvements, homely in either sense, and count our stores, it was wonderful what a feeling of possession and permanence grew up in the hearts of the lords of Silverado. A bed had still to be made up for Strong, and the morning's water to be fetched, with clinking pail; and as we set about these household duties, and showed off our wealth and conveniences before the stranger, and had a glass of wine, I think, in honour of our return, and trooped at length one after another up the flying bridge of plank, and lay down to sleep in our shattered, moon-pierced barrack, we were among the happiest sovereigns in the world, and certainly ruled over the most contented people. Yet, in our absence, the palace had been sacked. Wild cats, so the Hansons said, had broken in and carried off a side of bacon, a hatchet, and two knives.

Episodes in the Story of a Mine

No one could live at Silverado and not be curious about the story of the mine. We were surrounded by so many evidences of expense and toil, we lived so entirely in the wreck of that great enterprise, like mites in the ruins of a cheese, that the idea of the old din and bustle haunted our repose. Our own house, the forge, the dump, the chutes, the rails, the windlass, the mass of broken plant; the two tunnels, one far below in the green dell, the other on the platform where we kept our wine; the deep shaft, with the sun-glints and the water-drops; above all, the ledge, that great gaping slice out of the mountain shoulder, propped apart by wooden wedges, on whose immediate margin, high above our heads, the one tall pine precariously nodded – these stood for its greatness; while the dog-hutch, bootjacks, old boots, old tavern bills, and the very beds that we inherited from bygone miners, put in human touches and realised for us the story of the past.

I have sat on an old sleeper, under the thick madronas near the forge, with just a look over the dump on the green world below, and seen the sun lying broad among the wreck, and heard the silence broken only by the tinkling water in the shaft, or a stir of the royal family about the battered palace, and my mind has gone back to the epoch of the Stanleys and the Chapmans, with a grand *tutti* of pick and drill, hammer and anvil, echoing about the canyon; the assayer hard at it in our dining-room; the carts below on the road, and their cargo of red mineral bounding and thundering down the iron chute. And now all gone – all fallen away into this sunny silence and desertion: a family of squatters dining in the assayer's office, making their beds in the big sleeping-room erstwhile so crowded, keeping their wine in the tunnel that once rang with picks.

But Silverado itself, although now fallen in its turn into decay, was once but a mushroom, and had succeeded to other mines and other flitting cities. Twenty years ago, away down the glen on the Lake County side there was a place, Jonestown by name, with two thousand inhabitants dwelling under canvas, and one roofed house for the sale of whiskey. Round on the western side of Mount Saint Helena, there was at the same date a second large encampment, its name, if it ever had one, lost for me. Both of these have perished, leaving not a stick and scarce a memory behind them. Tide after tide of hopeful miners have thus flowed and ebbed about the mountain, coming and going, now by lone prospectors, now with a rush. Last in order of time came Silverado, reared the big mill, in the valley, founded the town which is now represented, monumentally, by Hanson's, pierced all these slaps and shafts and tunnels, and in turn declined and died away.

> Our noisy years seem moments in the being
> Of the eternal Silence.

As to the success of Silverado in its time of being, two reports were current. According to the first, six hundred thousand dollars were taken out of that great upright seam, that still hung open above us on crazy wedges. Then the ledge pinched out, and there followed, in quest of the remainder, a great drifting and tunnelling in all directions, and a great consequent effusion of dollars, until, all parties being sick of the expense, the mine was deserted, and the town decamped. According to the second version, told me with much secrecy of manner, the whole affair, mine, mill, and town, were parts of one majestic swindle. There had never come any silver out of any portion of the mine; there was no silver to come. At midnight trains of packhorses might have been observed winding by devious tracks about the shoulder of the mountain. They came from far away, from Amador, or Placer, laden with silver in 'old cigar boxes'. They discharged their load at Silverado, in the hour of sleep; and before the morning they were gone again with their mysterious drivers to their unknown source. In this way, twenty thousand pounds' worth of silver was smuggled in under cover of night, in these old cigar boxes; mixed with Silverado mineral; carted down to the mill; crushed, amalgamated, and refined, and despatched to the city as the proper product of the mine. Stock-jobbing, if it can cover such expenses, must be a profitable business in San Francisco.

I give these two version as I got them. But I place little reliance on either, my belief in history having been greatly shaken. For it chanced that I had come to dwell in Silverado at a critical hour; great events in its history were about to happen – did happen, as I am led to believe; nay, and it will be seen that I played a part in that revolution myself. And yet from first to last I never had a glimmer of an idea what was going on; and even now, after full reflection, profess myself at sea. That there was some obscure intrigue of the cigar-box order, and that I, in the character of a wooden puppet, set pen to paper in the interest of somebody, so much, and no more is certain.

Silverado, then under my immediate sway, belonged to one whom I will call a Mr Ronalds. I only knew him through the extraordinarily distorting medium of local gossip, now as a momentous jobber; now as a dupe to point an adage; and again, and much more probably, as an ordinary Christian gentleman like you or me, who had opened a mine and worked it for a while with better and worse fortune. So, through a defective window-pane, you may see the passer-by shoot up into a hunchbacked giant or dwindle into a pot-bellied dwarf.

To Ronalds, at least, the mine belonged; but the notice by which he held it would run out upon the 30th of June – or rather, as I suppose, it had run out already, and the month of grace would expire upon that day, after which any American citizen might post a notice of his own, and make Silverado his. This, with a sort of quiet slyness, Rufe told me at an early period of our acquaintance. There was no silver, of course; the mine 'wasn't worth nothing, Mr Stevens,' but there was a deal of old iron and wood around, and to gain possession of this old wood and iron, and get a right to the water, Rufe proposed, if I had no objections, to 'jump the claim.'

Of course, I had no objection. But I was filled with wonder. If all he wanted was the wood and iron, what, in the name of fortune, was to prevent him taking them? 'His right there was none to dispute.' He might lay hands on all to-morrow, as the wild cats had laid hands upon our knives and hatchet. Besides, was this mass of heavy mining plant worth transportation? If it was, why had not the rightful owners carted it away? If it was, would they not preserve their title to these movables, even after they had lost their title to the mine? And if it were not, what the better was Rufe? Nothing would grow at Silverado; there was even no wood to cut; beyond a sense of property, there was nothing to be gained. Lastly, was it at all credible that Rolands would forget what Rufe remembered? The days of grace were not yet over: any fine morning he might appear, paper in hand, and enter for another year on his inheritance. However, it was none of my business; all seemed legal; Rufe or Ronalds, all was one to me.

On the morning of the 27th, Mrs Hanson appeared with the milk as usual, in her sun bonnet. The time would be out on Tuesday, she reminded us, and bade me be in readiness to play my part, though I had no idea what it was to be. And suppose Ronalds came? we asked. She received the idea with derision, laughing aloud with all her fine teeth. He could not find the mine to save his life, it appeared, without Rufe to guide him. Last year, when he came, they heard him 'up and down the road hollerin' and a raisin' Cain.' And at last he had to come to the Hansons in despair, and bid Rufe, 'Jump into your pants and shoes, and show me where this old mine is, anyway!' Seeing that Ronalds had laid out so much money in the spot, and that a beaten road led right up to the bottom of the dump, I thought this a remarkable example. The sense of locality must be singularly in abeyance in the case of Ronalds.

That same evening, supper comfortably over, Joe Strong busy at work on a drawing of the dump and the opposite hills, we were all out on the platform together, sitting there, under the tented heavens, with the same sense of privacy as if we had been cabined in a parlour, when the sound of brisk footsteps came mounting up the path. We pricked our ears at this, for the tread seemed lighter and firmer than was usual with our country neighbours. And presently, sure enough, two town gentlemen, with cigars and kid gloves, came debouching past the house. The looked in that place like a blasphemy.

'Good evening,' they said. For none of us had stirred; we all sat stiff with wonder.

'Good evening,' I returned; and then, to put them at their ease, 'A stiff climb,' I added.

'Yes,' replied the leader; 'but we have to thank you for this path.'

I did not like the man's tone. None of us liked it. He did not seem embarrassed by the meeting, but threw us his remarks like favours, and strode magisterially by us towards the shaft and tunnel.

Presently we heard his voice raised to his companion. 'We drifted every sort of way, but couldn't strike the ledge.' Then again: 'It pinched out here.' And once more: 'Every miner that ever worked upon it says there's bound to be a ledge somewhere.'

These were the snatches of his talk that reached us, and they had a damning significance. We, the lords of Silverado, had come face to face with our superior. It is the worst of all quaint and of all cheap ways of life that they bring us at last to the pinch of some humiliation. I liked well enough to be a squatter when there was none but Hanson by; before Ronalds, I will own, I somewhat quailed. I hastened to do him fealty, said I gathered he was the Squattee, and apologised. He threatened me with ejection, in a manner grimly pleasant – more pleasant to him, I fancy, than to me; and then he passed off into praises of the former state of Silverado. 'It was the busiest little mining town you ever saw': a population of between a thousand and fifteen hundred souls, the engine in full blast, the mill newly erected; nothing going but champagne, and hope the order of the day. Ninety thousand dollars came out; a hundred and forty thousand were put in, making a net loss of fifty thousand. The last days, I gathered, the days of John Stanley, were not so bright; the champagne had ceased to flow, the population was already moving elsewhere, and Silverado had begun to wither in the branch before it was cut at the root. The last shot that was fired knocked over the stove chimney, and made that hole in the roof of our barrack, through which the sun was wont to visit slug-a-beds towards afternoon. A noisy last shot, to inaugurate the days of silence.

Throughout this interview, my conscience was a good deal exercised; and I was moved to throw myself on my knees and own the intended treachery. But then I had Hanson to consider. I was in much the same position as Old Rowley, that royal humorist, whom 'the rogue had taken into his confidence.' And again, here was Ronalds on the spot. He must know the day of the month as well as Hanson and I. If a broad hint were necessary, he had the broadest in the world. For a large board had been nailed by the crown prince on the very front of our house, between the door and window, painted in cinnabar – the pigment of the country – with doggerel rhymes and contumelious pictures, and announcing, in terms unnecessarily figurative, that the trick was already played, the claim already jumped, and Master Sam the legitimate successor of Mr Ronalds. But no, nothing could save that man; *quem deus vult perdere, prius dementat.* As he came so he went, and left his rights depending.

Late at night, by Silverado reckoning, and after we were all abed, Mrs Hanson returned to give us the newest of her news. It was like a scene in a ship's steerage: all of us abed in our different tiers, the single candle struggling with the darkness, and this plump, handsome woman, seated on an upturned valise beside the bunks, talking and showing her fine teeth, and laughing till the rafters rang. Any ship, to be sure, with a hundredth part as many holes in it as our barrack, must long ago have gone to her last port. Up to that time I had always imagined Mrs Hanson's loquacity to be mere incontinence, that she said what was uppermost for the pleasure of speaking, and laughed and laughed again as a kind of musical accompaniment. But I now found there was an art in it. I found it less communicative than silence itself. I wished to know why Ronalds had come; how he had found his way without Rufe; and why, being on the spot, he had not refreshed his title. She talked interminably on, but her replies were never answers. She fled under a cloud of words; and when I had made sure that she was purposely eluding me, I dropped the subject in my turn, and let her rattle where she would.

She had come to tell us that, instead of waiting for Tuesday, the claim was to be jumped on the morrow. How? If the time were not out, it was impossible. Why? If Ronalds had come and gone, and done nothing, there was the less cause for hurry. But again I could reach no satisfaction. The claim was to be jumped next morning, that was all that she would condescend upon.

And yet it was not jumped the next morning, nor yet the next, and a whole week had come and gone before we heard more of this exploit. That day week, however, a day of great heat, Hanson, with a little roll of paper in his hand, and the eternal pipe alight; Breedlove, his large, dull friend, to act, I suppose, as witness; Mrs Hanson, in her Sunday best; and all the children, from the oldest to the youngest; – arrived in a procession, tailing one behind another up the path. Caliban was absent, but he had been chary of his friendly visits since the row; and with that exception, the whole family was gathered together as for a marriage or a christening. Strong was sitting at work, in the shade of the dwarf madronas near the forge; and they planted themselves about him in a circle, one on a stone, another on the waggon rails, a third on a piece of plank. Gradually the children stole away up the canyon to where there was another chute, somewhat smaller than the one across the dump; and down this chute, for the rest of the afternoon, they poured one avalanche of stones after another, waking the echoes of the glen. Meantime we elders sat together on the platform, Hanson and his friend smoking in silence like Indian sachems, Mrs Hanson rattling on as usual with an adroit volubility, saying nothing, but keeping the party at their ease like a courtly hostess.

Not a word occurred about the business of the day. Once, twice, and thrice I tried to slide the subject in, but was discouraged by the stoic apathy of Rufe, and beaten down before the pouring verbiage of his wife. There is nothing of the Indian brave about me, and I began to grill with impatience. At last, like a highway robber, I cornered Hanson, and bade him stand and deliver his business. Thereupon he gravely rose, as though to hint that this was not a proper place, nor the subject one suitable for squaws, and I, following his example, led him up the plank into our barrack. There he bestowed himself on a box, and unrolled his papers with fastidious deliberation. There were two sheets of note-paper, and an old mining notice, dated May 30th, 1879, part print, part manuscript, and the latter much obliterated by the rains. It was by this identical piece of paper that the mine had been held last year. For thirteen months it had endured the weather and the change of seasons on a cairn behind the shoulder of the canyon; and it was now my business, spreading it before me on the table, and sitting on a valise, to copy its terms, with some necessary changes, twice over on the two sheets of note-paper. One was then to be placed on the same cairn – a 'mound of rocks' the notice put it; and the other to be lodged for registration.

Rufe watched me, silently smoking, till I came to the place for the locator's name at the end of the first copy; and when I proposed that he should sign, I thought I saw a scare in his eye. 'I don't think that'll be necessary,' he said slowly; 'just you write it down.' Perhaps this mighty hunter, who was the most active member of the local school-board, could not write. There would be nothing strange in that. The constable of Calistoga is, and has been for years, a bed-ridden man, and if I remember rightly, blind. He had more need of the emoluments than another, it was explained; and it was easy for him to 'depytize', with a strong accent on the last. So friendly and so free are popular institutions.

When I had done my scrivening, Hanson strolled out, and addressed Breedlove, 'Will you step up here a bit?' and after they had disappeared a little while into the chaparral and madrona thicket, they came back again, minus a notice, and the deed was done. The claim was jumped; a tract of mountainside, fifteen hundred feet long by six hundred wide, with all the earth's precious bowels, had passed from Ronalds to Hanson, and, in the passage, changed its name from the 'Mammoth' to the 'Calistoga'. I had tried to get Rufe to call it after his wife, after himself, and after Garfield, the Republican Presidential candidate of the hour – since then elected, and, alas! dead – but all was in vain. The claim had once been called the Calistoga before, and he seemed to feel safety in returning to that.

And so the history of that mine became once more plunged in darkness, lit only by some monster pyrotechnical displays of gossip. And perhaps the most curious feature of the whole matter is this: that we should have dwelt in this quiet corner of the mountains, with not a dozen neighbours, and yet struggled all the while, like desperate swimmers, in this sea of falsities and contradictions. Wherever a man is, there will be a lie.

Toils and Pleasures

I must try to convey some notion of our life, of how the days passed and what pleasures we took in them, of what there was to do and how we set about doing it, in our mountain hermitage. The house, after we had repaired the worst of the damages, and filled in some of the doors and windows with white cotton cloth, became a healthy and a pleasant dwelling-place, always airy and dry, and haunted by the outdoor perfumes of the glen. Within, it had the look of habitation, the human look. You had only to go into the third room, which we did not use, and see its stones, its sifting earth, its tumbled litter; and then return to our lodging, with the beds made, the plates on the rack, the pail of bright water behind the door, the stove crackling in a corner, and perhaps the table roughly laid against a meal, – and man's order, the little clean spots that he creates to dwell in, were at once contrasted with the rich passivity of nature. And yet our house was everywhere so wrecked and shattered, the air came and went so freely, the sun found so many portholes, the golden outdoor glow shone in so many open chinks, that we enjoyed, at the same time, some of the comforts of a roof and much of the gaiety and brightness of *al fresco* life. A single shower of rain, to be sure, and we should have been drowned out like mice. But ours was a Californian summer, and an earthquake was a far likelier accident than a shower of rain.

Trustful in this fine weather, we kept the house for kitchen and bedroom, and used the platform as our summer parlour. The sense of privacy, as I have said already, was complete. We could look over the dump on miles of forest and rough hilltop; our eyes commanded some of Napa Valley, where the train ran, and the little country townships sat so close together along the line of the rail. But here there was no man to intrude. None but the Hansons were our visitors. Even they came but at long intervals, or twice daily, at a stated hour, with milk. So our days, as they were never interrupted, drew out to the greater length; hour melted insensibly into hour; the household duties, though they were many, and some of them laborious, dwindled into mere islets of business in a sea of sunny day-time; and it appears to me, looking back, as though the far greater part of our life at Silverado had been passed, propped upon an elbow, or seated on a plank, listening to the silence that there is among the hills.

My work, it is true, was over early in the morning. I rose before anyone else, lit the stove, put on the water to boil, and strolled forth upon the platform to wait till it was ready. Silverado would then be still in shadow, the sun shining on the mountain higher up. A clean smell of trees, a smell of the earth at morning, hung in the air. Regularly, every day, there was a single bird, not singing, but awkwardly chirruping among the green madronas, and the sound was cheerful, natural, and stirring. It did not hold the attention, nor interrupt the thread of meditation, like a blackbird or a nightingale; it was mere woodland prattle, of which the mind was conscious like a perfume. The freshness of these morning seasons remained with me far on into the day.

As soon as the kettle boiled, I made porridge and coffee; and that, beyond the literal drawing of water, and the preparation of kindling, which it would be hyperbolical to call the hewing of wood, ended my domestic duties for the day. Thenceforth my wife laboured single-handed in the palace, and I lay or wandered on the platform at my own sweet will. The little corner near the forge, where we found a refuge under the madronas from the unsparing early sun, is indeed connected in my mind with some nightmare encounters over Euclid and the Latin Grammar. These were known as Sam's lessons. He was supposed to be the victim and the sufferer; but here there must have been some misconception, for whereas I generally retired to bed after one of these engagements, he was no sooner set free than he dashed up to the China-man's house, where he had installed a printing press, that great element of civilisation, and the sound of his labours would be faintly audible about the canyon half the day.

To walk at all was a laborious business; the foot sank and slid; the boots were cut to pieces, among sharp, uneven, rolling stones. When we crossed the platform in any direction, it was usual to lay a course, following as much as possible the line of waggon rails. Thus, if water were to be drawn, the water-carrier

left the house along some tilting planks that we had laid down,
and not laid down very well. These carried him to that great
highroad, the railway; and the railway served him as far as to
the head of the shaft. But from thence to the spring and back
again he made the best of his unaided way, staggering among
the stones, and wading in low growth of the calycanthus, where
the rattlesnakes lay hissing at his passage. Yet I liked to draw
water. It was pleasant to dip the grey metal pail into the clean,
colourless, cool water; pleasant to carry it back, with the water
lipping at the edge, and a broken sunbeam quivering in the
midst.

But the extreme roughness of the walking confined us in
common practice to the platform, and indeed to those parts of
it that were most easily accessible along the line of rails. The
rails came straight forward from the shaft, here and there
overgrown with little green bushes, but still entire, and still
carrying a truck, which it was Sam's delight to trundle to and
fro by the hour with various ladings. About midway down the
platform, the railroad trended to the right, leaving our house
and coasting along the far side within a few yards of the
madronas and the forge, and not far off the latter, ended in a
sort of platform on the edge of the dump. There, in old days,
the trucks were tipped, and their load sent thundering down the
chute. There, besides, was the only spot where we could
approach the margin of the dump. Anywhere else, you took
your life in your right hand when you came within a yard and a
half to peer over. For at any moment the dump might begin to
slide and carry you down and bury you below its ruins. Indeed,
the neighbourhood of an old mine is a place beset with dangers.
For as still as Silverado was, at any moment the report of rotten
wood might tell us that the platform had fallen into the shaft;
the dump might begin to pour into the road below; or a wedge
slip in the great upright seam, and hundreds of tons of mountain
bury the scene of our encampment.

I have already compared the dump to a rampart, built
certainly by some rude people, and for prehistoric wars. It was
likewise a frontier. All below was green and woodland, the tall
pines soaring one above another, each with a firm outline and
full spread of bough. All above was arid, rocky, and bald. The
great spout of broken mineral, that had dammed the canyon up,
was a creature of man's handiwork, its material dug out with a

pick and powder, and spread by the service of the trucks. But nature herself, in that upper district, seemed to have had an eye to nothing besides mining; and even the natural hillside was all sliding gravel and precarious boulder. Close at the margin of the well leaves would decay to skeletons and mummies, which at length some stronger gust would carry clear of the canyon and scatter in the subjacent woods. Even moisture and decaying vegetable matter could not, with all nature's alchemy, concoct enough soil to nourish a few poor grasses. It is the same, they say, in the neighbourhood of all silver mines; the nature of that precious rock being stubborn with quartz and poisonous with cinnabar. Both were plenty in our Silverado. The stones sparkled white in the sunshine with quartz; they were all stained red with cinnabar. Here, doubtless, came the Indians of yore to paint their faces for the warpath; and cinnabar, if I remember rightly, was one of the few articles of Indian commerce. Now, Sam had it in his undisturbed possession, to pound down and slake, and paint his rude designs with. But to me it had always a fine flavour of poetry, compounded out of Indian story and Hawthornden's allusion:

> Desire, alas! desire a Zeuxis new,
> From Indies borrowing gold, from Eastern skies
> Most bright cinoper . . .

Yet this is but half the picture; our Silverado platform has another side to it. Though there was no soil, and scarce a blade of grass, yet out of these tumbled gravel-heaps and broken boulders, a flower garden bloomed as at home in a conservatory. Calycanthus crept, like a hardy weed, all over our rough parlour, choking the railway, and pushing forth its rusty, aromatic cones from between two blocks of shattered mineral. Azaleas made a big snow-bed just above the well. The shoulder of the hill waved white with Mediterranean heath. In the crannies of the ledge and about the spurs of the tall pine, a red flowering stone-plant hung in clusters. Even the low, thorny chaparral was thick with pea-like blossom. Close at the foot of our path nutmegs prospered, delightful to the sight and smell. At sunrise, and again late at night, the scent of the sweet bay trees filled the canyon, and the down-blowing night wind must have borne it hundreds of feet into the outer air.

All this vegetation, to be sure, was stunted. The madrona was here no bigger than the manzanita; the bay was but a stripling shrub; the very pines, with four or five exceptions in all our upper canyon, were not so tall as myself, or but a little taller, and the most of them came lower than my waist. For a prosperous forest tree, we must look below, where the glen was crowded with green spires. But for flowers and ravishing perfume, we had none to envy: our heap of road-metal was thick with bloom, like a hawthorn in the front of June; our red, baking angle in the mountain, a laboratory of poignant scents. It was an endless wonder to my mind, as I dreamed about the platform, following the progress of the shadows, where the madrona with its leaves, the azalea and calycanthus with their blossoms, could find moisture to support such thick, wet waxy growths, or the bay tree collect the ingredients of its perfume. But there they all grew together, healthy, happy, and happy-making, as though rooted in a fathom of black soil.

Nor was it only vegetable life that prospered. We had, indeed, few birds, and none that had much of a voice or anything worthy to be called a song. My morning comrade had a thin chirp, unmusical and monotonous, but friendly and pleasant to hear. He had but one rival: a fellow with an ostentatious cry of near an octave descending, not one note of which properly followed another. This is the only bird I ever knew with a wrong ear; but there was something enthralling about his performance. You listened and listened, thinking each time he must surely get it right; but no, it was always wrong, and always wrong the same way. Yet he seemed proud of his song, delivered it with execution and a manner of his own, and was charming to his mate. A very incorrect, incessant human whistler had thus a chance of knowing how his own music pleased the world. Two great birds – eagles, we thought – dwelt at the top of the canyon, among the crags that were printed on the sky. Now and again, but very rarely, they wheeled high over our heads in silence, or with a distant, dying scream; and then, with a fresh impulse, winged fleetly forward, dipped over a hilltop, and were gone. They seemed solemn and ancient things, sailing the blue air: perhaps coeval with the mountain where they haunted, perhaps emigrants from Rome, where the glad legions may have shouted to behold them on the morn of battle.

But if birds were rare, the place abounded with rattlesnakes – the rattlesnakes' nest, it might have been named. Wherever we brushed among the bushes, our passage woke their angry buzz. One dwelt habitually in the wood-pile, and sometimes, when we came for firewood, thrust up his small head between two logs, and hissed at the intrusion. The rattle has a legendary credit; it is said to be awe-inspiring, and, once heard, to stamp itself for ever in the memory. But the sound is not at all alarming; the hum of many insects and the buzz of the wasp convince the ear of danger quite as readily. As a matter of fact, we lived for weeks in Silverado, coming and going, with rattles sprung on every side, and it never occurred to us to be afraid. I used to take sun-baths and do calisthenics in a certain pleasant nook among the azalea and calycanthus, the rattles whizzing on every side like spinning-wheels, and the combined hiss or buzz rising louder and angrier at any sudden movement; but I was never in the least impressed, nor ever attacked. It was only towards the end of our stay, that a man down at Calistoga, who was expatiating on the terrifying nature of the sound, gave me at last a very good imitation; and it burst on me at once that we dwelt in the metropolis of deadly snakes, and that the rattle was simply the commonest noise in Silverado. Immediately on our return, we attacked the Hansons on the subject. They had formerly assured us that our canyon was favoured, like Ireland, with an entire immunity from poisonous reptiles; but, with the perfect inconsequence of the natural man, they were no sooner found out than they went off at score in the contrary direction, and we were told that in no part of the world did rattlesnakes attain to such a monstrous bigness as among the warm, flower-dotted rocks of Silverado. This is a contribution rather to the natural history of the Hansons, than to that of snakes.

One person, however, better served by his instinct, had known the rattle from the first; and that was Chuchu, the dog. No rational creature has ever led an existence more poisoned by terror than that dog's at Silverado. Every whiz of the rattle made him bound. His eyes rolled; he trembled; he would be often wet with sweat. One of our great mysteries was his terror of the mountain. A little away above our nook, the azaleas and almost all the vegetation ceased. Dwarf pines not big enough to be Christmas trees grew thinly among loose stone and gravel scaurs. Here and there a big boulder sat quiescent on a knoll, having paused there till the next rain in his long slide down the mountain. There was here no ambuscade for the snakes, you could see clearly where you trod; and yet the higher I went, the more abject and appealing became Chuchu's terror. He was an excellent master of that composite language in which dogs communicate with men, and he would assure me, on his honour, that there was some peril on the mountain; appeal to me, by all that I held holy, to turn back; and at length, finding all was in vain, and that I still persisted, ignorantly foolhardy, he would suddenly whip round and make a bee-line down the slope for Silverado, the gravel showering after him. What was he afraid of? There were admittedly brown bears and California lions on the mountains; and a grizzly visited Rufe's poultry yard not long before, to the unspeakable alarm of Caliban, who dashed out to chastise the intruder, and found himself, by the moonlight, face to face with such a tartar. Something at least there must have been: some hairy, dangerous brute lodged permanently among the rocks a little to the north-west of Silverado, spending his summer thereabout, with wife and family.

And there was, or there had been, another animal. Once, under the broad daylight, on that open stony hillside, where the baby pines were growing, scarcely tall enough to be a badge for a MacGregor's bonnet, I came suddenly upon his innocent body, lying mummified by the dry air and sun: a pigmy kangaroo. I am ingloriously ignorant of these subjects; had never heard of such a beast; thought myself face to face with some incomparable sport of nature; and began to cherish hopes of immortality in science. Rarely have I been conscious of a stranger thrill than when I raised that singular creature from the stones, dry as a board, his innocent heart long quiet, and all warm with sunshine. His long hind legs were stiff, his tiny forepaws clutched upon his breast, as if to leap; his poor life cut short upon that mountain by some unknown accident. But the kangaroo rat, it proved, was no such unknown animal; and my discovery was nothing.

Crickets were not wanting. I thought I could make out exactly four of them, each with a corner of his own, who used to make night musical at Silverado. In the matter of voice they far excelled the birds, and their ringing whistle sounded from rock to rock, calling and replying the same thing, as in a meaningless opera. Thus, children in full health and spirits shout together, to the dismay of neighbours; and their idle, happy, deafening vociferations rise and fall, like the song of the crickets. I used to sit at night on the platform, and wonder why these creatures were so happy; and what was wrong with man that he also did not wind up his days with an hour or two of shouting; but I suspect that all long-lived animals are solemn. The dogs alone are hardly used by nature; and it seems a manifest injustice for poor Chuchu to die in his teens, after a life so shadowed and troubled, continually shaken with alarm, and the tear of elegant sentiment permanently in his eye.

There was another neighbour of ours at Silverado, small but very active, a destructive fellow. This was a black, ugly fly – a bore, the Hansons called him – who lived by hundreds in the boarding of our house. He entered by a round hole, more neatly pierced than a man could do it with a gimlet, and he seems to have spent his life in cutting out the interior of the plank, but whether as a dwelling or a storehouse, I could never find. When I used to lie in bed in the morning for a rest – we had no easy-chairs in Silverado – I would hear, hour after hour, the sharp cutting sound of his labours, and from time to time a dainty shower of sawdust would fall upon the blankets. There lives no more industrious creature than a bore.

And now that I have named to the reader all our animals and insects without exception – only I find I have forgotten the flies – he will be able to appreciate the singular privacy and silence of our days. It was not only man who was excluded: animals, the song of birds, the lowing of cattle, the bleating of sheep, clouds even, and the variations of the weather, were here also wanting; and as, day after day, the sky was one dome of blue, and the pines below us stood motionless in the still air, so the hours themselves were marked out from each other only by the series of our own affairs, and the sun's great period as he ranged westward through the heavens. The two birds cackled a while in the early morning; all day the water tinkled in the shaft, the bores ground sawdust in the planking of our crazy palace – infinitesimal sounds; and it was only with the return of night that any change would fall on our surroundings, or the four crickets begin to flute together in the dark.

Indeed, it would be hard to exaggerate the pleasure that we took in the approach of evening. Our day was not very long, but it was very tiring. To trip along unsteady planks or wade among shifting stones, to go to and fro for water, to clamber down the glen to the Toll House after meat and letters, to cook, to make fires and beds, were all exhausting to the body. Life out of doors, besides, under the fierce eye of day, draws largely on the animal spirits. There are certain hours in the afternoon when a man, unless he is in strong health or enjoys a vacant mind, would rather creep into a cool corner of a house and sit upon the chairs of civilisation. About that time, the sharp stones, the planks, the upturned boxes of Silverado, began to grow irksome to my body; I set out on that hopeless, never-ending quest for a more comfortable posture; I would be fevered and weary of the staring sun; and just then he would begin courteously to withdraw his countenance, the shadows lengthened, the aromatic airs awoke, and a indescribable but happy change announced the coming of the night.

The hours of evening, when we were once curtained in the friendly dark, sped lightly. Even as with the crickets, night brought to us a certain spirit of rejoicing. It was good to taste the air; good to mark the dawning of the stars, as they increased their glittering company; good, too, to gather stones, and send them crashing down the chute, a wave of light. It seemed, in some way, the reward and fulfilment of the day. So it is when men dwell in the open air; it is one of the simple pleasures that we lose by living cribbed and covered in a house, that, though the coming of the day is still the most inspiriting, yet day's departure, also, and the return of night refresh, renew, and quiet us; and in the pastures of the dusk we stand, like cattle, exulting in the absence of the load.

Our nights were never cold, and they were always still, but for one remarkable exception. Regularly, about nine o'clock, a warm wind sprang up, and blew for ten minutes, or maybe a quarter of an hour, right down the canyon, fanning it well out, airing it as a mother airs the night nursery before the children sleep. As far as I could judge, in the clear darkness of the night, this wind was purely local: perhaps dependent on the configuration of the glen. At least, it was very welcome to the hot and weary squatters; and if we were not abed already, the springing up of this Lilliputian valley-wind would often be our signal to retire.

I was the last to go to bed, as I was still the first to rise. Many a night I have strolled about the platform, taking a bath of darkness before I slept. The rest would be in bed, and even from the forge I could hear them talking together from bunk to bunk.

A single candle in the neck of a pint bottle was their only illumination; and yet the old cracked house seemed literally bursting with the light. It shone keen as a knife through all the vertical chinks; it struck upward through the broken shingles; and through the eastern door and window, it fell in a great splash upon the thicket and the overhanging rock. You would have said a conflagration, or at the least a roaring forge; and behold, it was but a candle. Or perhaps it was yet more strange to see the procession moving bedwards round the corner of the house, and up the plank that brought us to the bedroom door; under the immense spread of the starry heavens down in a crevice of the giant mountain, these few human shapes, with their unshielded taper, made so disproportionate a figure in the eye and mind. But the more he is alone with nature, the greater man and his doings bulk in the consideration of his fellow-men. Miles and miles away upon the opposite hilltops, if there were any hunter belated or any traveller who had lost his way, he must have stood, and watched and wondered, from the time the candle issued from the door of the assayer's office till it had mounted the plank and disappeared again into the miners' dormitory.

The End

STEVENSON AND HIS CRITICS

AN INLAND VOYAGE

Stevenson's first book received a generous welcome from the reviewers who were united in their agreement that a new literary talent had been discovered. The mood was struck by P. G. Hamerton in *Academy*, 22 June 1878 when he declared that Stevenson was 'one of the most perfect writers living, one of the very few who may yet do something that will become classical.' Hamerton also paid tribute to Stevenson's open personality and to the surefooted naturalness of his writing.

The theme was taken up by another influential literary critic, William Ernest Henley, who had been befriended by Stevenson in Edinburgh in 1875 while undergoing medical treatment for tuberculosis. The enthusiasm of his unsigned review owes much to the fact that not only was he an early admirer of Stevenson's work, but the two men had collaborated in writing several stage plays.

> The book is a small one; you can read it in an hour; but that hour must be for you so full and varied and sweet, that it's odds but you are the better and happier for it, and it's odds that but you will thank your stars for having brought you into contact with such a clear, humane, delightful spirit as his who gives it to you.
>
> He is humorous, philosophical, picturesque by turns: but he is never sentimental; and he is always human. And his English, which has a savour about it as of exquisite homespun – the delicate linen woven of fine, white, high-bred fingers – enables him to be all this with a quite beautiful ease and directness.
>
> W. E. Henley, unsigned review in *London*, 25 May 1878

Similar enthusiasm was voiced by Sidney Colvin, another friend and early admirer. At the time he was Slade Professor of Fine Art at Cambridge and had met Stevenson in 1873 at Cockfield Rectory, Suffolk, the home of his cousin Mrs Maud Babington.

Colvin was Stevenson's earliest literary mentor and a vital influence in his development as a writer.

> This brilliant and entertaining writer may at one moment show himself too raw in youth, and at another his words may seem to carry in them an echo of Heine, or at another of Sterne; but we shall acknowledge that he has both gifts and promise, and one inestimable gift in especial – charm.
> Sidney Colvin, unsigned review in *Athenaeum*, 1 June 1878

The only discordant note was struck by the *Saturday Review*, whose anonymous critic complained that 'a little of his mannerism goes a long way, and we frankly confess that he has now and then put us out of temper. The more so because, if he had been less pompously formal, he would have written a more entertaining little book.' The review ended with the thought that the book was blighted by a 'disturbing affectation' and another critic in the *Examiner* of 25 May 1878 found the work 'ostentatious.' Of the criticism, Stevenson wrote to his mother in September 1878: 'What rubbish these reviewers did talk! It is not badly written, thin, mildly cheery and strained.'

TRAVELS WITH A DONKEY IN THE CÉVENNES

Pleased though Stevenson was with the reception given to *An Inland Voyage*, he did take the criticisms to heart and his prose style was less florid in his second travel book. A reviewer in *Saturday* approved of 'the modulated beauties of a simple prose' (21 June 1879); and even the normally critical Grant Allen was moved to praise the book.

> His Inland Voyage struck the key-note of his literary gamut; and the new volume of travel with which he now favours us, has the self-same happy ring, the self-same light and graceful touch, as if Mr Stevenson were rather a Frenchman born out of due place, than a Scotsman of the Scots. I shall not attempt to quote any specimen passage from his delightful travels, because, as in all such work, the setting is everything, and the intrinsic worth a minor consideration. Mr Stevenson is a stylist who lays himself out for the mastery of style. He has succeeded in placing himself high among those whose object it is rather to say well than merely to say.'
> Grant Allen, *Fortnightly Review*, July 1879

The point was taken up by an anonymous reviewer in *Fraser's Magazine*. While commenting favourably on Stevenson's prose style, he argued that the book owed its success to the author's ability to draw himself into the narrative. Later, Stevenson was to be criticised for allowing his personality to intrude in his early books, but at the time of publication the device was thought to represent 'spontaneousness and ease':

> It is all about himself, but it is not egotistical in the evil meaning of the word. We never feel that we are hearing too much of him, or find his details impertinences or at the least *hardly* ever, to use the guarded language of the popular poet. Though the idea of the expedition is altogether over-fine and superior in its very rudeness, our young author is never priggish. He is perfectly unaffected in his affectation. The innocent vanity of his satisfaction in doing something no one has thought of doing before *is* quite innocent and pleasant, and in no way harms the impression produced in our minds that he is a quite charming companion, full of good feeling and good taste, as well as of sense and spirit, and with a quite exceptional gift of literary expression.
>
> Unsigned review, *Fraser's Magazine*, September 1879

THE SILVERADO SQUATTERS

Four years later Stevenson published a different kind of travel book about his experiences in California and as his biographer Jenni Calder notes, by then he was a changed man: 'The man emerging in the pages of *The Amateur Emigrant* and living in *The Silverado Squatters* has a substance, an acquaintance with sorrow, an engagement with life, that the companion of Cigarette and Modestine had not yet discovered.' (Jenni Calder, *RLS: A Life Study*, 1980) The shift was not just due to the passing of the years. By 1883 Stevenson had married Fanny Osbourne and was living in France with her and Lloyd, her son from a previous marriage. He had family responsibilities and had to write to earn his keep but, more importantly, he had matured and the transformation showed in his writing.

By then, too, he had enjoyed his first popular success with *Treasure Island* and the critics were inclined to treat him differently. From being a young man of some promise he had become a writer of note and the first full critical assessment of his work was written by William Archer, the distinguished drama critic and translator of the work of Henrik Ibsen. In a long critical article, 'Robert Louis Stevenson: His Style and His Thought' (*London*, November 1885) he used the recent publication of *The Silverado Squatters* to object that Stevenson was only interested in literature 'for its own sake' and that 'lightness of touch' in his natural descriptions was no substitute for more profound feelings.

The charge was answered by Henry James who argued that the emotional side of Stevenson's writing could be seen in his creation of characters who emerged fully fledged with all the strengths and weaknesses of common humanity. He also admired his delineation of landscape and his ability to recreate moods. Although he preferred 'Across the Plains', Stevenson's account of his journey across the United States which had been published in *Longman's Magazine* in 1883, James admired *The Silverado Squatters* for its 'half-humorous, half-tragical recital':

> The Silverado Squatters describes a picnicking episode, undertaken on grounds of health, on a mountain-top in California; but this free sketch, which contains a hundred humorous touches, and in the figure of Irvine Lovelands one of Mr Stevenson's most veracious portraits, is perhaps less vivid, as it is certainly less painful, than those other pages in which, some years ago, he commemorated the twelvemonth he spent in America – the history of a journey from New York to San Francisco in an emigrant-train, performed as the sequel to a voyage across the Atlantic in the same severe conditions. Henry James, 'Robert Louis Stevenson', *Century Magazine*, April 1888

In the years following Stevenson's death in 1894 a critical reaction set in against his literary reputation. Much of it was prompted by the over-promotion of the gallantry he displayed during a life-long fight against illness. As Paul Maxiner notes in his study of Stevenson's reputation, the efforts did more harm than good:

> It became increasingly difficult for readers of taste and discrimination to see Stevenson as loveable, owing to ambitious efforts of family and friends, admirers and chance acquaintances, to promote him, to remove all blemishes from the portrait, purge him of all human dross, and enshrine every utterance, however fragmentary or jejeune,

within the impressive covers of the Edinburgh Edition – by doing
everything, in short, within their power to hasten immortalisation.
(*Robert Louis Stevenson: The Critical Heritage*, 1981)

Although much of the disquiet was reserved for the novels,
Frank Swinnerton went further by arguing that Stevenson had
to be considered in relation to his works only and that the
modern reader had to disregard the personality which intruded
in his earlier books.

> It is sufficient here to maintain that Stevenson's literary reputation,
> as distinct from the humanitarian aspect of his fortitude, is seriously
> impaired. It is no longer possible for a serious critic to place him
> among the great writers, because in no department of letters –
> excepting the boy's book and the short story – has he written work
> of first-class importance. His plays, his essays, his romances – all are
> seen nowadays to be consumptive.
> Frank Swinnerton, *R. L. Stevenson* (1914)

In time Swinnerton's strictures were themselves re-assessed but
they address the problem which faced earlier reviewers of *An
Inland Voyage* and *Travels with a Donkey*: the imaginative
reconstruction of his personality and its prominent place in the
narrative. As they had noted at the time, such literary decoration
was an indication of the author's 'charm', but in the longer term
its self-conscious use pointed him in the wrong direction. And
yet, as Jenni Calder points out, the travel books were not
without significance because they recorded facts which altered
his life: 'There is little doubt that he changed direction, and that
France and America and the Pacific had everything to do with
the change.'

SUGGESTIONS FOR FURTHER READING

The fullest and most complete bibliographic work is Roger C. Swearingen, *The Prose Writings of Robert Louis Stevenson: A Guide* (London: Macmillan, 1980). Also of continuing interest is W. F. Prideaux's pioneering study: *A Bibliography of the Works of Robert Louis Stevenson*, rev. ed. (London: Hollings, and New York: Scribner's 1971).

The first biography, *The Life of Robert Louis Stevenson* (London: Macmillan, 1901), was written by Stevenson's cousin Graham Balfour who visited Samoa in 1892. Although he attempted to present a balanced and objective account, and to some extent succeeded, Balfour wrote the book with the help of Fanny Osbourne and found it impossible to be completely dispassionate. When it was published, W. E. Henley attacked it vigorously in a review in *Pall Mall Magazine* (December 1901) which gained notoriety for his jibe that Balfour had created a 'Seraph in Chocolate, this barley-sugar of a real man.'

This was followed by John A. Steuart's *Robert Louis Stevenson: Man and Writer* (London: Low, 1924) and by George S. Hellman's *The True Stevenson: A Study in Clarification* (Boston: Little, Brown and Co., 1925), both of which were written as correctives to Balfour. By then Frank Swinnerton had published his *R. L. Stevenson: A Critical Study* (London: Martin Secker, 1914) which judged Stevenson to be a second-rate writer; and although these charges were answered by G. K. Chesterton's *Robert Louis Stevenson* (London: Hodder & Stoughton, 1927) it was not until the second half of the 20th century that Stevenson was re-assessed by a new generation of critics:

Bell, Ian, *Dreams of Exile: Robert Louis Stevenson – A Biography* (Edinburgh: Mainstream, 1992). A thorough examination of Stevenson's family and social background.

Calder, Jenni, *RLS: A Life Study* (London: Hamish Hamilton, 1980). Examines the influences of Stevenson's life on his work and contains a lively re-assessment of his literary importance.

Daiches, David, *Robert Louis Stevenson* (Glasgow: McLellan, 1947). A sympathetic study of Stevenson's work and its relevance to the Scottish literary tradition.

Eigner, Edwin, *Robert Louis Stevenson and Romantic Tradition*

(Princeton: Princeton University Press, 1966). Places Stevenson's work within the tradition of the 19th century Gothic novel.

Furnas, J. C. *Voyage to Windward: The Life of Robert Louis Stevenson* (London: Faber and Faber, 1952). The first authoritative critical biography. Unrivalled in its treatment of Stevenson's life and literary reputation.

Kiely, Robert, *Robert Louis Stevenson and the Fiction of Adventure* (Cambridge, Massachusetts: Harvard University Press, 1965). Contains useful comparisons with the work of Joseph Conrad and assesses Stevenson as a serious novelist.

Knight, Alanna, *The Robert Louis Stevenson Treasury* (London: Shepherd-Walwyn, 1985). The complete reference book on the life and work of Robert Louis Stevenson.

Maxiner, Paul (ed.), *Robert Louis Stevenson: The Critical Heritage* (London: Routledge & Kegan Paul, 1981). Traces the critical response to Stevenson's work between 1878 and 1914.

Smith, Janet Adam, *Robert Louis Stevenson* (London: Duckworth, 1937). A briskly written, no-nonsense account of Stevenson's life and work and the first reliable antidote to the earlier hagiographies.

ACKNOWLEDGEMENTS

The publishers and the editor are grateful for permission to quote from the following:

Jenni Calder, *RLS: A Life Study*, London, Hamish Hamilton, 1980 (The Peters Fraser and Dunlop Group); Paul Maxiner (ed.) *Robert Louis Stevenson: The Critical Heritage*, London, Routledge & Kegan Paul, 1981; Frank Swinnerton, *R. L. Stevenson: A Critical Study*, London, Martin Secker, 1914.

CLASSIC FICTION
IN EVERYMAN

**The Impressions of
Theophrastus Such**
GEORGE ELIOT
*An amusing collection of character
sketches, and the only paperback
edition available*
£5.99

Frankenstein
MARY SHELLEY
*A masterpiece of Gothic terror in
its original 1818 version*
£3.99

East Lynne
MRS HENRY WOOD
*A classic tale of melodrama,
murder and mystery*
£7.99

**Holiday Romance and
Other Writings for Children**
CHARLES DICKENS
*Dickens's works for children,
including 'The Life of Our Lord'
and 'A Child's History of England',
with original illustrations*
£5.99

The Ebb-Tide
R. L. STEVENSON
*A compelling study of ordinary
people in extreme circumstances*
£4.99

The Three Impostors
ARTHUR MACHEN
*The only edition available
of this cult thriller*
£4.99

Mister Johnson
JOYCE CARY
*The only edition available of this
amusing but disturbing twentieth-
century tale*
£5.99

The Jungle Book
RUDYARD KIPLING
*The classic adventures of Mowgli
and his friends*
£3.99

Glenarvon
LADY CAROLINE LAMB
*The only edition available of the
novel which throws light on the
greatest scandal of the early nineteenth century – the infatuation of
Caroline Lamb with Lord Byron*
£6.99

**Twenty Thousand Leagues
Under the Sea**
JULES VERNE
*Scientific fact combines with
fantasy in this prophetic tale
of underwater adventure*
£4.99

All books are available from your local bookshop or direct from:
Littlehampton Book Services Cash Sales, 14 Eldon Way, Lineside Estate,
Littlehampton, West Sussex BN17 7HE (*prices are subject to change*)

To order any of the books, please enclose a cheque (in sterling) made payable to
Littlehampton Book Services, or phone your order through with credit card details (Access,
Visa or Mastercard) on 01903 721596 (24 hour answering service) stating card number
and expiry date. (*Please add £1.25 for package and postage to the total of your order.*)

In the USA, for further information and a complete catalogue call 1-800-526-2778

CLASSIC NOVELS
IN EVERYMAN

The Time Machine
H. G. WELLS

One of the books which defined 'science fiction' – a compelling and tragic story of a brilliant and driven scientist
£3.99

Oliver Twist
CHARLES DICKENS

Arguably the best-loved of Dickens's novels. With all the original illustrations
£4.99

Barchester Towers
ANTHONY TROLLOPE

The second of Trollope's Chronicles of Barsetshire, and one of the funniest of all Victorian novels
£4.99

The Heart of Darkness
JOSEPH CONRAD

Conrad's most intense, subtle, compressed, profound and proleptic work
£3.99

Tess of the d'Urbervilles
THOMAS HARDY

The powerful, poetic classic of wronged innocence
£3.99

Wuthering Heights and Poems
EMILY BRONTË

A powerful work of genius – one of the great masterpieces of literature
£3.99

Pride and Prejudice
JANE AUSTEN

Proposals, rejections, infidelities, elopements, happy marriages – Jane Austen's most popular novel
£2.99

North and South
ELIZABETH GASKELL

A novel of hardship, passion and hard-won wisdom amidst the conflicts of the industrial revolution
£4.99

The Newcomes
W. M. THACKERAY

An exposé of Victorian polite society by one of the nineteenth-century's finest novelists
£6.99

Adam Bede
GEORGE ELIOT

A passionate rural drama enacted at the turn of the eighteenth century
£5.99

All books are available from your local bookshop or direct from:
Littlehampton Book Services Cash Sales, 14 Eldon Way, Lineside Estate,
Littlehampton, West Sussex BN17 7HE (*prices are subject to change*)

To order any of the books, please enclose a cheque (in sterling) made payable to
Littlehampton Book Services, or phone your order through with credit card details (Access,
Visa or Mastercard) on 01903 721596 (24 hour answering service) stating card number
and expiry date. (*Please add £1.25 for package and postage to the total of your order.*)

In the USA, for further information and a complete catalogue call 1-800-526-2778

SHORT STORY COLLECTIONS
IN EVERYMAN

The Strange Case of Dr Jekyll and Mr Hyde and Other Stories
R. L. STEVENSON
An exciting selection of gripping tales from a master of suspense
£1.99

Nineteenth-Century American Short Stories
edited by Christopher Bigsby
A selection of the works of Henry James, Edith Wharton, Mark Twain and many other great American writers
£6.99

The Best of Saki
edited by MARTIN STEPHEN
Includes Tobermory, Gabriel Ernest, Svedni Vashtar, The Interlopers, Birds on the Western Front
£4.99

Souls Belated and Other Stories
EDITH WHARTON
Brief, neatly crafted tales exploring a range of themes from big taboo subjects to the subtlest little ironies of social life
£6.99

The Night of the Iguana and Other Stories
TENNESSEE WILLIAMS
Twelve remarkable short stories, each a compelling drama in miniature
£4.99

Selected Short Stories and Poems
THOMAS HARDY
Hardy's most memorable stories and poetry in one volume
£4.99

Selected Tales
HENRY JAMES
Stories portraying the tensions between private life and the outside world
£5.99

The Best of Sherlock Homes
ARTHUR CONAN DOYLE
All the favourite adventures in one volume
£4.99

The Secret Self 1: *Short Stories by Women*
edited by Hermione Lee
'A superb collection' The Guardian
£4.99